ROUTLEDGE LIBRARY EDITIONS: EARLY YEARS

Volume 1

THE ROLE OF SUBJECT KNOWLEDGE IN THE EARLY YEARS OF SCHOOLING

THE ROLE OF SUBJECT KNOWLEDGE IN THE EARLY YEARS OF SCHOOLING

Edited by
CAROL AUBREY

LONDON AND NEW YORK

First published in 1994 by The Falmer Press

This edition first published in 2023
by Routledge
4 Park Square, Milton Park, Abingdon, Oxon OX14 4RN

and by Routledge
605 Third Avenue, New York, NY 10158

Routledge is an imprint of the Taylor & Francis Group, an informa business

© 1994 Selection and editorial material copyright Carol Aubrey

All rights reserved. No part of this book may be reprinted or reproduced or utilised in any form or by any electronic, mechanical, or other means, now known or hereafter invented, including photocopying and recording, or in any information storage or retrieval system, without permission in writing from the publishers.

Trademark notice: Product or corporate names may be trademarks or registered trademarks, and are used only for identification and explanation without intent to infringe.

British Library Cataloguing in Publication Data
A catalogue record for this book is available from the British Library

ISBN: 978-1-032-34369-3 (Set)
ISBN: 978-1-032-34461-4 (Volume 1) (hbk)
ISBN: 978-1-032-34468-3 (Volume 1) (pbk)
ISBN: 978-1-003-32228-3 (Volume 1) (ebk)

DOI: 10.4324/9781003322283

Publisher's Note
The publisher has gone to great lengths to ensure the quality of this reprint but points out that some imperfections in the original copies may be apparent.

Disclaimer
The publisher has made every effort to trace copyright holders and would welcome correspondence from those they have been unable to trace.

The Role of Subject Knowledge in the Early Years of Schooling

Edited by

Carol Aubrey

 The Falmer Press

(A member of the Taylor & Francis Group)
London • Washington, D.C.

UK   The Falmer Press, 4 John Street, London, WC1N 2ET
USA   The Falmer Press, Taylor & Francis Inc., 1900 Frost Road, Suite 101,
          Bristol, PA 19007

© Selection and editorial material copyright Carol Aubrey 1994

All rights reserved. No part of this publication may be reproduced, stored in a retrieval system, or transmitted, in any form or by any means, electronic, mechanical, photocopying, recording or otherwise, without permission in writing from the Publisher.

First published 1994

A catalogue record for this book is available from the British Library

Library of Congress Cataloging-in-Publication Data are available on request

ISBN 0 7507 0194 3 (cased)
ISBN 0 7507 0195 1 (paper)

Jacket design by Isabel

Typeset in 10/12pt Garamond
by Graphicraft Typesetters Ltd., Hong Kong

Contents

Plate 1		vii
Preface		ix
Glossary		xi
Chapter 1	Overview of Advances in Understanding of Learning and Teaching of Subject Knowledge *Carol Aubrey*	1
Chapter 2	Subject Knowledge: The Case for English *Linda Thompson*	14
Chapter 3	Knowledge About Drama *Peter Millward*	29
Chapter 4	Can Teachers Use and Make More Explicit their Knowledge of How Writing Works to Help Children Become Writers? *Deirdre Pettitt*	41
Chapter 5	Construction of Mathematics in the Early Years *Carol Aubrey*	53
Chapter 6	The Challenge of Science *Rosemary Feasey*	73
Chapter 7	Teaching History in the Infant Classroom *Deirdre Pettitt*	89
Chapter 8	A Sense of Place: Geography/Environmental Education in the Early Years *Joy Palmer*	105
Chapter 9	'I Can't Teach Music — So We Just Sing' *Coral Davies*	119

Contents

Chapter 10	Teachers' Understanding of Children's Drawing *Jennifer Buckham*	133
Chapter 11	Physical Education as a Specialist Subject *Pauline Wetton*	168
Chapter 12	Subject Knowledge in the Early Years: The Case of Religious Education *David Day and Elizabeth Ashton*	178
Chapter 13	The Role of Subject Knowledge *Carol Aubrey*	188

Notes on Contributors   195

Index   198

Plate 1: Black Cat by a Fish Pond by Isabel (6 years 4 months)

Preface

The *Education Reform Act* of 1988 constitutes the most radical piece of educational legislation for England and Wales since the Education Act of 1944. Of its wide-ranging implications for educational organization and practice, those relating to the imposition of a centrally-directed National Curriculum are of particular relevance to this book. The Act requires all maintained schools, that is county and voluntary schools, and the new category of grant-maintained schools, to provide for all pupils, within the years of compulsory schooling, a basic curriculum. The requirements of Section 1 (2) are satisfied if it is a balanced and broadly-based curriculum which:

(a) promotes the spiritual, moral, cultural, mental and physical development of pupils at the school and of society; and
(b) prepares such pupils for the opportunities, responsibilities and experiences of adult life.

Section 3 designates three core subjects and foundation subjects which must be taught. The core subjects are mathematics, English and science. The foundation subjects include the core subjects, art, geography, history, music, physical education, technology, and (at secondary stage) a modern language. Welsh is a core subject for Welsh-speaking schools and a foundation subject in non-Welsh-speaking schools in Wales. Religious education is included in Section 2 (1) (a) as part of the 'basic' curriculum, without being subject to the particular conditions attached to the core and foundation subjects. Related Attainment Targets, Programmes of Study and arrangements for assessment at the Key Stages of 7, 11, 14 and 16 were settled in the form of Orders.

By age 7 years most (80 per cent) of children will have reached levels 1, 2 and 3 according to their assessed performance. Under the 1944 Education Act legal control of the curriculum in maintained schools was devolved to the local educational authorities and the governors of aided schools. In practice, responsibility for the curriculum became that of the headteacher and senior members of staff, with local authority advisors exerting a strong influence.

Preface

Until the National Curriculum was introduced, schools and individual class teachers exercised considerable autonomy in curriculum planning, with no set timetable for individual subjects, except typically for activities taking place outside the classroom such as PE or music, or events organized on a whole-school basis, such as school assembly.

The Education Reform Act has set out the responsibilities of the local authorities and school governors for ensuring that the National Curriculum is enforced and the the Education Act 1992 required that all maintained schools be inspected every four years, with the reports, including plans for acting on inspectors' criticisms, published for parents. Having set in motion mechanisms for producing Programmes of Study, Attainment Targets and procedures for testing and the assessment, the Secretary of State must keep the National Curriculum under review. The local authorities must implement the National Curriculum and have regard to it in undertaking their statutory duties. Governing bodies, who are responsible for oversight of the school curriculum must produce a curriculum policy document for parents showing how they intend to meet the requirements of the National Curriculum. Headteachers have the responsibility to see the National Curriculum policy is carried out, using the Attainment Targets as a structure for planning and the Programmes of Study as a basis for more detailed consideration of schemes of work. This includes deciding *how* the subjects of the National Curriculum shall be taught, in conjunction with cross-curricular themes which thread through the curriculum.

Under the Education Act 1993 the Secretary of State has new powers to specify assessment arrangements and confer special functions on governing bodies and headteachers. The National Curriculum Council (NCC) and the School Examinations and Assessment Council (SEAC) are abolished and replaced by the School Curriculum and Assessment Authority.

Glossary

Assessment Arrangements
: The arrangements for assessment will demonstrate what pupils have achieved with respect to subject-specific attainment targets at the end of each Key Stage. A variety of methods of assessment will be involved, including both formal (standard assessment tasks) and continuous assessment by teachers.

Attainment Targets
: For each core and foundation subject objectives set out the knowledge, skills and understanding that pupils of diverse attainments are expected to develop from ages 5–16 years. Each attainment target is organized in terms of ten levels of attainment and each level is defined in terms of appropriate statements of attainment.

Basic Curriculum
: This is the National Curriculum and religious education.

Core Subjects
: These are English, mathematics and science.

Foundation Subjects
: These comprise English, mathematics, science, technology, history, geography, music, art and physical education; and also (for secondary-age pupils) a modern foreign language.

Key Stages
: There are four Key Stages: from the beginning of compulsory education to 7 years; 7–11 years; 11–14 years; and 14 years to the end of compulsory education. At the end of these four stages performance is defined in terms of specific attainment targets and levels of attainment and formally reported.

Glossary

Levels of Attainment	As noted above there are ten levels of achievement within each attainment target through which it is expected children will progress during compulsory education.
Profile Components	For the purpose of assessment and reporting groups of attainment targets within a subject are brought together.
Programmes of Study	These concern the content, skills and processes which must be taught to pupils during each Key Stage in order to meet the objectives identified in the attainment targets.
Statements of Attainment	These are the specific objectives defined for each of the ten levels of attainment within the Statutory Orders provided for each subject.
TGAT	Task Group on Assessment and Testing.

All pupils have the same statutory entitlement to a broad and balanced curriculum, including access to the National Curriculum but in some cases, such as pupils with special educational needs, it may be necessary to make exceptional arrangements.

Chapter 1

Overview of Advances in Understanding of Learning and Teaching of Subject Knowledge

Carol Aubrey

Introduction

The task of the primary school teacher has changed fundamentally in terms of planning and monitoring progress and in ensuring progression in the subjects of the National Curriculum, regardless of the way the curriculum is organized. The Department of Education and Sciences (DES) commissioned a discussion document entitled *Curriculum Organisation and Classroom Practice in Primary Schools* (Alexander, Rose and Woodhead, 1992) which was intended to stimulate fresh debate about such issues as the role of subject knowledge and the deployment of subject specialism in the primary school. This called for both more 'sharply-focused and rigorously planned topic work and for an increase in single-subject teaching'. The problem of shortage of subject expertise in the primary school was described as 'acute' and the report advocated that every primary school should in principle have direct access to specialist expertise in all nine National Curriculum subjects and in religious education. The authors recommended the introduction of semi-specialist and specialist teaching to primary schools to strengthen the existing, rather rigidly conceived roles of class teacher and consultant and to introduce greater flexibility in staff deployment. Current priorities for initial training, they suggested, should be the acquisition and strengthening of subject expertise, as well as the systematic training in a broad range of classroom organizational strategies and teaching techniques.

The more recent publication of two reports from National Curriculum Council (NCC) and the Office for Standards in Education (OFSTED) on the anniversary of the 1992 discussion paper signalled yet further changes to both primary schooling and initial training. In many respects the two latest reports merely confirmed and reemphasized the major issues raised by the original discussion paper. In terms of teaching methods the need for a broad repertoire of teaching strategies with some strategies, like whole class teaching and single subject work, having a greater prominence together with the competent

1

deployment of a range of teaching skills such as questioning, explaining, direct instruction, assessment and feedback, merely echoed the previous document.

With respect to subject knowledge the three documents are in accord: a proper knowledge of subject matter across the National Curriculum range and the suitable deployment of subject expertise, through whatever combination of generalist, semi-specialist and specialist teaching or subject consultation, is fundamental to effective instruction. The growing awareness of National Curriculum 'overload' is acknowledged by all documents. Less consensus concerning the role of resourcing and the means to increasing teachers' subject knowledge, however, has been obtained. The aim of this book is to begin a proper discussion about the nature of subject knowledge which, so far, has been little examined in the British debate with its current focus on curriculum organization and classroom practice.

The Role of Subject Knowledge: A New Emphasis?

As primary schools now begin to reassess the role of subject knowledge, educational research has already shifted attention away from what teachers *do*, towards a focus on the knowledge that teachers hold, the way in which this is organized, and the different forms of knowledge which inform their teaching. Research interest of the 1960s and 1970s in general features of classroom processes, time use and teacher effectiveness, in relation to children's achievement gains, gave way in the 1980s to more detailed and qualitative analyses of curriculum topics, even individual lessons, which took account of teacher's own goals and intentions, as well as children's existing understandings, explanations and problem-solving strategies, their errors and misconceptions. It was Shulman (1986) who noted that subject knowledge was missing from research on teaching and called for attention to this area.

Shulman (*ibid*) suggested that knowledge of subject discipline and pedagogy are combined to form a special form of professional understanding, or content-specific pedagogy. Teachers, for their part, construct this from knowledge and beliefs about what content is to be taught and how this can be represented to children in ways that they will understand. Children, in turn, construct their own understanding of what has been taught. In this process, new insights are created for both teacher and learner.

In the context of this increased emphasis on teachers' knowledge of, and beliefs about subject matter, the learner is seen as actively constructing understanding from teaching activities which take account of the social context of learning, the learner's existing knowledge and goals for learning.

Teachers' Knowledge of Subject Matter

Until recently teachers' subject knowledge has been largely assumed and, hence, teachers' learning of subject content is a relatively new area for investigation. The *Knowledge Growth in Teaching Program* at Stanford University (Wilson, Shulman and Richert, 1987), for instance, has been investigating beginning secondary teachers' knowledge of subject matter which, it is argued, is a prerequisite to their understanding of their subject for teaching. Through their early attempts as new teachers to teach their subject, new knowledge of children's learning, of the curriculum, of the setting in which they work is formed. This is pedagogical content knowledge.

But what constitutes effective subject knowledge? How can teachers increase knowledge of the subjects they teach? Should teacher education simply provide subject content to be taught or should new teachers be provided with a liberal education which, in itself, stimulates general critical reflection and some sense of intellectual enquiry (Dewey, 1904; Peters, 1977). Knowing about a subject, however, means knowing about the fundamental activities and discourse of a particular discipline, showing an awareness of competing perspectives and central ideas within this field, as well as understanding how seemingly incompatible views can be justified and validated. According to Wilson, Shulman and Richert (1987) teachers must understand both the substantive and syntactic structure of their subject. Grossman, Wilson and Shulman (1989) have suggested that knowing one's subject for teaching implies several sorts of knowing: knowing what factual information, central concepts, organizing principles and ideas make up the discipline (content knowledge); knowing the explanatory models or paradigms, the conceptual tools used to guide enquiry conducted in the field, or make sense of data (substantive knowledge); and knowing the relevant forms of methodology, the ways in which new knowledge is brought into the field, including the 'canons of evidence and proof and rules governing how they are applied' (syntactic knowledge). Content knowledge may, for instance, influence the teachers' analysis of textbooks, the choice of curriculum material used, the structuring of planning and the conduct of teaching. Substantive knowledge can have a powerful influence on what and how teachers choose to teach. Teachers may have acquired such knowledge of their discipline mainly through their undergraduate studies and may, depending on the course they followed, hold differing conceptions of subject knowledge. Kuhn's (1970) analysis of scientific theories, for instance, showed how a dominant theoretical structure may hold sway until it is displaced eventually by a new structure which offers an alternative view. On the other hand, in more interpretive studies such as history or English, a number of models of explanation can co-exist and teachers may present a story or historical event, for instance, from a social or political perspective according to their own interests or biases. Consideration of substantive structures, however, is not complete without attention to the knowledge of means employed to conduct enquiry within a discipline (syntactic knowledge). The study of art, for instance, will include aesthetics and art criticism, just as the study of literature will entail literary criticism.

Through conducting their own enquiries, the artist, the English specialist, the scientist, the historian, or the mathematician, will learn what evidence is legitimate and acceptable. Such knowledge is essential to ensure that teachers have the means to keep informed of new developments within their field and to critically evaluate it. Inadequate syntactic knowledge may lead to misrepresentation of the subject in teaching and may affect teachers' ability to learn new knowledge in their fields.

From the point of view of teaching, the consideration of ways of understanding characteristic of the major disciplines and the means for making these accessible to young children, is essential. The explanatory power of the Grossman, Wilson and Shulman (1989) model with respect to pedagogical subject knowledge may be best judged in the context of a more detailed consideration of particular subjects of the National Curriculum. Blyth (1991), for instance, in discussing approaches to primary humanities, identified major aspects of development — concepts, skills, values and attitudes.

With respect to developing concepts, Blyth distinguished between the substantive and methodological. Substantive concepts concern general ideas about organizing content and knowledge, where early questions about a particular castle, for example, lead to reasoning about other castles built at the same, then other times, and finally lead to the concept of general physical defensive strategies. Methodological concepts relate to ways of handling and analyzing content and knowledge such as continuity/change concepts where children progressively build up understanding of timescale. These two kinds of concepts, substantive and methodological, may be considered to comprise the substantive knowledge base of primary humanities. In terms of syntactic knowledge, Blyth identified three 'thinking skills' which he regarded as relatively distinctive to the humanities: the evaluation of diverse evidence; the capacity to decide the more probable explanation of events where certainty is unattainable; and the exercise of empathy, or the capacity to think imaginatively about people who inhabit, or who inhabited other life-spaces. Associated attitudes and values in primary humanities may relate to the child's personal and moral development, to more specific attitudes towards the value of objectivity in study and to attitudes towards forms of study, for instance to the collaboration in, or the sharing of, tasks.

Learning in science is, perhaps, less straightforward from the point of view of the Grossman *et al*, model. Harlen (1991) has noted that whilst there are various views of science the view which underlies current educational thinking, including the National Curriculum, is one which conceives learning science as the deepening of understanding of the biological and physical aspects of the world. It entails the process of reaching an understanding of the world, that is the testing of ideas and theories by scientific methods, as well as the ideas and generalizations derived from this process and used to make sense of everyday events and phenomena.

Children use their existing ideas to make sense of new classroom activities and subsequently will be encouraged to test these ideas against the evidence. The dependence of such activities on the ways in which ideas are tested by 'science process skills' is of considerable importance. These skills may include making an observation, planning an investigation or contributing to a group account. The consideration of scientific activities serves also to emphasize the interrelatedness of concepts and process skills through which they are developed. Such ideas which are tested out and, hopefully extended may relate to processes of life, earth and atmosphere, types and uses of materials, forces or sound and music. Harlen noted, for instance, the average 7-year-old might be expected to be aware that the length of the day and the position of the sun in the sky change during a year, whilst a 16-year-old might be expected to have an idea of the Earth as part of the solar system, which explains annual changes in day length and average temperature.

The conceptual framework proposed by Grossman, Wilson and Shulman (1989) may be useful for the consideration of teacher subject knowledge and pedagogical subject knowledge in a number of subjects. The case of science, however, as Carlsen (1991) has observed and as the above account serves to illustrate, demonstrates the difficulty, in practice, of distinguishing between substantive and syntactic knowledge structures, where considerable overlap occurs. At a practical level teachers differ not only in their curriculum planning, teaching and assessment but in their knowledge of subject matter and in their beliefs about what is involved in learning and teaching subjects. Subject knowledge does make a difference and effective teachers know how to select content and to identify key points. They know how to present topics to children in ways that they understand which suggests that a teacher also needs to understand the subject in *contextually* appropriate ways. Where subject knowledge is richer, deeper and better-integrated it is more likely that the teacher will be confident and more open to children's ideas, contributions, questions and comments. This is not to under-estimate the problems of identifying and responding in appropriate ways to the disparate understandings of a large class of pupils. A teacher skilful enough to recognize the scientific merit of an unexpected comment and to encourage the child to share the reasons for making such a response may experience more difficulty in dealing with an individual misconception without confusing the rest of the class!

A teacher's subject knowledge and pedagogical subject knowledge, however, may differ within a subject, as well as across subjects. To expect teachers to have adequate subject knowledge across all the nine subjects of the National Curriculum will be neither fair nor realistic. Suffice it to say that where knowledge is limited the teacher may rely more on scheme work, text books and in occupying pupils with individual work.

Those who teach children in the early years may, however, regard other criteria such as the way young children learn and develop at a particular stage as more important. Clearly taking account of young children's interests, preferred activities and out-of-school experiences as these relate to teaching subject matter is vitally important. Early years teachers may have different orientations to different subjects, as well as different knowledge bases, adopting a child-centred approach to, for instance, children's literature and history and a fact-centred approach to mathematics and science. Smith and Neale

(1991) in their staff development programmes have identified a number of orientations towards primary science which entail different beliefs about the discipline of science, the nature of school science and learning and teaching science. These are as follows: discovery, processes, didactive/content mastery, and conceptual change orientations. A discovery orientation will stress enquiry, discovering with the five senses, with children trying out ideas and drawing their own conclusions. Teachers for their part will provide interesting material and activities to stimulate curiosity. A processes orientation will emphasize learning the steps for the scientific method, with children observing, collecting data, testing hypotheses, inferring and drawing conclusions. A content mastery orientation will stress known facts and laws, the assimilation of new information and teacher evaluation. A conceptual change orientation stresses fundamental concepts, the evolution of ideas and opportunities provided for children to construct and reorganize their own knowledge through problem solving and the consideration of alternative views.

Subject knowledge, in fact, cannot be easily distinguished from beliefs. It cannot be directly observed and, thus, is not easily verifiable. One would hope, in addition, that it is not static but dynamic and continually subject to change with professional development.

Given the central role of subject knowledge in teaching and learning it is important to consider why so many primary teachers might seem more comfortable to emphasize their generalist role across subjects rather than their subject specialist role. Taking account of the diverse routes into primary teaching which have been offered to the current teaching force during the last thirty years or so, the diverse nature and length of such training courses, the varying degree to which post-experience training has been made available within schools and the local authority, this should come as no surprise. The situation is complicated further by the diverse learning experiences to which recruits to the teaching profession have been exposed. On the one hand there have been a wide range of undergraduate programmes provided by colleges and universities, on the other hand graduate entrants, bring a variety in breadth and depth of subject matter knowledge to their postgraduate training, depending on the particular degree course that they have followed. Since the National Curriculum was introduced, however, the Council for the Accreditation of Teacher Education (CATE) has provided precise guidelines to training institutions with respect to recruitment of candidates with relevant length and depth of subject study.

An assumption is emerging in this chapter, however, that teachers' subject knowledge is acquired solely through their undergraduate study. Just as children's, young adults' knowledge and understanding is acquired in out-of-school setting as much as in formal teaching situations and is, similarly, constructed from everyday experience and activities in meaningful social contexts. Teachers, themselves, are products of primary and secondary schools in which pupils commonly lack deep understanding of subject matter. Furthermore Lortie (1975) demonstrated that children, through thousands of hours spent in school, acquire attitudes towards teaching and learning particular subjects. It should be noted that student teachers have been learning subjects in schools for thirteen years before they enter undergraduate study as well as forming views about subjects, topics and activities and the nature of academic success and failure. Young children's early make-believe games about schools provide examples of attitudes towards schooling as do student teachers' evaluations of teacher education courses at a later stage! Ball and McDiamid (1990) have suggested that whether pre-college learning is a greater influence on subject matter knowledge than college studies is an open and empirical question. In this respect the proposed weakening of students' subject knowledge base by increasing school-based teacher education should raise good cause for concern. Whilst classroom experience may deepen their understanding of the curriculum, young learners and pedagogy, deepening of a new teacher's subject knowledge may *not* occur. Ball and McDiamid (1990) have concluded that there is mounting evidence that undergraduate students of mathematics and science, whether or not intending teachers, can satisfactorily meet course requirements without developing conceptual understanding of subject matter. Ball and Feiman-Nemser (1988) in the area of mathematics have cited the experience of a student teacher learning the conceptual basis of numeration and place value through a combination of teaching the topic and working through the text book. Whether the acquisition of subject knowledge from school text books is reliable is another matter.

There *is* evidence to suggest that trainee teachers' subject knowledge is transformed, however, during training and when they start teaching — by children, by the school curriculum and by the context in which they teach. Calderhead and Miller (1985) have indicated that teachers interweave knowledge of subjects with particular knowledge of classroom realities to create 'action-relevant' knowledge.

Finally, as Brophy (1991) has suggested, teachers' personal beliefs about learning and teaching may affect profoundly their work in classrooms. These are derived from their own experience of learning and teaching and may be wholly implicit, influencing the teachers' work in ways that they are not aware of.

Children's Early Learning

The home is the child's first learning environment. Here first perceptions of the social and physical world are formed and linguistic competence, early mathematical knowledge and cultural understandings acquired. Everyday living provides the context for learning about growing up in a particular cultural group. It is a link to the past and future through shared understandings with trusted adults, and a bridge to the wider world.

Meanings constructed by the child through interactions in physical and social experiences are derived from or 'embedded' in the situations and activities in which they are produced. Natural language has a fundamental role in supporting social communication and in representing the child's growing experience. At first language is rooted in, and accompanies ongoing contextualized, social activity. Between this early and undifferentiated use of speech is an intermediate, 'egocentric' phase where speech not only accompanies activity but transforms it through its planning and guiding function. Later as Vygotsky noted (Kozulin, 1986) speech is internalized and the child begins to differentiate the representational aspects of speech from the communicative. Language can now be used to mediate, as well as represent action, to plan and self-regulate.

Whilst the meanings constructed by the child through these interactions in the physical and social world are personal, knowledge and thinking are derived from the situations and activities in which they are produced. Language plays a crucial role in the transmission of culture to the child, first in the family and with peers, later with teachers in school. Wells (1985) suggested that some of the differences between children's rate of initial language learning could be accounted for by differences in the quality of linguistic interaction they experience. A 'supportive' style was characterized by an attitude of reciprocity, where the adult picked up and extended the child's previous utterance or ongoing activity and matched language to the shared focus of attention, expressing an interest in what the child was doing or communicating and helping to extend understanding of this shared topic. In general the adult treated the child as an equal partner, supporting or extending the child's contributions and providing a joint construction adjusted to the child's level of development. Bruner (1983) described the adult's provision of a 'Language Acquisition Support System' (LASS) which framed or structured early exchanges until the child could take an independent part. By contrast to this 'supportive' style, Wells described a 'teaching' style where the adult took the lead, asked questions which required the child to display knowledge, led to evaluation and the frequent experience of being inadequate by adult standards. Whatever the quality of early care received, however, the social origins of cognition and the role of instruction in leading development is central. Further, as Wells (1985) has noted, the medium of instruction in the home and at school is language and as such justifies the serious attention of anyone working in education.

Play, games and books, too, provide opportunities for extending the child's social, linguistic, scientific and physical world. Vygotsky described how play provided a context for separating objects from the meaning normally given them by words and how, in turn, the possibility of a new attitude to reality is created. In play, for example, a stick may stand for a horse and be ridden. Through social role play children create an imaginary situation and a new world of meaning to guide their actions.

From the study of young children's early drawing Matthews (1987) noted some of the child's earliest representations and expressive structures in singing, jumping, running, shouting, mark-making and constructing with bricks may go unnoticed as such. Yet within these activities, whether engaged in simultaneously or in succession, children explore semiotic possibilities of actions which provide the beginning of symbol or sign use. Matthews observed a general 'inability to comprehend an entire family of interrelated representational processes in early childhood' and noted the 'scant attention which psychologists had paid to an important level of early representation and expression'.

The lack of attention to the contribution that psycho-motor behaviour may make to development is, perhaps, most marked in Western psychology. The French philosopher and psychologist Henri Wallon (see Aubrey, 1987), in fact constructed a major developmental theory which sought to identify the relationship among movement, emotion and mind. For him, emotion in its physiological aspects and social contexts provided the conditions for the creation of personality and representation, and the origins of thinking. Emotion was a language before language, expressed first through movement, and becoming social through adaptation to others. For Wallon, representation began in this early distinction between self and other which was a prelude to personality.

Bruner (1966) claimed that the young learner's cognitive growth was influenced by the development of representations through action (the enactive mode), through imagery (the iconic mode) and through symbols (the symbolic mode). As Kaput (1987) noted, representation can be used to support personal thinking about ideas and to communicate them to others. Lesh (1979) has also suggested a number of modes of representation in addition to real-life situations and spoken symbols. These are manipulative aids, pictures and written symbols all of which children experience in the pre-school years and which, as shown in the writer's chapter on mathematics, play a significant role in school learning.

The world of school, however, as shown by Donaldson (1978) and Tizard and Hughes (1984) is discontinuous with the rest of the child's world. It is a 'decontextualized' world, only indirectly linked with the child's existing experience, where new meanings must be more explicitly negotiated. It is a world where children learn new roles and responsibilities in new relationships with new adults. Although both the home and the school have an educational function, as Wells (1985) noted, school complements the home's informality through the introduction of more formal ways of acquiring knowledge. Scardamalia and Bereiter (1989) also emphasized that whilst children may enter school with elementary linguistic or numerical competencies, acquired in supportive environments the role of education is to go beyond supporting 'natural' competence. In this regard of particular concern are those children whose home environments have not supported the development of such early competencies.

Children's Subject Knowledge

With children's learning, as with teachers', an association between subject matter knowledge and performance is well-established.

Research in the area of development of subject matter knowledge supports the view that effective learners bring more applicable knowledge to new learning tasks than do less successful ones. 'Expert' learners bring more detailed and elaborated representations of knowledge domains than non-experts. A major purpose of this book is to provide definitions of the young learner's acquisition and use of knowledge and skills in different domains.

Flavell (1985) has summarized the differences between knowledge of experts and novices as more domain-specific concepts embedded in a richer, interrelated network. Differences also lie in more efficient planning and effective learning strategies. Schema theory, mentioned by Linda Thompson (chapter 2), is widely used in conjunction with understanding how young learners gain knowledge from the written and spoken text (Scardamalia and Bereiter, 1986). A 'schema' is a unit of knowledge which the individual internalizes about objects, situations, events and actions or an organized structure which summarizes knowledge about cases or instances, linked on the basis of their similarity or difference. It is brought into play to help the learner make sense of new situations on the basis of knowledge of existing ones. Children develop schema for 'story grammar', for instance, or grasp of the structure of narratives, which helps the listener to notice characters, settings, problem definition and resolution. This occurs before starting school if children have had enough experience of listening to stories.

This recent emphasis on the development of domain-specific knowledge has even called into question the notion of general change and developmental theory, in particular, Piaget's (again, see Flavell, 1985). As understanding of the development of knowledge within a domain increases, children are seen as moving from novice to expert in different subject areas.

There are a number of implications which arise from these views. The organization of children's knowledge will differ and its organization will influence how they respond to new knowledge. Knowledge structures will change as a result of new learning. Prior knowledge will always provide the basis for the construction of new knowledge.

The importance of relating new knowledge to existing knowledge is emphasized in the present writer's chapter on mathematics where links between formal, school mathematics and the rich, informal mathematics acquired in out-of-school settings are considered. Strategies for counting and knowledge of simple addition and subtraction problems are examples of such informal knowledge (Gellman and Gallistel, 1978; Carpenter, Fennema and Peterson, 1987). Similarly the importance in effective teaching of identifying the child's existing state of knowledge in order to promote change in, for instance, scientific concepts has been considered by Anderson and Roth (1989).

Teachers need to know how children understand different scientific concepts and why they fail to make connections between personal and scientific knowledge if they are to help them develop knowledge which can be used to describe, explain, predict and control their world. The view that most children hold about the working of batteries, for example, has been termed by Anderson

(1980) as the 'consumer model'. Batteries make an electric current and bulbs use it. Electricians and physicists, however, maintain a 'circular flow model' where the current flows out of one battery terminal and back into the other. In order to develop scientific knowledge which is coherent and integrated with personal knowledge of the world, children must modify some beliefs about the working of batteries, as well as strengthen and reorganize others. Since writing this chapter the writer's own attention has been drawn to two further facts:

(i) teachers seem often to ask students to teach children to build simple circuits with switches, bulbs and buzzers;
(ii) students, themselves, are liable still to hold the 'consumer model' view of working batteries.

In this regard there is some evidence to suggest that teachers' understanding of subjects they teach reveals gaps and misconceptions like those of their pupils.

Returning to children's subject knowledge the importance of using children's existing knowledge and problem-solving strategies as a basis for planning future instruction is highlighted as well as the need to provide problem-solving tasks with 'real life' applications. The implications for teaching methods of adopting such an approach are considerable. With respect to the particular focus of this chapter such an approach requires the development of considerable knowledge, in this case about science and about the development of children's knowledge within the domain of science.

The following chapters consider the role of teacher and pupil knowledge from a range of perspectives. They share a focus in National Curriculum subjects which schools are required to teach. The view of learning and teaching presented carries implications for classroom instruction which will be developed more fully in a later chapter.

References

ALEXANDER, R., ROSE, J. and WOODHEAD, C. (1992) *Curriculum Organisation and Classroom Practice in Primary Schools — A Discussion Paper*, London, HMSO.
ANDERSON, B. (1980) 'Pupils' understanding of some aspects of energy transfer', unpublished manuscript cited in McDIARMID, G.W., BALL, D.L. and ANDERSON, C.W. (1989) 'Why staying one chapter ahead doesn't really work! Subject specific pedagogy', in MAYNARD, M.C. (Ed) *Knowledge Base for the Beginning Teacher*, Oxford, Pergamon.
ANDERSON, C.W. and ROTH, K.J. (1989) 'Teaching for meaningful and self-regulated learning of science', in BROPHY, J. (Ed) *Advances in Research on Teaching*, Vol. 1, Greenwich, CT, JAI Press, pp. 265–309.
AUBREY, C. (1987) 'La Vie et L'oeuvre d'Henri Wallon', *Educational Studies*, 13, 3, pp. 281–92.

BALL, D.L. and FEIMAN-NEMSER, S. (1988) 'Using textbooks and teachers' guides: A dilemma for beginning teachers and teacher educators', *Curriculum Inquiry*, 18, pp. 401–23.
BALL, D.L. and McDIARMID, G.W. (1990) 'The subject-matter preparation of teachers', in HOUSTON, W.R. (Ed) *Handbook of Research on Teacher Education*, New York, Macmillan, pp. 437–49.
BLYTH, A. (1991) 'The assessment of humanities', in HARDING, L. and BEECH, J.R. (Eds) *Educational Assessment of the Primary School Child*, Windsor, NFER-Nelson.
BROPHY, J. (Ed) (1991) Introduction to Vol. 2. *Advances in Research on Teaching*. Greenwich, CT, JAI Press.
BRUNER, J.S. (1966) *Towards a Theory of Instruction*, New York, W.W. Norton and Co Inc.
BRUNER, J.S. (1983) *Child's Talk*, Oxford, Oxford University Press.
CALDERHEAD, J. and MILLER, E. (1985) 'The integration of subject matter knowledge in student teachers' classroom practice', paper presented at the annual meeting of the British Educational Research Association, Sheffield.
CARLSEN, W.S. (1991) 'Subject-matter knowledge and science teaching: A pragmatic perspective', in BROPHY, J. (1991) *Advances in Research on Teaching*. Greenwich, CT, JAI Press Inc.
CARPENTER, T.P., FENNEMA, E. and PETERSON, P.L. (1987) 'Teachers pedagogical content knowledge in mathematics', paper presented at the annual meeting of the American Educational Research Association, Washington, DC.
DEWEY, J. (1904) 'The relation of theory to practice in education', in ARCHAMBAULT, R. (Ed) *John Dewey on Education*, Chicago, IL, University of Chicago, pp. 316–38.
DONALDSON, M. (1978) *Children's Minds*, London, Fontana.
FLAVELL, J.H. (1985) *Cognitive Development* (2nd edn) Englewood Cliffs, NJ, Prentice Hall.
GELLMAN, R. and GALLISTEL, C.R. (1978) *The Child's Understanding of Number*, Cambridge, MA, Harvard University Press.
GROSSMAN, P.L., WILSON, S.M. and SHULMAN, L.S. (1989) 'Teachers of substance: Subject matter knowledge for teaching', in REYNOLDS, M.C. (Ed) *The Knowledge Base for the Beginning Teacher*, Oxford, Pergamon Press.
HARLEN, W. (1991) 'The assessment of science', in HARDING, L. and BEECH, J.R. (Eds) *Educational Assessment of the Primary School Child*, Windsor, NFER-Nelson.
KAPUT, J.J. (1987) 'Representation systems as mathematics', in JANVIER, C. (Ed) *Problems of Representation in the Teaching and Learning of Mathematics*, Hillsdale, NJ, Erlbaum, pp. 159–95.
KOZULIN, A. (1986) *Thought and Language. Lev Vygostsky*, Cambridge, MA, MIT Press.
KUHN, T.S. (1970) *The Structure of Scientific Revolutions*, Chicago, IL, University of Chicago Press.
LESH, R. (1979) 'Mathematical learning disabilities: Considerations for identification, diagnosis and remediation', in LESH, R., MIERKIEWICS, D. and KANTOWSKI, M.G. (Eds) *Applied Mathematical Problem Solving*, Columbus, OH, ERIC/SMEAR.
LORTIE, D. (1975) *Schoolteacher: A Sociological Study*, Chicago, IL, University of Chicago Press.
MATTHEWS, D. (1987) 'The young child's early representation and drawing', in BLENKIN, G.W. and KELLY, A.V. (Eds) *Early Childhood Education. A Developmental Curriculum*, London, Paul Chapman Publishing.

NATIONAL CURRICULUM COUNCIL (1993) *The National Curriculum at Key Stages 1 and 3*, York, NCC.

OFFICE FOR STANDARDS IN EDUCATION (1993) *Curriculum Organisation and Classroom Practice in Primary Schools: A Follow-up Report*, London, DFE Publications Centre.

PETERS, R.S. (1977) *Education and the Education of Teachers*, London, Routledge and Kegan Paul.

SCARDMAMALIA, M. and BEREITER, C. (1986) 'Research on written composition', in WITTROCK, M.C. (Ed) *Handbook of Research on Teaching*, New York, Macmillan.

SCARDAMALIA, M. and BEREITER, C. (1989) 'Conceptions of teaching and approaches to core problems', in MAYNARD, M.C. (Ed) *Knowledge Base for the Beginning Teacher*, London, Pergamon.

SMITH, D.C. and NEALE, D.C. (1991) 'The construction of subject-matter knowledge in primary science teaching', in BROPHY, J. (Ed) (1991) *Advances in Research on Teaching*, Greenwich, CT, JAI Press.

SHULMAN, L.S. (1986) 'Those who understand: Knowledge growth in teaching', *Educational Researcher*, February, pp. 4–14.

TIZARD, B. and HUGHES, M. (1984) *Young Children Learning*, London, Fontana.

WELLS, G. (1985) *Language, Learning and Education*, Windsor, NFER-Nelson.

WILSON, S.M., SHULMAN, L.S. and RICHERT, A.E. (1987) '150 Ways of knowing: Representation of knowledge in teaching', in CALDERHEAD, J. (Ed) *Exploring Teaching Thinking*, London, Cassell, pp. 104–24.

Chapter 2

Subject Knowledge: The Case for English

Linda Thompson

We are always seeking more effective ways of teaching children in school and more appropriate ways of preparing people for the teaching profession. In pursuit of these goals the term *subject knowledge* is being increasingly used. This chapter will explore what this term means for the teaching of English during the early years of schooling.

What Do We Mean by the Subject Knowledge of English?

What do we mean when we talk about the subject knowledge of English? Do we mean a body of subject specific knowledge or do we mean an accumulation of facts, information and skills? Indeed, if we did mean the latter, what would these be? It is of course easier to pose these questions than it is to find satisfying answers. Various typologies of knowledge exist. Discussions on the topic of subject knowledge in the school curriculum include reference to procedural, conceptual, analogical, logical and received knowledge. However, none of these help with clarifying what is meant by the term *the subject knowledge of English*.

Current descriptions of the psychological and social dimensions of language use draw on a common vocabulary which includes terms like *schemata* (Bartlett, 1932); *frames* (Bateson, 1972) and *scripts* (Schank and Abelson, 1977). These terms are now well-established and will be taken as a starting point for exploring what is meant and understood as the subject knowledge of the English language.

Schemata, Frames and Scripts

The term schema was originally used by Bartlett (1932) to describe organizational or contextual structures. People anticipate social events, situations and indeed other people and their behaviour, in terms of previous experiences of similar contexts, events and situations. For example, on the basis of the experience of the first day at school, children construct expectations about subsequent experience of schooling. These schemata or *structures of expectation* (Tannen, 1979) encourage the anticipation of future events and expectations of likelihood based on previous experiences of similar or dissimilar events. In developing these expectations, individuals nurture personal beliefs and value systems. These include for example, assumptions and expectations about a variety of things, people, places, roles and responsibilities including what to say and how to behave appropriately in given situations. For example, after only a short time in school, children become aware of the specific behaviour expected of children at school. They quickly learn to become pupils (Willes, 1983). Schemata also play an important role in guiding people's behaviour in situations which require highly regulated and ritualized patterns of behaviour, for example, doctor-patient encounters, pupil-teacher interactions, telephone conversations, and service encounters like waiter/waitress-customer interactions. These situations, like all language situations, are bound by the norms of behaviour specific to the culture and society in which they occur. They are culture bound and context dependent. However, what is appropriate behaviour in one context between participants may not necessarily be appropriate to a different context even with the same participants. For example, a group of children would be expected to behave differently in different contexts even within the school setting, for instance, in the classroom and in the playground.

Frames are another aspect of the subject knowledge of language use. The notion of interactive frames was first explored by Bateson (1972). The term has also been used by discourse analysts (Sinclair and Coulthard, 1975; Tannen and Wallat, 1982) to show the ways in which people signal significant developments during conversation. For example:

Anyway (frame) I'd better be off now

indicates the intention to terminate an interaction while:

Well (frame) how are things going?

indicates the opposite intention.

Similarly, the concept of scripts contributes to the subject knowledge of language. These emerged from attempts by computer scientists to create programs which were capable of understanding human language. It soon became clear that computers, while capable of recognizing a word like school, would not be able to associate with the use of that word all of the elements of the word which would represent the human construct of its meaning. The concept of scripts accounts for the cognitive connections made by individuals to construct a semantic map, or personal understanding of words. In everyday conversations these connections are made at the intuitive level of language use and individuals remain unaware of the processes in which they are engaged. Schank and Abelson (1977) defined scripts as 'a predetermined, stereotyped sequence of actions that defines a well-known situation'.

Schemata, scripts and frames are important sets of knowledge for language learners. They include the social dimension of language use and stress the interdependence of language use and social behaviour. They respect the strict rules which govern language use and accompanying appropriate social behaviour and account for the development of social cognition as an aspect of language learning.

Metalinguistic Awareness, Subject Knowledge, KAL or What?

Various terms have been coined to discuss the nature of learning and teaching English as a curriculum subject. Do the various terms have any shared elements or do they each represent different perspectives on a common theme? This section will outline the most commonly used terms in the discussion and attempt to identify similarities and differences between them.

Terms used include, *metalinguistic awareness, language awareness* and *knowledge about language* (KAL). Although variously described, these terms do share common elements. Levelt *et al*, (1978, p. 5) used the term language awareness to mean implicit knowledge which has become explicit. Read (1978, p. 70) reinforced this definition by suggesting that language awareness is focusing one's attention on something which one already knows, while Tinkel (1985, p. 39) extended these definitions to include an element of external facilitation in the process of developing awareness by suggesting that language awareness involves exploring already possessed intuitive language abilities. Donmall (1985) favoured the term language awareness and defined it as 'a person's sensitivity to and conscious awareness of the nature of language and its role in human life' (p. 7). Her definition included a developing awareness of the pattern, contrast, system, units, categories and rules of language use together with the ability of the individual to reflect upon these aspects of language form and function. It is a view which typifies the British Language Awareness Movement, within which there:

> is considerable emphasis on reflecting on and talking about language, and a clear implication that the teaching of languages involves talking about language in an illuminating way. This requires the establishment of a common, acceptable and adequate metalanguage that is accessible to both teachers and learners. (James and Garrett, 1991, p. 7)

This definition introduces another facet into the subject knowledge debate, namely, the idea that there should be a language for talking about language.

This idea is not wholly novel in the development of English language teaching in British primary schools, although it has recently been raised to a higher profile in discussions about curriculum content. It was, however, in 1975 that the influential Bullock Report (DES, 1975) first suggested that a conscious knowledge of the structure and working of the English language is necessary if it is to be used effectively by children. The idea was picked up and developed in subsequent official curriculum documents on the aims of English teaching (DES, 1984, 1986) which identified:

> a (fourth) aim which applies to all modes of language. That is to teach pupils about language, so that they achieve a working knowledge of its structure and the variety of ways in which meaning is made, so that they have a vocabulary for discussing it, so they can use it with greater awareness, and because it is interesting. (DES, 1986, p. 3)

However, it was not until the publication of the Kingman Report, an enquiry into the teaching of English language, in 1988 that this aspect of the English curriculum was raised to the current high public and professional profile. The terms of reference of the Committee were as follows.

1 To recommend a model of the English language, whether spoken or written which would:
   (i) serve as a basis of how teachers are trained to understand how the English language works;
   (ii) inform professional discussion of all aspects of English teaching.
2 To recommend the principles which should guide teachers on how far and in what ways the model should be made explicit to pupils, to make them conscious of how language is used in a range of contexts.
3 To recommend what, in general terms, pupils need to know about how the English language works and in consequence what they should have been taught, and be expected to understand, ... at ages 7, 11 and 16. (DES, 1988a, p. 73)

The report outlined age-related expectations of pupil performance and knowledge about language. Of particular interest and significance to early years' teachers are those outlined for age 7 (*ibid*, pp. 55–6).

Ironically, a report which set out to inform professional discussion on all aspects of the teaching of English spawned public debate, most of which remained ill-informed about the content of the actual report and mis-focused on teaching style rather than curriculum content.

The curriculum area of English is unique among school curriculum subjects in that there has already been this official pronouncement on the content if not the teaching methods required by the National Curriculum. It is therefore important at this stage to probe some of the assumptions on which the report and its recommendations are based. It is claimed that:

> Learning about language is necessary as a means to increasing one's ability to use and respond to it; it is not an end in itself. It should arise from the activities of talking, listening, writing and reading for real purposes; and take the form of encouraging children's curiosity about language. (DES, 1986, p. 14)

Despite the Kingman Report and its recommendations there remains confusion over explicit teaching of Knowledge About Language (KAL) and in particular the emphasis placed on grammar. It has already been recognized that formal exercises in the analysis and classification of language contributes little to the individual child's ability to use it (*ibid*, para 3.3). There is little evidence from the Kingman Report to support those who have argued for a return to formal grammar teaching as the basis for an English curriculum. However, the Report does suggest that if some attention is given to examining and discussing the structure of the language which pupils *already* use (my emphasis) to speak, write, read or listen to for real purposes, then their awareness of the possibilities of language use can be sharpened. This emphasis is important. Current discussions about the role of subject knowledge in the school curriculum have sometimes suggested it as an alternative primary pedagogy (cf. Alexander *et al*, 1992). It is important to keep clear the distinction between the curriculum content and the teaching methods appropriate to the age, interests and needs of particular children.

The Kingman Report reaffirms a number of views on the teaching of English. It suggests that pupils should learn such grammatical terminology as is useful to them for the discussion of language. But the report cautions that the nature and extent (what and how much) terminology is taught at any given stage must depend on how much the children can assimilate with understanding and what they can apply to purposes they see to be meaningful and interesting. The report further acknowledges that the least able language users are also those least likely to be able to understand the terminology and hence those least likely to find this of personal interest or use. Throughout the report there is sensitivity to the child as the centre of curriculum.

However laudable the recommendations of the Kingman Report are, a word of caution seems appropriate. At present there is little empirical evidence to support either the recommendations or the central tenet that KAL contributes to raising standards of language use for all individuals. Without this support the recommendations may remain potentially interesting possibilities for teachers to explore in the English curriculum but could not wisely be used as the foundation for planning curriculum content and the training needs of the teaching profession.

KAL or Con in Descriptions of Child Language Development

It may be possible to ignore the subject knowledge which children have already acquired when they begin school at 4 years old (or earlier) in some

Subject Knowledge: The Case for English

subject areas, for example, maths and science, but it is less easy to deny even young learners some knowledge of language. They constantly offer proof of their proficiency: Children talk! But is the ability to talk, to perform, sufficient evidence of competence? Chomsky (1980, p. 54) would claim not. It is true that a child speaking is demonstrating intuitive knowledge of the language system but this should not be taken as evidence for the existence of other forms of knowledge about language. When two people talk to each other they communicate ideas via a system of sounds (phonology), words (lexis) within a highly organized structure (grammar). Although at some level, all of these levels are processed by both the speaker and the listeners, neither are necessarily conscious of that processing. Language users, adult or child, do not necessarily have an overt, explicit or conscious knowledge of what they are doing or how they are doing it.

Chomsky recognized this distinction between what individuals can do and their understanding of what they are doing as *linguistic performance* and *linguistic competence*. Linguistic performance on the one hand is an individual's use of language and linguistic competencies, the deep-seated mental state below the level of conscious language use which allows even young children to generate a large set of utterances when they talk. Competence, derived from the innate biological function of a *Language Acquisition Device* (LAD) is intuitive and unique to human beings. It is the competence which Chomsky equated with subject knowledge. Performance on the other hand is language behaviour which can sometimes be determined by non-linguistic (psychological or physiological) factors. Chomsky considered these individual factors combine with wider social attitudes and value systems to influence an individual speaker's actual performance. It should, however, be borne in mind that Chomsky originally used language to demonstrate an individual's knowledge of systems and rules, the parameters and principles, the configurations of the mind for which the structure of language (or grammar) simply serves as evidence. Too frequently this has been misunderstood or misrepresented as knowledge of the grammar system being a prerequisite for language learning. It may account for the narrow focus of much foreign and native language teaching.

Similarly, there is of course the danger that metalinguistic awareness, knowledge of the forms, structure and communicative force of language, together with an ability to talk about it to others, may be equally misrepresented as a prerequisite to any language teaching.

There is a complementary description of language use offered by Hymes (1972) who extended Chomsky's definition to include the use of language in social contexts. He suggested that to learn a language it is insufficient to be merely grammatically competent in the Chomskyan sense, i.e. to know the grammatical rules, the phonological (sound) system and lexis (words) of the language being used. In learning to speak a language the child (or adult) must also be able to demonstrate a *communicative competence*. This he defined as knowing:

> when to speak and when not to, what to talk about, with whom, when, where and in what manner to interact. (p. 277)

To demonstrate a knowledge of language a child therefore needs to have not only a knowledge of the rules of the language system but also a knowledge of the rules which govern social behaviour. Hymes' notion of communicative competence includes Chomsky's concepts of grammatical and pragmatic competence plus the category of performance. Hence, for Hymes a child must not only be able to demonstrate knowledge of grammar, phonology and lexis but must also be able to use this knowledge and behave appropriately in social contexts. However, even appropriate behaviour cannot be taken as indicative of anything more than intuitive knowledge. Romaine (1989, p. 10) identified an incoherence in the term communicative competence and suggested a more integrated approach to language description which does not attempt to describe tacit knowledge and communicative ability separately.

Perhaps it is that individuals depend upon both tacit and social knowledge when they use language. Hymes (1972, p. 282) set out four parameters for this: possibility, feasibility, appropriateness and attestedness in actual performance. Widdowson (1989) however posed an interesting challenge to this when he asked:

> Is it possible for somebody to have knowledge in respect of what Hymes calls possibility, that is to say of the formal properties of a language, and fail to have ability in respect of appropriateness? (p. 130)

To which he suggested Chomsky (1980) might reply:

> I assume that it is possible in principle for a person to have full grammatical competence and no pragmatic competence, hence no ability to use language appropriately, though its syntax and semantics are intact. (p. 54)

The TGAT Report (DES, 1988b) reminds teachers that testing lies at the heart of the National Curriculum. The statements above from Widdowson and Chomsky pose an interesting professional challenge to those responsible for designing tests to monitor children's language abilities. What should be tested and how? (This does not seem the place to pose the most interesting question of all, why!)

Testing, Testing, Testing: How do Children Demonstrate their Subject Knowledge?

There are a number of opinions on how a young child can demonstrate a subject knowledge of language. Widdowson (1989) suggested that it can be characterized in terms of the degree to which the knowledge is accessible to the individual speaker and the degree to which they can analyze the language which they are using. These combined abilities are sometimes referred to as metalinguistic awareness. *Metalinguistic awareness* involves high levels of two components: the ability to analyze linguistic knowledge into categories and the ability to control attentional procedures that select and process specific linguistic information (Bialystok and Ryan, 1985a and 1985b). Hence I would suggest there is tentative agreement that in order to be able to demonstrate an emerging subject knowledge of language young children must demonstrate an element of control over the language which they use.

There is evidence that children do demonstrate an awareness of both the form and function(s) of their language from a very early stage (Clark, 1978, p. 35). Children have demonstrated a realization of inadequate or inappropriate attempts at communicating as revealed through their spoken interaction when communication breaks down and attempts are made at repair strategies, such as reformulating utterances.

Perner (1988) suggested that to demonstrate metalinguistic awareness, an individual should not only be able to focus and reflect on language use but in addition should demonstrate some appreciation that it is language which is being reflected upon. The two components described by Bialystok and Ryan (1985a and 1985b) and outlined above concur with this view. The first of these components, the ability to analyze linguistic knowledge, is responsible for making explicit aspects of language structure such as phonemes, syllables and syntax; while the second component involves the ability to give explicit attention to language context. According to Bialystok (1986), it is only when an individual can demonstrate both of these abilities that evidence of metalinguistic awareness can be claimed. Garton and Pratt (1989) summarized metalinguistic awareness evident at four levels of language use: phonological awareness, word awareness, syntactic awareness and pragmatic awareness.

The lack of consensus in description of the development of metalinguistic awareness in young children should not be used as an argument against its existence or against its inclusion in a school curriculum. Lack of consensus should only suggest caution.

The Development of Subject Knowledge

A number of accounts of the subject knowledge of language use exist, including some descriptive models of development. Clark (1978) presented the case for developing awareness as an integral part of language acquisition, as evidenced through language play (rhymes, puns and riddles) speech repair strategies and explicit judgments about the appropriateness of linguistic forms in given contexts. Karmiloff-Smith (1979, 1984 and 1986) suggested an alternative account. She claimed to have identified three distinct phases in the learning of linguistic forms. Phase 1 is dependent upon implicit procedures in the production of specific linguistic forms, when one form may then be used to perform a range of functions. Phase 2 is where the distinction between form and function is recognized and one common form may be used with several functions. During Phase 2 children may make mistakes in production which they monitor and correct unconsciously. Phase 3 marks an individual's progress towards a conscious access of the components and procedures of redescription. It is the consciousness element contained in this third phase that Karmiloff-Smith defined as metalinguistic awareness. Her model is not directly linked to any particular age or stage of cognitive development. An individual child may operate simultaneously at different phases. Yet the model she suggests is hierarchical and linear. Phase 3 can only occur after the two preceding levels are mastered.

A third account of metalinguistic awareness has been offered by Tunmer, Pratt and Herriman (1984). Their explanation is that metalinguistic awareness is a cognitive process which occurs after the age of 5 years once the individual has passed the concrete operational stage of development. Their view is influenced strongly by Piagetian theory and terminology. Their description is characterized by the use that individuals make of control processes when making explicit judgments about language. Children's speech repair strategies are not included in this data set because they are regarded as automatic, unconscious processes rather than evidence of a conscious control over the language. Birdsong (1989, pp. 16–19) outlined a summary overview of a number of accounts of age related metalinguistic development which he presents as metalinguistic activity and ability.

Hence it can be seen from a number of accounts that there is tentative agreement on one aspect of emergent knowledge about language, namely, that in order to be able to say that a child has achieved a given level of explicit language awareness three factors should prevail; firstly, the child should be able to demonstrate use of the language in their personal repertoire i.e. to use it when they talk; secondly, the child should be able to extemporate from personal use and demonstrate a degree of control or versatility in the language used; and thirdly, there should be a language for talking about language, i.e. a metalanguage.

There are times when even young children demonstrate this developing competence in the classroom. For example, the repair strategies (self-correction) which learners demonstrate when they read aloud would seem to demonstrate both an element of metalinguistic awareness combined with the ability to control some aspects of the related language performance.

If metalinguistic abilities are to provide the subject knowledge base of the English language, opportunities for supporting and teaching them must be provided within the school curriculum.

Opportunities for Metalinguistic Development in the Classroom

What therefore are the implications of these descriptive accounts of metalinguistic development for classroom teachers? I suggest that there are a number of opportunities for developing metalanguage and metalinguistic awareness in the classroom. Many of these opportunities already exist in the form of the common place activities which are to be found concentrated in the familiar learning domains of the nursery and reception class, domains such as the dressing up box, the writing corner, the book corner, the pretend corner, sand tray, water trough, to name just a few. These activities all provide pupils with the opportunities to explore a range of roles. The home corner can be used to practise familiar routines of everyday family life (whatever the composition of the family might be). Rearranging the home corner to a cafe, hospital, optician or a number of other social contexts provides the teacher with the opportunity to model the patterns of language use appropriate to these contexts which may be unfamiliar to the child. Creative play in these learning domains provides pupils with the opportunities to practise new and familiar roles together with appropriate language use in these contexts. Activities at the water trough, sand tray, junk modelling area provide opportunities for the teacher to introduce the language specific to these activities which will help to lay the foundations for the subject-specific language which will be needed for learning across the curriculum in subject areas (like) maths, science and history.

The intrinsic merit of these and similar activities may be considered sufficient justification for including them as learning activities in the classroom. However, further justification can be found from the link between metalinguistic development and general success at school. This has been explained by the role which an enhanced knowledge of metalinguistic development plays in developing literacy. In the study of young children learning in the inner city, Tizard *et al*, (1988) found a significant correlation between children's overt knowledge of the alphabet and awareness of print and later literacy proficiency. There is little evidence to support claims that the study of language confers cognitive advantage and there is little to support those who argue for its inclusion in terms of the enhanced social or psychological benefits which it is claimed it will bring pupils. Indeed it is a pity to argue for its inclusion in the curriculum in these terms as the study of language is patently self-justifying (James and Garrett, 1991, p. 19).

Learners and Teachers: Separate Words for Separate Worlds?

Underlying most of the discussions on subject knowledge has been the assumption that a pupil's learning is dependent in some ways, upon the subject knowledge of the teacher. Frequently missing from these descriptions and subsequent discussions has been the acknowledgement of the ways in which learners arrive at their own forms of knowledge and the possibility that they may independently, perhaps through their own actions and experiences arrive at learning, however defined. Current discussions therefore, with the focus on teachers' subject knowledge is a focus on declarative knowledge which may be imparted or transmitted by any agent external to the learner. There is the possibility that these agents may include inanimate learning aids, such as, books, computers, televisions, audio and video tape recordings etc., as well as human teachers of children.

Central to current discussions about subject knowledge is the notion that the teacher (human or inanimate) needs to be more knowledgeable than the learner. This would seem to preclude the possibility of learning as a joint venture and the possibility of teaching itself being a learning process. Yet this would seem to conflict with successful current primary practice which includes, for example, peer tutoring and collaborative group work. It would also seem to undermine the widely-held view that teaching something to another person is a process whereby an individual may arrive at a better personal understanding of that which is being taught. To force a dichotomy between the experiences of teaching and learning (and therefore inevitably between teachers and learners?) may not be the best foundation for forging further education policy and practice. The English language itself reinforces the divide between the processes of learning and teaching, with separate words from separate semantic bases to conceptualize the processes (this is not the case in all languages, Arabic and Swedish are two such examples). While little can be done in the short term to change established use of the language, current discussions raise the more immediate and practical questions, like, how much English does an individual need to know to teach it (successfully) and what is required of learners before they can be judged to have learnt it (successfully)?

It is in the exploration of these questions in relation to the curriculum area of English which demonstrates the potential flaws in subject knowledge as a rationale for teaching children, planning the curriculum and the preparing individuals for the teaching profession. Inherent in the current discussions linking subject knowledge with the professional preparation of teachers is the assumption that there is a link between an individual's primary knowledge repertoire and their ability to teach. This is based on a to date, unfounded premise that an adult can conceptually organize, represent and communicate a personal knowledge repertoire in such a way as to encourage and support a child's learning and understanding. The transfer of an individual's primary knowledge base to another person may however be less straightforward.

Subject Knowledge, the Teacher and the Profession

The introduction of the 1988 Education Reform Act and the subsequent changes in the school curriculum carry implications for initial and in-service teacher education. This section will outline some of the changes perceived as necessary as a result of these developments. Since 1986 the Council for the Accreditation of Teacher Education (CATE) has required that entrants to the teaching profession be able to demonstrate minimum competence in core subjects of English and maths as demonstrated through examination grades at GCSE or 'O' level. As the result of recent changes, current examinations do not adequately cater for the specific needs of entrants to the teaching profession. Moreover, these examination grades have been taken as a bench mark of subject competence and now seem a naively low level expectation.

A more appropriate level of subject competence could be judged by a new examination, *English For Teachers*, administered nationally, specifically designed to assess competence in three aspects of personal use of English: written, spoken and a knowledge of the form and structure of the language. This examination could be taken either at the same time as other national examinations, or later, in the case of mature entrants to the profession.

Changes in the content of the school curriculum since the introduction of the National Curriculum in 1988 have implications for the organization and content of initial teacher education courses however they are perceived. If teachers are to be expected to include the KAL dimension in their classroom work, it would seem appropriate to reconsider the content of initial teacher education. The Bullock Report (DES, 1975, p. 336) stated the necessity for all teachers in training, irrespective of the age range they intend to teach, to complete a substantial core course in language and reading.

To prepare early years' teachers more adequately for their professional role initial education courses should now include the KAL dimension (a knowledge of the forms and structure of spoken and written language) together with more emphasis placed on the understanding of processes involved in child language development and with a particular emphasis on literacy development.

Changes in post-experience teacher education course are now needed. There are currently in schools a number of teachers who qualified before the introduction of the National Curriculum and the attendant increased interest in subject expertise. To meet the professional needs of these teachers English should be included in the Grant for Education and Training (GEST) priorities for INSET funding. These courses could particularly address issues arising from the descriptions of language use which have emerged in the last decade and which have recently been given practical vitality in the form of the LINC teaching materials.

The image of the teacher as the font of all knowledge is bound up with the role and status of teachers in society. Within such a value system it is therefore important that teachers do possess more knowledge than those whom they are teaching. Indeed it is frequently expected that teachers will also possess a vast bank of knowledge beyond that which they will need to teach a particular subject. This expectation is reflected in the current organization of primary schools where one class teacher is responsible for teaching across a range of subject areas. The recent call for subject specialist teaching in primary schools (Alexander *et al*, 1992) reinforces the idea that individuals do have limits to their capacity for learning. Teachers cannot be expected to acquire the subject knowledge necessary to teach the National Curriculum across a range of subject areas but children are expected to learn across the same range of subject areas. The profession should think hard before accepting (the as yet, largely unsubstantiated) arguments for a greater emphasis on subject specialism as a step towards ameliorating standards of pupil achievement. Subject specialism may be misunderstood (or misrepresented) as the basis for enhancing professional prestige (and career prospects) of selected groups. This could lead to divides within the profession between generalists and subject specialists. At a time when a move away from the security of centrally-negotiated national pay scales seems a possibility, nursery and infant school teachers (the majority of whom are women) may find themselves professionally vulnerable.

Final Thoughts

Subject knowledge is a current focus in the debate on education. It would however be an opportunity missed if this current interest was used to build subject boundaries and emphasize subject separateness. We need now to build bridges, forge links and make connections across disciplines so that we arrive at a better *understanding* of what we already know. At present too little is known about the way in which young children learn and the role of external agencies in supporting (or thwarting) them in those processes.

The current focus on subject knowledge is a welcome debate on the nature and purpose of the school curriculum. If the influence of Rousseau (1712–1778) is no longer to prevail in the British primary school curriculum the questions we should be exploring are not only what is to replace it but why?

References

ALEXANDER, R., ROSE, J. and WOODHEAD, C. (1992) *Curriculum Organisation and Classroom Practice in Primary Schools*, London, HMSO.
BARTLETT, G. (1932) *Remembering*, Cambridge, Cambridge University Press.
BATESON, G. (1972) 'A theory of plan and phantasy', in BATESON, G. (Ed) *Steps to an Ecology of Mind*, New York, Chandler, pp. 150–167.
BIALYSTOK, E. and RYAN, E.B. (1985a) 'A metacognitive framework for the development of first and second language skills', in FORREST-PRESSLEY, D.L. *et al*, (Eds) *Metacognition, Cognition and Human Performance*, Orlando, Academic Press, pp. 207–252.
BIALYSTOK, E. and RYAN, E.B. (1985b) 'Towards a definition of metalinguistic skill', *Merrill-Palmer Quarterly*, 31, pp. 229–59.
BIALYSTOK, E. (1986) 'Factors in the growth of linguistic awareness', *Child Development*, 57, pp. 498–510.
BIRDSONG, D. (1989) *Metalinguistic Performance and Interlinguistic Competence*, Berlin, Springer-Verlag.
CHOMSKY, N. (1980) *Rules and Representations*, New York, Columbus University Press.

CLARK, E.V. (1978) 'Awareness of language: Some evidence from what children say and do', in SINCLAIR, A. *et al*, (Eds) *The Child's Conception of Language*, Berlin, Springer-Verlag.
DES (1975) *The Bullock Report: A Language for Life*, London, HMSO.
DES (1984) *English 5–16*, London, HMSO.
DES (1986) *English 5–16*, (2nd edn), London, HMSO.
DES (1988a) *The Kingman Report: Report of The Committee of Enquiry into The Teaching of English Language*, London, HMSO.
DES (1988b) *National Curriculum. Task Group on Assessment and Testing Report*, London.
DONMALL, B.G. (Ed) (1985) *Language Awareness, NCLE Reports and Papers 6*, London, CILT.
GARTON, C. and PRATT, C. (1989) *Learning to be Literate*, Oxford, Basil Blackwell.
HAKES, E.G., EVANS, J.S. and TUNMER, W.E. (1980) *The Development of Metalinguistic Abilities in Children*, Berlin, Springer-Verlag.
HYMES, D. (1972) 'Competence and performance in linguistic theory', in HUXLEY, R. and INGAMS, E. (Eds) *Language Acquisition: Models and Methods*, New York, Academic Press.
JAMES, C. and GARRETT, P. (Eds) (1991) *Language Awareness in The Classroom*, London, Longman.
KARMILOFF-SMITH, A. (1979) *A Functional Approach to Child Language: A Study of Determines and Reference*, Cambridge, Cambridge University Press.
KARMILOFF-SMITH, A. (1984) 'Children's problem solving', in LAMB, M., BROWN, A. and ROGOFF, R. (Eds) *Advances in Developmental Psychology*, Vol. 3, Hillsdale, NJ, Lawrence Erlbaum.
KARMILOFF-SMITH, A. (1986) 'From meta-process to conscious access: Evidence from children's metalinguistic and repair data', *Cognition*, 23, pp. 95–147.
LEVELT, W., SINCLAIR, A. and JARVELLA, R.J. (1978) 'Causes and functions of linguistic awareness in language acquisition: Some introductory remarks', in SINCLAIR, A., JARVELLA, R. and LEVELT, W. (Eds) *The Child's Conception of Language*, Berlin, Springer-Verlag, pp. 1–14.
PERNER, J. (1988) 'Developing semantics for theories of mind: From propositional attitudes to mental representations', in ASHINGTON, J., HARRIS, P.L. and OLSON, D.R. (Eds) *Developing Theories of Mind*, Cambridge, Cambridge University Press.
READ, C. (1978) 'Children's Awareness of Language with Emphasis on Sound Systems', in SINCLAIR, A. *et al*, (Eds) *The Child's Conception of Language*, Berlin, Springer-Verlag, pp. 65–82.
ROMAINE, S. (1989) *The Language of Children and Adolescents*, Oxford, Basil Blackwell.
SCHANK, R. and ABELSON, R. (1977) *Scripts, Plans, Goals and Understanding*, Hillsdale, NJ, Lawrence Erlbaum.
SINCLAIR, J.M. and COULTHARD, R.M. (1975) *Towards an Analysis of Discourse*, London, Oxford University Press.
SINCLAIR, A., JARVELLA, R.V. and LEVELT, W. (1978) *The Child's Conception of Language*, Berlin, Springer-Verlag.
TANNEN, D. (1979) 'What's in a frame?', in FREEDLE, R.O. (Ed) *New Directions in Discourse Processing*, Vol. 2, Norwood, NJ, Ablex, pp. 137–183.
TANNEN, D. and WALLATT, C. (1982) 'Interactive frames and structure schemes in interaction: Examples from a paediatric examination', Paper presented at Seminar on Natural Language Comprehension, St. Paul, Les Durances, France.

TINKEL, A.J. (1985) 'Methodology related to language awareness', in DONMALL, B.G. (Ed) *Language Awareness*, National Congress on Language in Education (NCLE), Report 7, Paper 6, London, Centre of Information for Language Teaching (CILT), pp. 37–45.

TIZARD, B. *et al*, (1988) *Young Children at School in the Inner City*, London, Lawrence Erlbaum.

TUNMER, W., PRATT, C. and HERRIMAN, M. (Eds) (1984) *Metalinguistic Awareness in Children: Theory, Research and Implications*, Berlin, Springer-Verlag.

WIDDOWSON, H.G. (1989) 'Knowledge of language', *Applied Linguistics*, 10, 2, pp. 128–37.

WILLES, M. (1983) *Children into Pupils: A Study of Language in Early Schooling*, London, Routledge and Kegan Paul.

Chapter 3

Knowledge About Drama

Peter Millward

What do we mean when we speak of subject knowledge? What do we need to know about a subject in order to teach it? We need to know about the matter of the subject (the people of history or mathematical concepts) and we need to know about the way the subject works (historical method or mathematical processes). We need, as teachers, to know how children make sense of the subject: how they know about history or mathematics and how they manage to do history or mathematics. These are things we need to know. But drama may not be quite like history or mathematics.

Drama as a Subject

It is not easy to see drama as a school subject with a distinctive body of knowledge which teachers could know about. Drama is not one of the foundation subjects of the National Curriculum and has to depend on its place in the English documents in order to be treated as a worthwhile area of study. Unfortunately, this may not be the securest of havens, for the subject matter of English is not immediately apparent (Protherough *et al*, 1989, chapter 3) and drama, as it is featured in the programmes of study for English (DES, 1989, p. 24), does not look very much like a subject. Drama in Key Stage 1 looks rather more like a way of working: a method of teaching or a tool for learning. It is hardly possible to point to role play, mantle of the expert, hotseating and so forth (*ibid*, C6) without seeming to focus on teaching and learning activities. There is no hint here of dramatic content. In Key Stage 2 this dramatic activity is developed to include performance type drama (Bolton, 1979) but there is still no attempt to describe the subject matter of drama. Indeed, that which one might consider to be the proper content of drama (playscripts, for instance, or the history of the theatre or stagecraft) is hardly the stuff of the early years curriculum. It might be quite easy to identify the skills in drama and very difficult to point to a knowledge base for drama. We may not be surprised that drama is not a foundation subject for we may begin to feel that it is not really a subject at all. We may even wonder what it is doing in a book about subject knowledge.

Of course we might find ourselves in this doubtful state because we are seeking a knowledge base in the wrong place. We might be peering around in drama when we should be looking at the experiences we create, and live through, in drama. It is more than just interesting that people who write about drama in education often present their ideas through case studies and sample lessons (Wagner, 1979; Neelands, 1984; Heathcote, 1984; Bolton, 1992, for example). It seems that all of these writers have to provide some content in order to show how drama works. It looks as though the subject matter of drama is separate from the activity (in the way that a book is always about something) and that doing drama means engaging with a subject in a dramatic way. In reading these accounts one quickly gets the impression that the subject content of drama is located in the children's lives and that the purpose of drama is to help them to make more sense of their experiences (both within and without school). Drama looks very like a collection of practices for exploring our social experiences and for exploring the subject matter of our lives. This is hardly surprising; after all, it is the way that drama has ever worked in society. We need not be apologetic or defensive when drama is called a tool for learning; neither should we be overly concerned if people wish to deny it status as a subject. What is important, is that we appreciate how drama can be used to develop children's understanding, for then we might see how it can work to make formal knowledge part of a child's social experience. Drama can help children to understand subjects differently, but it can also help them to fold those subjects into the fabric of their lives. There is a sense in which drama can help to make more personal the formal knowledge presented to early years children, and the drama teacher (or the teacher using drama) has the opportunity to engage with young children in the 'guided reinvention of knowledge' (Wells, 1987, p. 218).

We are likely to be disappointed if we try to relate what teachers need to know about drama to the subject matter of drama. A more promising approach would be to focus on the communicative process of dramatic discourse, and this might helpfully be explored by looking at the way drama relates to the everyday world of the child's experience and how it connects with the subjects of the formal curriculum. This will mean looking, as well, at the nature of the relationship between teachers and pupils who are working to present the social life in a dramatic way. These relationships are at the heart of drama in education. They are powerful and dynamic, and they are relationships which we, as teachers, need to know about.

The Relationship Between Dramatic and Everyday Experience

One of Carol Aubrey's key concerns in the first part of this book is to emphasize the active engagement of young children in contributing to social contexts which give meaning to their lives (chapter 1, pp. 7–8). If children manage to make sense of the world about them (and, like most adults, they generally do) then it must be done by taking part in the everyday business of social living. Children construct the world around them even as they are bound by it and they do this, primarily, through their use of language. They learn what it means to contribute in an appropriate manner by being attentive to one another and mindful of the way the world works. Their contributions (in language and actions) are made appropriate in the manner through which they are presented and in the way through which they are received. The process is characterized by collaboration and negotiation and a concern to maintain a sense of identity in an (apparently) shared in common and meaningful world. This is not just an account of the social dimension to learning (Vygotsky, 1978) but also an account of the way in which we make the social world visible (and hence meaningful) to ourselves and each other. It is an account of how we construct our lives as well as an account of how we learn about our lives. Consider, for a moment, the context of the infant classroom made visible (and meaningful) in the words and actions of teachers and pupils. Consider the narrowly-defined context of teacher/pupil talk (Willes, 1983) and consider how the roles of teachers and pupils are contained in, whilst they are yet described by, the manner in which they engage with each other through their language and their actions. Consider the reflexive quality of the words which are used to 'indicate' the context even as they are made meaningful by taking account of that context. The managed, collaborative quality of the engagement is immediately apparent. We are not simply teachers and pupils. Rather do we have to continually present to ourselves and to one another our 'teacherness' and our 'pupilness' and we do that through our use of language and through the ways in which we engage with one another. The teacher/pupil context, the context of the classroom, is continually managed and so is every other aspect of our social experience. We present our daily lives through the use of conventional rules and procedures embedded in our language and in our actions and featured in our culture. They are the rules by which we demonstrate that we are teaching or shopping or having an argument (Edwards and Mercer, 1987, p. 32). Furthermore, these contexts are managed from moment to moment and at no time can we simply say they exist and expect them to be (Harré, 1983). We might feel that they have an existence beyond the work that we do to make them visible, but that is because we generate and live through familiar contexts which can be produced and reproduced without a thought (Bolton, 1992). Whether it is apparent or not, all of these everyday contexts have to be continually sustained and that demands a continual presentation of the everyday experience. We are all involved and no one can escape responsibility by doing nothing. The everyday world has to be kept ever before our eyes (Handel, 1982).

We may feel that this account of the way we construct our everyday lives is rather like our everyday understanding of drama. It seems likely that most of us would agree, for example, about the managed quality of our dramatic contexts. Most of us would agree that they are sustained by the words and actions of those involved (and by the interpretations of those who stand and watch). Most of us would agree that the presentation of dramatic experience is a collaborative engagement in which participants are attentive to one another and to the developing context of which they are a part. Indeed, this looks very much like the description we have just given of everyday life and it may be apparent that drama is not just about the stuff of our daily lives but draws upon the same culturally-bound methods and procedures which are used to make our lives visible, meaningful and available to be shared. All of this might be made clearer if we look at a very ordinary extract taken from a piece of drama. Here is an example of Dorothy Heathcote (a very extraordinary drama teacher) edging some early years children into drama. She is in the process of shifting attention from everyday to make-believe contexts and both contexts are illuminated by her words.

Two children are sitting on chairs. They are a king and queen and they have lost their baby. The teacher has suggested that the remaining children and herself should be citizens who might help to find the missing baby. The following piece of dialogue then occurred.

1 *Teacher*: Are we going to help them?
2 *Children*: Yes.
3 *Teacher*: Would you like to stand up? Would you mind
4   first coming to the palace with me? Shall
5   we go together? (Heathcote, 1972)

We need to know very little about this tiny and unremarkable fragment of drama in order to appreciate that the words serve to present the everyday and dramatic contexts and that they are meaningful in both the everyday and dramatic contexts. The teacher's first question, 'Are we going to help them?' (1), can be seen as a question asked by a teacher of her pupils 'Are we going to help them (by taking part in the drama)?' or as a question by the teacher in role as a leading citizen and directed towards a group of citizens, 'Are we going to help them (find their baby?)'. The question indicates both contexts (the make-believe and the everyday), and both are indicated and available at the same time. The children's response, 'Yes' (2), can also be seen as agreement by the pupils to take part in the drama or as agreement within the drama to help the teacher in the role as the leading citizen. In both cases it represents agreement to take part ('Yes [we will take part in the drama]' or 'Yes [we will help them find their baby]' — meaning that they are taking part). The teacher's questions which follow can be taken in both contexts even as they illuminate both contexts. The first, 'Would you like to stand up?' (3) suggests that she is marking the everyday context of teachers and pupils preparing for drama but it would not be inappropriate within the dramatic context. The other two questions (3) suggest the dramatic context but would certainly work in the everyday context of teacher and early years pupils preparing for drama. What is important, of course, is that there are no instructions accompanying these questions which tell the children how they should be taken. It is up to them to actively make sense of the words by constructing a context within which they are made sensible. Furthermore, it is quite possible for the children to interpret them in different ways and for some of the children to be working within the drama whilst others are preparing to get into drama. It is important, as well, to appreciate that whilst the teacher might be quite clear in her own mind which context she is seeking to present through her words, it is not enough to ensure that they are taken in that way. We cannot simply 'mean' something, for the way in which words and actions are made meaningful depends as much on the way in which they are taken. This is the sense in which context is 'essentially a mental phenomenon' and the 'common knowledge of the speakers invoked by the discourse' (Edwards and Mercer, 1987, p. 160). It is a collaborative business and all are involved. Social experience has to be constructed and presented in both everyday and make-believe contexts.

At this early stage in the drama, and when it is just coming to life, the teacher's words are working to construct two quite distinct social contexts. Some of her words edge into the everyday teaching context whilst some are firmly rooted in the make-believe context of the princess and her palace; all of them can be interpreted in both contexts. This is significant, for it means that drama of this kind cannot be seen as some kind of imitative activity (a pale shadow of life itself) but rather as the very stuff of life, both in its focus of interest and its procedures for making contexts visible. Later, and as the drama gets more clearly established, the words will work to give primacy to the dramatic context; though even then, the everyday context — of a teacher and a group of children doing drama — will nearly always be recoverable (Millward, 1990).

Of course drama is different from everyday life but the major part of that difference lies in our agreement to treat it as make-believe. We do this by demonstrating that it is make-believe. This is in contrast with our presentation of everyday contexts in which we play down the make-believe and managed quality. We see dramatic contexts as make-believe because the participants are seen to be attentive to the methods and practices by which they create those contexts, and they are the same methods and practices which, generally speaking, we fail to mark in our everyday lives (Bolton, 1992, chapter 1). Drama is different from everyday life in that we are aware of managing the dramatic context and are treated as managing the dramatic context. In our ordered, regular and familiar lives there is little sense of this managed quality. In drama, it is as if we are adopting Britton's more reflective 'spectator' role whilst yet being participants (Britton, 1972, chapter 3). This is important, for it reaches to the heart of the significance of drama. Drama is life-like in that it is true to the practices through which our social life is made visible, but it is different from life in that it demands an extra level of awareness. Drama puts us in touch with our lives and in touch with the ways in which we construct our lives. There is a reflective edge to all dramatic experience, a 'distancing process' (Bruner, 1986, p. 127) which enables the learner to focus on his or her learning.

Young children create contexts in their imaginative play and in their drama in the way that they present contexts in their everday lives; they are 'at home' with this kind of activity. The interesting question is no longer directed towards uncovering the differences between everyday and make-believe experience, but rather towards wondering how it is that we demonstrate that we are treating certain aspects of our managed experience as being real (and as existing beyond the work we do to present and sustain them). This is likely to be too great a knot for us to untie just now, but we might at least appreciate that part of the answer must lie in the way in which we manage to show that we are not only 'living through' our drama but are also aware of the dramatic quality of this living through experience. There is, as well, an aesthetic dimension to our drama.

Drama and Subject Knowledge

In an early draft of the proposals offered to the National Curriculum Council by the History Working Party, and at a stage when drama was seen as a helpful way of developing children's historical understanding, an important caveat was introduced. Whilst promoting drama as a valuable tool for learning about history, the working party expressed concern that it might be seen as just an opportunity for the children to dress up and play at being, say, kings and queens. Clearly, they felt that such an activity would do little to develop the children's understanding of history. They were surely right. What they did not say, was that it would probably do very little, as well, to help them make sense of drama. Dressing up might be heaps of fun but it is not drama and it is not history. When drama is used to develop children's understanding in history, the contributions made by the teacher and the children must work within the dramatic context whilst yet being faithful to the demands of historical enquiry. Recreating scenes from history might be very enjoyable and might be challenging on all kinds of levels, but such activities are likely to emphasize the 'illustrative/performance' type of drama (Bolton, 1992, p. 23) rather than 'dramatic playing' which has the existential and dynamic quality which puts the children in touch with their own lives. Unfortunately, it seems as if this is what may yet happen in history. Whilst drama is presented in the history documents as an opportunity to 'help pupils understand the motives and behaviour of people in the past' (DES, 1991, C11), it is linked to the communication of historical knowledge and understanding rather than to the development of historical enquiry. The emphasis is upon the 'illuminative/performance' type of drama in which, for instance, children should be helped to 'show understanding of an event through mime' or encouraged to 'act out a story about the past' (DES, 1991, C16), and not upon 'dramatic play'. The non-statutory guidance for Key Stage 1 in history emphasizes the performance quality in drama whilst in the

Knowledge About Drama

English documents for Key Stage 1 it is the existential quality which is being stressed. This is not helpful, for the dramatic activity should illuminate both the dramatic and the historical contexts and in ways that are sensitive to the demands of drama and to the understanding of history. It is difficult for early years children to achieve this whilst working in the performance mode (Bolton, 1992, p. 23). Not only is it important that the drama teacher knows about history but that he/she is prepared to develop the spirit of historical enquiry and that is more likely to be achieved with early years children whilst working in the dramatic playing mode. This, of course, is a nice challenge for the teacher who means to use drama to help the children make sense of history, for it will need to be done through the meaning-making activity of dramatic playing rather than by putting on plays for assemblies (perhaps to show others what we have learned).

Here is a tiny example from a piece of drama with a group of reception-aged children. The children are trying to help the teacher (who is in role as one of their neighbours) get in touch with the police by telephone. They have found a box and they are having some difficulty in deciding what ought to be done with it. One of the children suggests they telephone the police, and the teacher in role as one of a group of neighbours asks for the telephone number. Someone says 999. The teacher in role dials the number, is connected to the police and asks for advice about the box. It is clear that the police are not pleased and the teacher in role gets quite agitated as he talks to them:

```
1    Teacher:   I'm sorry ... sorry to have bothered you ... no ...
2               it's all right ... no ... sorry ... sorry.
3               (He replaces the receiver)
4               That was wrong.
5               You told me to ring the police ... 999 and that's
6               for an emergency. This isn't an emergency/
7    Andrew:                                              888
8    Teacher:                                                  is it?
9    Andrew:    It might be 888.
10   Michael:   It's not ... it's ... em/
11   Teacher:   Can anyone remember? Does anyone/
12   Andrew:                                       777 ... for not
13              quite an emergency.
```

An extract like this is amusing as well as illuminating. The drama was not being used to develop the children's understanding of mathematics, but it does enable us to see how contributions in drama can work to elaborate the dramatic context as well as, in this case, mathematical understanding. Andrew is drawing on his knowledge of numbers and number value to indicate the context they are managing through their drama. He is using his mathematical knowledge to illuminate the dramatic context and show it to be less than a full-scale 999 emergency. At the same time, and reflexively, the context in which Andrew talked about the numbers ('not quite an emergency') gave the numbers significance. His words are appropriate within the dramatic context and appropriate in terms of his mathematical understanding. They also tell the teacher something about the child's view of the dramatic context and his appreciation of number value. Even a tiny bit like this can show the dynamic quality of the learning that is possible when drama and mathematics are linked in this way, for the learning has a special quality. Andrew's contribution is appropriate within the drama even though it is wrong (in that 888 will not get the kind of police who would be pleased to help them with their problem). It is for this reason that it does not threaten the drama and the children are shortly making contact with a special group who use the 777 number. At the same time, his words demonstrate a mathematical concern for numbers and, whilst the justification for using 777 might be inadequate, it is based on a certain level of understanding and a respect for numbers (the significance of greater and lesser numbers, for example). Once again, it is not inappropriate. What we see here is the child using his formal knowledge of mathematics to present a personal contribution to a context which he is collaboratively engaged in developing. It has that 'living through', spontaneous, existential quality and it is a lovely example of a child making formal knowledge work in his world and on his terms. His use of formal mathematical knowledge is imaginative and generative. He applies his knowledge in an original way. His knowledge is used to enrich his life and to enrich the lives of those sharing in the presentation of the dramatic context (and that includes those who read this chapter and recreate and enjoy the dramatic context for themselves). For what we have here is a completed relationship. The drama is the link between the child's experience of everyday life and the formal structures of mathematics. His words, '777 for not quite an emergency', draw upon everyday life and the subject knowledge of mathematics and they are used to create a dramatic context within which the participants feel at home and within which they can fare forward. This connects with a particular account of understanding as 'knowing how to go on from here' (Wittgenstein, 1978, para. 154), and it seems important that we should seek to generate situations in which young children can use their knowledge to illuminate their lives. We are headed towards a 'cultural communicative model of education' (Edwards and Mercer, 1987) in which,

> children are helped and guided into an active, creative participation in their culture (within which) education is seen as the development of joint understanding. (p. 36)

The child's words are produced in a context which is familiar to the children. It is familiar in the way that it has been collaboratively constructed (a persistent feature of their lives) and in the way that it reflects their lives (they brought the neighbours and the police into the drama, for example). His words are produced in the context but then serve to sustain and develop the context. In a short while, and as a result of this child's contributions, the drama will move away into new directions as the participants get in touch with the 777 service ('the not quite emergency service') and talk with policemen and policewomen who can tell you how to handle missing boxes. You might be interested to know that they also deal with kittens up trees, children stuck in railings and parents and teachers who act unfairly. Vygotsky (1978) considered it is an essential feature of learning that the child be able to interact with people in his/her environment and in cooperation with peers (p. 90). Drama offers people the opportunity to show they know more than they think they know.

Drama and the Relationship Between the Children and their Teacher

At the heart of the link between the child's everyday life and the formal structures of subject knowledge is the teacher and, most potently, the teacher in role. When the teacher is working in role, and within the drama, he/she is using the dramatic context to guide the children's experiences and to guide the course of their understanding. It is at this point that the teacher is able to support the children in their learning for it is at this point, and within a shared in-common context, that he/she is most likely to be attentive to their levels of understanding and most likely to be in touch with the child's level of potential development (Vygotsky, 1978, p. 86). It is within this collaboratively developed context that Bruner's ideas about teacher support and 'scaffolding' (Bruner, 1983) are readily applicable. The teacher in role is not just taking part in the drama but teaching through a role in the drama. It means contributing to the dramatic context whilst keeping one foot firmly in the classroom. The extent to which at any moment, for example, Dorothy Heathcote emphasized her role as the children's teacher or her role as a leading citizen with a bit of a problem is likely to vary, but if the 'teacher presence' is too apparent then the dramatic role will be threatened. Furthermore, if the teacher's role is threatened then so, too, are the roles of the other participants. If the teacher does not take part properly there will be no dramatic context and no drama. The teaching might carry on, of course, and it might be very effective, but the drama would have been snuffed out. If the teacher is concerned to work through drama with the children, then he/she has to look after the dramatic context and that must be the first concern. However, it cannot be the only concern. It is possible to imagine, for instance, and at the other extreme, the teacher getting 'lost' in the dramatic context and being so involved that all traces of the teacher role have disappeared. There is no place for this kind of indulgence in dramatic playing in schools for the drama would have lost its purpose and could no longer serve the interests of the children's education. As teachers we need to know that anyone working in role to develop the children's understanding has to teach (and be seen and treated as a teacher) whilst yet contributing to the management of the dramatic context. It all sounds very difficult and rather puzzling, but it happens quite easily when you teach in role.

It should be apparent that a teacher wanting to use dramatic playing as a teaching and learning opportunity, has to accept real constraints on the way he/she can relate to the children. One of the ways in which dramatic (or everyday) contexts are made visible is by marking the relationships which are developed between participants (even as these relationships are made visible within a specified and developing context). Whilst the pupil/teacher relationship is characteristic of teaching contexts (and helps to describe those contexts) it will do little to present a dramatic context in which, say, an influential member of the court is trying encourage the king and queen to make decisions about their lost baby. The only contexts presented through teacher/pupil relationships (and the only contexts within which they are visible) are teacher/pupil contexts (either everyday or dramatic). The drama teacher has to 'play down' the teacher/pupil relationship in order to build up the relationship that might exist between a queen and one of her courtiers. The drama teacher has to contribute appropriately to the dramatic context (as, of course, do all the participants) and that means treating the participants in ways which uphold their roles (as kings or queens or courtiers) and not their places as pupils in school. To do anything else would be to threaten the drama. Different roles may provide different opportunities for the teacher to draw upon her 'teacher/pupil relationships' in the presentation of her dramatic role (consider, for instance, the opportunity provided by a role as a leading citizen helping the king and queen). However, these 'teacher/pupil relationships' cannot be allowed to characterize the dramatic relationship for then not only would the chief minister disappear but so, too, the king and the queen, and the drama would die. All that would be left would be a rather disappointed teacher and a group of early years children trying to get some drama going. The teacher in role has to accept a different relationship with the children and a relationship which is sensitive to the developing dramatic context (and that might mean being interrupted by a reception child in role as a neighbour). If this new relationship is not accepted (by the teacher and the children) then there will be no drama and no opportunity to teach through the drama. The dramatic context has to be preserved as an opportunity for teaching and learning and the shift in relationships between teachers and learners gives the children responsibility for creating and sustaining contexts in which they feel at home. If the teacher gets too heavy-handed the drama will crumble before his/her eyes.

It is also important to appreciate that the teacher cannot make the children do drama (anymore than a child can be made to engage in symbolic play). Dramatic play depends upon the agreement of the participants to treat the context of their play as real. You cannot make a child talk to another as though she were a queen; you can only invite them to do so, invite them to take part. Each of the teacher's questions in the first extract was directed towards getting the children's agreement to take part ('Are we going to help them?', 'Would you like . . . ?', 'Would you mind . . . ?', 'Shall we go . . . ?'). If the teacher is to get the children's agreement and if that agreement is to be realized as they take part in the drama and manage to contribute appropriately, then he or she has to make sure that the context of the drama is interesting, engaging and recognizable to the children. The context has to touch their lives.

Dramatic play is different from everyday life and the 'living through' quality of drama is different. But the difference lies not in the nature of drama but in our agreement to treat dramatic discourse as make-believe and as managed from moment to moment. This managed, 'make-believe' quality describes the way we present the everyday social life (though it is rarely explicit and may not easily be recoverable) and it may not be surprising that young children who are clearly experiencing the joy of constructing their own lives should be able to slip so easily into areas of dramatic discourse. If teachers are to use drama to develop children's experience of living and put them in touch with the way they construct their lives, then they must do so from within the dramatic context. They must engage with the children in ways that are attentive to the patterns in their language and the patterns of their lives. Only then may it be possible for them to help young children to make use of their formal knowledge in ways which enrich their dramatic and everyday experiences.

Knowledge about drama is knowing about relationships: relationships between everyday and make-believe discourse, relationships between subject knowledge and personal understanding and relationships between teachers and children. It also means knowing about the possibilities for developing these relationships; it means finding common ground.

References

BOLTON, G. (1979) *Towards a Theory of Drama in Education*, London, Longman.
BOLTON, G. (1992) *New Perspectives on Classroom Drama*, Hemel Hempstead, Simon and Schuster.
BRITTON, J. (1972) *Language and Learning*, Harmondsworth, Penguin.
BRUNER, J. (1983) *Child's Talk*, London, Oxford University Press.
BRUNER, J. (1985) 'Vygotsky: A historical and conceptual perspective', in WERTSCH, J. (Ed) *Culture, Communication and Cognition: Vygotskian Perspectives*, Cambridge, Cambridge University Press.
BRUNER, J. (1986) *Actual Minds, Possible Worlds*, London, Harvard University Press.
DES (1989) *English in the National Curriculum*, London, HMSO.
DES (1991) *History in the National Curriculum*, London, HMSO.
EDWARDS, D. and MERCER, N. (1987) *Common Knowledge: The Development of Understanding in the Classroom*, London, Methuen.
HANDEL, W. (1982) *Ethnomethodology: How People Make Sense*, Eaglewood Cliffs, New Jersey, Prentice-Hall.
HARRÉ, R. (1983) 'An analysis of social activity', in MILLER, J. (Ed) *States of Mind*, London, BBC Publications.

HEATHCOTE, D. (1984) *Collected Writings on Drama in Education*, London, Hutchinson.
MILLWARD, P. (1990) 'Drama as a well-made play', *Language Arts*, 67, 2, pp. 151–62.
NEELANDS, J. (1984) *Making Sense of Drama*, London, Heinemann.
PROTHEROUGH, R. *et al*, (1989) *The Effective Teaching of English*, London, Longman.
VYGOTSKY, L. (1978) *Mind in Society: The Development of Higher Psychological Processes*, London, Harvard University Press.
WAGNER, B.J. (1979) *Dorothy Heathcote: Drama as a Learning Medium*, London, Hutchinson.
WELLS, G. (1987) *The Meaning Makers*, London, Hodder and Stoughton.
WILLES, M. (1983) *Children into Pupils: A Study of Language in Early Schooling*, London, Routledge and Kegan Paul.
WITTGENSTEIN, L. (1978) *Philosophical Investigations*, Oxford, Blackwell.

Video Recording

HEATHCOTE, D. (1972) 'Making Magic: Drama with 6-year-old children'. The original recording is in the University Library, University of Newcastle, UK.

Chapter 4

Can Teachers Use and Make More Explicit their Knowledge of How Writing Works to Help Children Become Writers?

Deirdre Pettitt

Introduction

It is almost a convention when writing about learning to write to ask why school children spend so much time writing when comparatively few adults write a great deal in their daily lives. This is not a good reason for not learning to write of course. Some children may become poets or novelists. Some may aspire to the dizzy heights of the PhD or the gossip columnist. Much of the power to run or change society resides in the hands of those who can express their thoughts coherently in writing or pay others to do this for them. At the more obvious level everyone's life chances are likely to be better if they can for example write a reasonable job application. So learning how to write ensures that opportunities at all levels are open to those who can succeed at writing well for particular purposes. More idealistically it could be hoped that children could also learn that writing, at least some of the time can be an intrinsically rewarding and exciting experience. Additionally there is the practical reason that society expects that education should include being able to write and that its representatives have enshrined this expectation in the National Curriculum. All these reasons are obvious. Alongside them, however, runs the power of writing to clarify thought and the use of writing to learn across the curriculum. In writing what we think we know, we find out what we do not know and struggle with meaning. Wells (1986) puts this succinctly:

> But perhaps the most important reason for advocating a strong emphasis on writing right from the start is its potential as a tool for learning... Writing is, par excellence, the activity, in which we wrestle with thoughts and words, in order to discover what we mean.

He adds the following quotation having been unable to track it to its source but feeling that it is very 'apt'. 'The process itself unfolds the truths which the mind learns. Writing informs the mind, it is not the other way around' (*ibid*).

Writing is not easy. The excitement and pleasure mentioned above are tempered by effort. The contributors to this volume have essayed to write appropriately for its audience and their efforts have been marked by thought, sweat and full wastepaper baskets. Writing appropriately for an audience requires that the text is easy to read by that audience. Easy to read, does not refer to the content which may be complex and difficult but to the expression of that content. It refers to how well the content is rendered intelligible to readers by the writer anticipating their needs. It requires attention to structure, syntax, punctuation and semantic features. It has to be cohesive within and across sentences and paragraphs and employ devices which remind the reader what has gone before and flags up what will follow. If the writer is writing about writing there is an extra feeling of vulnerability. Can she practice what she preaches?

Be that as it may, writing a chapter of a book of this sort demonstrates, to some extent, how writing works. It is an example of writing to learn as well as to share thoughts with others. Each contributor has had to assess and refine what they know or believe. They have had to justify what they write and look again at their evidence. More than that, they have had the discipline of putting their thoughts onto paper using the conventions of written English. This requires them to think how these conventions should be used. How we construct a text affects meaning and meaning affects how the text is constructed. Ideas become more powerful to the reader according to the syntactic choices as well as the words used by the writer. These choices are not automatic. Sentences may be constructed and then turned around for particular effect. If they have become too complex, they may be divided into two or more shorter sentences. However a writer does not think 'I have to make a different syntactic choice here'. *That* has become automatic. But not always. Notice here a deliberate flouting of a rule for emphasis. The emphasis is required because many adult learners, including undergraduates and postgraduates do not appear to have been enabled to construct writing coherently. If this is the case and we can surmise that it also applies to many children in school, there is a sad loss of a powerful tool for learning.

This is a matter for teachers of young children to consider, because as in many areas of the curriculum a good start is crucial and gives colleagues foundations on which to build. The problem is that many young children seem to get rather good at writing without being taught. Of course teaching includes the provision of the models for writing and stimuli which will be discussed later. Similarly it is agreed that building on how children are known to develop in their writing (Temple and Gillet, 1989) can and does work. Robin Alexander (1984) questioned notions like 'learning to read by reading' comparing this to 'learning to sit by sitting'. Nevertheless a good deal of learning to write does occur through writing. However the premise of this chapter is that learning to write should be taught as well as caught. (With acknowledgment to Peters, 1967, who used this phrase in the title of her book '*Spelling: Caught or Taught?*) Learning to write by writing is only justifiable if writing improves thereby. If children spend two years writing, perhaps with teacher-as-scribe and at the end of that period cannot write at all for themselves, action is needed. If able year 2 children are still putting 'and . . . and . . . and' to connect up their texts help is required. Writing is a complex process in which many different skills and concepts are brought together simultaneously. Perhaps it can be accepted that the most important elements are the content: the information, the story, the description; together with the purpose: to inform, to amuse, to record. The content is, of course, dependent on knowledge and experience. You cannot write what you do not know anything about. The purpose also requires experience; that is some knowledge about the recipient or some reasons for making a record. However, conveying content, as has been argued, requires management of structure, syntax and punctuation. For young children problems with the mechanics of writing — spelling and handwriting — also loom large.

Teachers are writers themselves but in order to help children they need to make their knowledge of the process explicit to themselves and perhaps to consider elements of how to write which may be less than obvious. This chapter is about that knowledge and how it might be translated appropriately for young children. Its focus will be on what the writer wants to convey and to whom; the content and how this is managed. Necessarily this has to include something about syntax and punctuation. Handwriting and spelling will not be included. They are important but it is more than likely that teachers are well-equipped to deal with these skills and would prefer discussion about the heart of writing: the content.

Speech and Writing

Children beginning to write in school are using what they already know about language which is considerable. There is a good deal of evidence that this knowledge is not only about speaking but also about writing (Ferreiro and Teberosky, 1982). However, leaving that aside for the moment, it is sensible to suppose that children tend to write what they would say. This is not entirely the case. Very quickly most young children realize that writing is different from speaking. If you ask many young children what they would say — for example about a picture — and then what they might write about it, there is often a clear difference in their replies. They begin to use a sentence-type structure when writing is mentioned. Their experience of hearing stories and observing the writing around them has been absorbed and they have begun to appreciate that there is a difference between speaking and writing. This difference is very important. Until this concept has been developed children are not likely to progress as far as they could as writers.

Speech, in the normal sorts of conversations with which children are familiar at home and in most interactions in school, does not use the syntax of the language in the same way as it is used in writing. This does not refer to informality, slang, dialect, choice of words or 'bad grammar'. It refers to how syntax is employed. In speech, for example, the sentence as it is found in writing rarely occurs. Kress (1982) points out that speech consists of 'chains' of clauses, which are often equal in status and 'weakly' connected. A conversation in a car illustrates what this means.

1   *Speaker A*:   in France// all the cars are damaged//um//at the front and at the side//new ones
2   *Driver*:   parking
3   *Speaker A*:   mm// they shunt backwards and forwards//laughs/ dunno about the sides/jumping red lights
4   *Speaker B*:   the police//they seem to spend most of their time watching traffic lights//we saw vans full//especially taxis and sports cars//red ones//they take hours//all the papers/they keep them in the dash//
5   *Driver*:   never argue with a French policeman

Note that 1 had no introduction. The driver knew that speakers A and B had just been to France. Utterance 2 is a question. It is clear to the conversationalists that in utterance 3 'they' were drivers, 'the sides' refers back to cars and 'jumping red lights' was a question. This made speaker B move onto French policemen, 'vans full' were vans full of police and 'papers' referred to insurance certificates, driving licences and the like. Apparently French policemen seem to have a particular down on red cars, sports cars and taxis. Written-down speech, as in this extract, is often barely intelligible but is perfectly well-understood by the participants.

It can be seen that not only are clauses 'weakly connected' in this sort of conversation but that shared meanings allow it to become extremely elliptical. The more familiar speakers are with each other the less they need to say to make meanings explicit. In a family two words say, 'Aunt Jane' can convey an encyclopaedia of meaning and the family may fall about laughing or become very grave depending on the situation conjured up. In writing shared meanings cannot be taken for granted. In speech the audience is present and participates. This is not just by speaking but by body language such as gestures, nods or looks of incomprehension.

In speech, intonation is crucial to meaning. Speech is not just the words which are said. It includes pauses, gestures and most important of all, the tunes of the language which make statements into questions, questions into orders and a host of other subtle changes from the words to the meaning. In writing explicitness and punctuation have to substitute for these spoken devices. Some spoken language comes closer to writing. This is often when what is spoken has been written down. A newsreader is reading a prepared text. A lecturer might also do but tends to depart from the written text to establish rapport with an audience which is there but generally does not respond by speaking except by invitation. The more people write the more likely it is that they may sometimes 'talk like a book'. However, these instances do not invalidate the argument that speaking is not like writing. Writers have to write for an absent audience and clearly writing as one speaks would normally be very confusing to a reader.

Given that this argument is accepted, it is not hard to see why young writers put 'and . . . and . . . and' to connect their clauses. These substitute for the 'ums' 'ers' and pauses with which we connect spoken language. It is also easy to understand why young writers find the sentence a difficult structure to use. Leaving aside the problems linguists have in defining a sentence, the sort of sentence required by writing is not often found in the spoken discourse with which children are familiar.

Implications for Teaching

Understanding the difficulties children may have does not always help teachers to decide what to do. Our current state of knowledge about how children can reinvent writing has led many teachers to 'process' or 'developmental' writing (Temple and Gillet, 1989). The following examples show how children's writing moves towards the adult model given help and encouragement.

> I sbr a rnbb shrd
> (I saw a rainbow ?)
> A man is huging fgm A sjmk
> (A man is hanging from a ?)
> I wot to look in my mgrr
> (I want to look in my mirror)
> The man has lot the ljyt on the car
> (The man has lit the light on the car)

Other teachers use more traditional methods, normally helping children to compose texts, acting, in the first instance as scribe and then gradually withdrawing support. Still others employ a mixture of methods. These would generally include starting by acting as a scribe but including opportunities for children to write for themselves from the outset. Opportunities to write, whatever teachers' main methods of teaching writing are, might include: writing corners, the shop, the clinic, the travel agent, the ticket office, a school, in fact all the ways with which ingenious teachers transform the environment. Some teachers also reverse the teacher-as-scribe process by writing in 'book writing' under children's early texts.

It is not intended to comment on these methods. Whatever method is used, however, it seems essential that teachers' interactions with the class, groups or individuals should include ways of informing children that writing is different from speaking and that it has to take account of an audience. When teachers work with children during or before the process such opportunities arise. Teachers also need to provide audiences for writing. Teachers themselves provide one of those audiences but this, although it is necessary, is not sufficient. Teachers know too much about the children or so children assume. Why tell teachers what they know? A favourite device for providing another audience in a reception or year 1 class is to have a doll, a puppet or a teddy bear to whom the children can write. (The downside is that teachers have to write the replies.) However, Teddy-as-audience, unlike teachers is unfamiliar with the children's lives and characteristics. His lack of comprehension is one way to underline the differences between speech and writing. He may perhaps go on holiday so that children cannot *tell* or show him anything. Letters of all kinds at all ages are of course, good ways of developing this sense of the needs of an unseen audience. Writing for younger children, books to be published for the class library, newspapers and magazines are obvious additions to the canon of ideas. These and other familiar ploys may be less than helpful however, if teachers do not use them to make the points which have been discussed.

The problem of using sentences is not easy to overcome. Children are likely to use the 'chains' mentioned above and it seems likely that working with them as they write is the major opportunity for making suggestions about connectives, where to end sentences and how to punctuate (Nicholls *et al*, 1989). Teachers may also write, on a flip chart for example, texts which children dictate, where they can discuss the necessary structure and why it is needed. It is probably not helpful to say that a sentence is a complete thought mainly because it often isn't. More profitable may be to have children read their writing aloud. Where to breathe or pause may be a better indicator of where to put a full stop than the 'complete thought' notion.

Working with children may also provide opportunities for suggesting the use of the cohesive devices such as pronouns or other different words for characters in successive sentences (*ibid*). Teachers do work with the youngest children but may do so less often as children become able to write for themselves a little or with some fluency. However, the discussions which can be held with groups of children before and as they write may be essential to their progress. It is also the case that the English Non-Statutory Guidance (NCC, 1990) advise that part of the assessment of children's work should be the observations and notes made of the process. This observation time can also be deployed for teaching by sharing the writing process with children.

Reading what has been written to teachers after the event of writing is also essential. However young children find it very hard and sometimes annoying to alter texts at that point. There are two suggestions which can be made here. One is that as well as reading to teachers children should be encouraged to read their texts to their friends both while they are writing and when they are finished. This sharing (also recommended in the Non-Statutory

Guidance (*ibid*) shifts the audience to one which is present but reading a text is not like conversation. Reading aloud as often as possible enables children to find out, not what they thought they wrote but what they have actually written and whether they themselves as the audience can understand it. If this reading is in the middle of their composition alterations are more likely to occur then than afterwards. Children planning and doing their writing together as soon as possible is also a process helpful to underlining the differences between speech and writing.

As well as all of this, teachers are naturally providing those important models for writing which include the material which children read and which is read to them.

Models for Writing

When we talk about creative writing it is necessary to consider that on the one hand any text children write is 'creative' in the sense that they create a piece of text which is new to them. So it may be unhelpful to reserve this term for texts which are thought to be 'poetic' or 'imaginative'. On the other hand the vast majority of writing and almost all of that done by young children must be very much a process of imitating the forms and conventions of the various genres that make up the whole of writing (Kress, 1982). A story (i.e. a fictional narrative) is the genre which children meet first and the one with which they are most comfortable. In the chapter on history the relationship between 'storying' as a way of thinking and story will be discussed. Here it is being stressed, rather obviously, that hearing and reading stories provides children with a 'story grammar' i.e. the form which a story normally takes, which they can use in their own writing. The child whose writing follows did not invent the format she uses very skilfully in year 1. She fails to hold the narrator constant thoughout the text and asked for help with spelling. Nevertheless, the surprise ending — yes she was going to be the monster's dinner — shows, not that she invented the idea of surprise endings but that she could use this device.

> *Frances, age 5 years*
> Once upon a time a little girl was in the woods picking flowers and suddenly she heard a noise it was a rustling noise and in the distance she could see Pink it was the pink Spotted Scrunch and he saw me and I saw him and he was a kind monster and he gave me a ride and it was very uncomfortable because he was spikey and he grinned and he said you are just in time for dinner.

Here we have a strong argument for reading constantly to children and to give them time to read, to provide models for writing quite apart from any of the many other reasons which could be advanced. However it is also an argument in favour of including in the curriculum, stories which are well-written and structured by skilled authors who write for childrens' entertainment and delight. Not all children are as good as Frances at making these stories their own in order to use them for writing. It cannot be stressed too much that care must be taken not to spoil stories as stories for children. However it may be possible, perhaps after a story, to draw attention to how authors set scenes, introduce characters, develop plots and use inferential meanings. 'It didn't say that. How do we know what happened?'

It follows perhaps, that the short story — which is what we normally ask children to write — should not be abandoned entirely in favour of the serial even in year 2. It also follows that we need to introduce and to distinguish between various other genres or types of writing and to provide and discuss models for those types which young children can begin to deal with. These might include: reported experience, descriptions, poems, letters, lists, instructions, reports of experiments in science or investigations in mathematics, recipes, guidebooks and many others. There are other formats too, which are related to writing. These include flow diagrams and cartoons (including strip cartoons and comics). Sometimes the written materials which can model these types can be found and read to children. Selected information books, very carefully selected newspaper reports and poems, of course, all provide models for writing. Teachers can augment these by asking children to share and contribute to the writing which the teachers do on displays. When teachers label scientific experiments — the data display or the stages of the activity — they can introduce the questions which are to be answered. 'What did we want to find out? What materials/equipment did we use? What did we do? What happened? What did we find out?' Then with the help of the children the answers can be written by the teacher. Other models might include teachers' own diaries, shopping lists and books of favourite recipes or poems.

Writing takes many forms and, as suggested above, each tends to use generally-accepted structures. Here again it may be necesary to do more than provide the models but also to discuss why they look as they do. Newspaper articles may be short and snappy to attract a quick read. Scientific reports convey information succinctly as opposed to descriptive writing of a poetic sort which conveys the author's feelings. Something of these differences is within the reach of young children if they are personally involved in trying to think about them with the aid of teachers. When children are asked to try to write in these different ways or choose to do so, the provision of audience and purpose also helps to determine a necessary format. It is not being argued that each and every type of writing has a limited and specific structure but that we recognize that certain sorts of structures meet certain sorts of demands. For example, it is usual and rarely has to be made explicit to children that a story or a report of experience will be written in mainly the past tense. Most descriptions are written in the present or present continuous tense. An example follows of a task which demands the rather rarer use of modal auxilliaries (will,

would, might etc.). The audience was a student teacher on a pre-course experience visit. The children discussed and then wrote:
What do you think Anthea will need to learn to be a teacher?

Gary, Year 2
She will need to know Whats right and whats wrong because if you asked if a sum was right and then you will not know the answer and you will not get the work done. And (crossed out) She will have to know what to do if there is a fire because if Anthea did not take us out we will get burnt or we might even die. Anthea will have to be taught by some one who nows (crossed out) knows what to do to be a teacher because if she did not get someone who new she would get it all wrong and she would not be a proper teacher.

To summarize, teachers need to be very aware of the different audiences and purposes of writing and the different forms which writing takes because of these audiences and purposes. They need to provide a variety of models, purposes and audiences but may need to go further and explain to children why writing takes various forms and how the children can employ different structures in their own writing. This can start, as in the examples of teachers writing in the classroom, *even* before children can write for themselves. Planning writing can also begin quite early on.

Planning Writing

One important device which novice writers (and others) use often, has been called a 'Knowledge telling strategy' (Bereiter and Scardamalia, 1985). These authors have worked mostly with older children in the American equivalent of top junior and secondary schools. They note that what frequently happens is

> (The writer thinks) Whatever the writing assignment translate it into a topic. Then tell all you know about the topic . . . it (the knowledge telling strategy) is clearly adaptive to school writing demands. It permits at least a minimally adequate response to any assignment for which the student has relevant knowledge, it turns the assignment into an aid to memory search . . . it virtually eliminates the need for goal directed planning or problem solving . . . it allows composition to proceed on more or less a sentence-by-sentence basis. . . .' (*ibid*, p. 102)

Of course this strategy can lead to some quite impressive writing. However such writing is not planned. It might be asked whether young children need to think about planning and whether, if they did, this would spoil a natural flow of ideas. On the second question, of course, no one would wish to disturb this flow. However it may become clear that some of the suggestions which will follow are not interference but aids which may help children to solve some of the problems that having to attend to the mechanics of writing and the ideas and putting these on paper involve. As to whether beginning to think about planning is necessary, the argument that writing helps one to think has already been outlined in the introduction. Futhermore we are looking ahead to using writing to learn across the curriculum. If writing is not planned it does not have the effect of becoming a tool for thinking and learning. Even the youngest children can be helped to think about writing; to begin to select what is important and to look for a structure, at least some of the time. At other times having a great idea or a need to recount an experience should be written about as it comes into the head.

It has already been suggested that teachers need to work with children before and during writing. On these occasions ideas can be planned, amended, included or rejected. It is also common practice for children to draw before they write. These drawings are more than enjoyable for their own sake. They help children to think about what they will write. The detail on the drawings can be a 'memory search' done before writing. They can be, in effect, a mode of planning. The natural extension to a single drawing is the equally familiar 'zig zag book'. This is a rectangular strip of card or thickish paper folded so that it is divided into pages. Children draw a sequence of pictures at the top of each page and write text underneath. This device also can promote planning. The pictures generally tell the complete story or sequence of events in recalled experience or class activity. Whilst writing in any of these forms without such an aid it is very common for children to get carried away with the very first part — going on the bus after a trip, for example — and fail to complete their account. The picture format and the limited spece for writing make the latter more specific and given time, children can meet the whole of their intentions. It is desirable not to put stringent time limits on to writing. Indeed, in this example, doing the illustrations and then coming back to the writing may provide fresh thinking. Older children might limit their drawings, perhaps just using a pencil. Then the drawings can come to be seen as aids to the writing and not complete illustrations. The drawing provides the 'memory search' mentioned above, includes details which might otherwise be omitted and frees the writer up to decide how to use what has become a plan for writing. After that the drawings might be returned to and coloured or otherwise elaborated.

Teachers often write words on the chalkboard or a flip chart which they think that children will need in their writing. Apart from being a spelling aid, teachers are also identifying for children the key words that will be needed. In effect they are planning for the children. A simple extension is not to put these words on show but to ask children to start their work with such a list. Here very familiar ideas are being used to illustrate how tried and tested activities can be used in ways in which teachers may see new possibilities. In no way is it suggested that every writing task should be planned. To get an idea and want to write it straight onto the paper while it is bubbling in the mind is another way to write but not the only one.

At the top end of the infant school a planning sheet might be used. For example:

Who am I writing for
What will it be about
What to I want to say?
or what do I know?   1
                     2
                     3
                     4
                     5
                     6

With older children such a sheet could be used by the children on their own. With younger children it would need teacher help. The children would need to be shown how to make brief notes. Additional sorts of questions that could be included for older children would need to be asked orally for infants, who could be asked what was most important and about the best order in which they might write. Of course any such sheet — which it is suggested should be used sparingly — would have to be adapted for the particular writing task.

Young children might also be given a printed sheet with the start of a story to brainstorm, with a partner, ideas with which to finish it. Children do plan, sometimes, in their heads although Bereiter and Scardamalia (1985) comment that elementary school children are 'frequently incredulous and unable to imagine what adults find to think about' when told that adults often think about writing for fifteen minutes or more before they start. Nevertheless a very simple ploy may be to suggest that children do take a little time to think before they write and especially that they share their ideas with their neighbours. Children may also be helped to plan if they compose texts together. The intention of sitting children in groups is presumably that this sort of thing can happen and children ought not to see writing as anti-social. It may be private but that is another matter.

Becoming a Writer

Perhaps the most important thing that should be borne in mind is that a writer rarely sits down, composes a text and that is the end of the matter. Writers, except possibly in a very informal letter to a close friend, write, rewrite, alter and polish. Children learning to be writers can be helped to see that most writing is provisional and alterable and that corrections and crossings out are part of the process. Even when children are dictating texts they can be encouraged to change their minds.

However, children do not like their best writing books to look messy. When they are using those books it takes a lot of persuasion to encourage them to cross out, even neatly, rather than rub out. If such persuasion were effective it would remove a lot of classroom disruption caused by looking for rubbers! However, it may be more profitable to have a good deal of writing done, not in books but on sheets of paper where it is clear that alterations are seen positively and commended. Showing children the sorts of alterations adult writers, perhaps teachers, make demonstrates how the process works. However, writing of this provisional sort is not likely to be profitable if each and every piece of rough work has to be painstakingly rewritten. Selected pieces can be rewritten after correction but for specific purposes; stories to be published as a classroom resource, open day displays, texts to go with displays on the wall or in the corridor and so forth. To demand that every text is rewritten may be a recipe for getting children to limit their work when they catch on.

Another advantage of rough work is that it is a mirror into children's progress and strategies. The Non-Statutory Guidance for English (NCC, 1990) suggest that files of children's writing are kept to assess progress. Carefully altered texts are not very helpful to that end. As the guidelines also suggest children themselves should be involved in their own assessment. To have a folder of ones own work enables children to see both their own progress and to suggest what they need to do to get better as writers.

Helping children to get better as writers has been the theme of this chapter. It has not been suggested that teachers could improve their subject knowledge by writing themselves. However, this might well be the case even if it were limited to teachers themselves trying out some of the tasks they set for children and if they are feeling brave, showing them to children.

References

ALEXANDER, R. (1984) *Primary Teaching*, Eastbourne, Holt, Rinehart and Winston.
BEREITER, C. and SCARDAMALIA, M. (1985) 'Children's difficulties in learning to compose', in WELLS, G. and NICHOLLS, J. (Eds) *Language and Learning: An Interactional Perspective*, London, Falmer Press.
DES (1990) *English in the National Curriculum (No. 2)*, London, HMSO.
FERREIRO, E. and TEBEROSKY, A. (1982) *Literacy Before Schooling*, London, Heinemann Educational Books Inc.
KRESS, G. (1982) *Learning To Write*, London, Routledge and Kegan Paul.
NCC (1990) *English, Non-Statutory Guidance*, York, NCC.
NICHOLLS, J., BAUER, A., PETTITT, D., REDGEWELL, V. and WATSON, G. (1989) *Beginning Writing*, Milton Keynes, Open University Press.
PETERS, M.L. (1967) *Spelling: Caught or Taught?* London, Routledge and Kegan Paul.
TEMPLE, C. and GILLET, J.W. (1989) *Language Art: Learning Processes and Teaching Practices*, London, Scott Foresman and Co.
WELLS, G. (1986) *The Meaning Makers: Children Learning Language and Using Language to Learn*, Portsmouth, Heinemann Educational Books Inc.

Chapter 5

Construction of Mathematics in the Early Years

Carol Aubrey

What does it mean to learn and teach mathematics in the early years? What mathematical knowledge and competences do young children bring to school and what sort of mathematical experiences should they receive in the early years of schooling? This chapter will consider these questions from three points of view: first, from the point of view of mathematics as a discipline; second, from the point of view of the child as a young learner; and third, from the point of view of classroom practice. We have already a substantial literature relating to the emergence of the young child's mathematical knowledge little of which has been very accessible to, or widely known by early years teachers. We have a small knowledge base relating to the teaching of specific, mathematical topics to particular groups of children such as addition and subtraction word problems for 6-year-olds. As yet we have very little knowledge about the co-ordination and utilization of teacher and pupil knowledge in classroom contexts. Teaching principles tend to have been inferred from research which has focused on what children can and cannot do in particular mathematical domains, and from accumulated experience in teaching young children. The main purpose of this chapter is to make more widely available some of what is already known about learning and teaching mathematics. The first section will consider the subject content of early years mathematics.

Mathematics as a Discipline

Studies of British classrooms (for instance, Bennett *et al*, 1984) have drawn attention to an over-emphasis on 'four rules', paper and pencil exercises and routine calculations which poorly match children's existing skills and understanding, just as HMI (1978) and Cockcroft (1982) criticized British mathematics education for its over-emphasis on computation and limited problem-solving in real-life situations. Since then developments in such areas as practical work, problem-solving and mathematical investigations have taken place, though

HMI (1991) has commented again recently on a lack of attention to the using and applying of mathematics at Key Stage 1 of the National Curriculum.

Since the Cockcroft Report (1982) the mathematics curriculum has been affected by the increased availability of calculators and microcomputers. The use of microtechnology has changed views about the kind of computation skills which are needed by children. As well as an ability to interpret the results of computation by such means comes the need for children to check results and, hence, estimation and a greater facility in mental arithmetic are required too. Whilst routine calculation rarely leads to application outside the conditions in which it is taught, number does indeed form a fundamental and central part of school mathematics.

In the early stages of school work, which is the concern of this book, children use number for counting, ordering and, in association with measurement of quantities, such as length, weight (mass) and time, once a unit has been established, will again apply counting. The study of shape and space (geometry) which provides pupils with a way to relate mathematics to the physical environment is important at all stages. Children learn to recognize and use properties of shape and recognize relationships between shapes. They locate, describe and represent position and mobility in space and, at a later stage, will find and use numerical relationships associated with space. Handling data from the simple collecting and recording of mathematical information in pictorial form to the later, and more complex analyses of data aided by the use of the microcomputer and calculator is important throughout this period. Algebra, too, is concerned with numerical relationships of various forms and is of growing importance through Key Stage 1 and beyond. Whilst each of the topics is, itself, hierarchically organized, children need opportunities and experiences which establish interrelationships among topics and cross-connections with other parts of the curriculum.

Major revision of the British mathematics curriculum has come with the introduction of the National Curriculum in 1989. This has broadened the mathematics curriculum to provide five strands: *Using and Applying Mathematics*, which involves making use of knowledge, skills and understanding of mathematics in real-life problems and investigation within mathematics itself; *Number*, which includes estimation and approximation, interpreting results and checking for reasonableness; *Algebra*, which involves recognition and use of symbolic and graphical representation to express patterns and relationships; *Shape and Space*, which includes recognition and use of properties of 2-D and 3-D shapes, and use of measurement, location and transformation in the study of space; and *Handling Data*, which entails collecting, processing, and interpreting data, estimation and use of probabilities.

Cockcroft (1982) suggested mathematics 'provides a means of communication which is powerful, concise and unambiguous'. Mathematics is thus a means of communication and pupils need opportunities to talk (and later, to read and write) about mathematical ideas and use mathematical language. Discussion helps the child clarify ideas and extend control of language and it reveals to the teacher understanding, misconceptions and areas of uncertainty.

As symbols and formal methods of calculation are learned through Key Stage 1 children gain in experience and competence in expressing mathematical ideas in a variety of ways, not only talking and writing and drawing, but making models and constructing graphs. They learn to calculate without stopping to consider what the symbols mean as facility is gained in the language of mathematics. If mathematics provides a means of communication which is precise, it can also become a source of difficulty. Ordinary language needs to be used in teaching to explain and interpret calculations and the introduction of symbols must be handled gradually. The terminology of sets which is one means of describing accurately, of noting similarities and differences and expressing the operation of rules, is popular with infant teachers and used widely in infant mathematics schemes. Mathematics is then a form of reasoning too.

Explanations are offered and proof considered, from the most informal discussion with young children to the most sophisticated higher order mathematical reasoning.

Beyond mathematics as communication, is mathematics as a problem-solving activity. It is through practical problem-solving and investigations relevant to pupils that they learn the importance of mathematics for a deeper understanding of the world in which they live. By the end of their primary years, for instance, they will be using measurement and data handling to carry out science investigations. In fact mathematics can make a contribution to the whole curriculum from the application of simple calculations, through measurement and data handling, and the application to the physical world through numerical relationships associated with shape and space.

There is ample evidence, as some of the writer's own work (Aubrey, 1993) shows that children bring into school a range of strategies for solving simple mathematical problems encountered in their everyday lives which should be cultivated rather than ignored. This suggests, too, that mathematics can be creative and pupils should continue to be encouraged to invent their own routines and procedures to check, explain and justify, and to compare with others, as questions of effectiveness in procedures are considered. The next section will consider in more detail the young child as a learner of mathematics: mathematics as communication; mathematics as representation; and mathematics as problem solving.

The Child as a Young Learner

Introduction

In investigating the young learner of mathematics the main source of enquiry is psychological literature in providing both a broad framework for the consideration of learning and development and for a more detailed analysis of the child's cognitive development in the domain of mathematics.

Traditionally the broad framework has been provided by Piagetian theory since Piaget examined the development of particular mathematical and scientific concepts over time such as number, geometry, space, time, causality and logical thinking. Taking measurement as one area which has received considerable attention, as an illustration, the majority of research concerning children and the stages of developing understanding has focused on readiness to learn (Piaget, Inhelder and Szeminska, 1960; Anderson and Cuneo, 1978; Hart, 1984). Many studies have been conducted in the style of Piaget and examined the developmental stage of the child. Carpenter (1976) provided a thorough review of the literature concerning readiness to learn measurement. Three foundational ideas will be considered here: transitivity, conservation and unit of measure.

Transitivity is a notion of comparison. If three pieces of wool are of different length and $a > b > c$, then $a > c$. Young children may not draw this conclusion until they have had considerable measurement experience. Conservation relates to children's understanding that physical quantities, for instance length, weight or volume remain unchanged despite apparent changes, for example, in appearance. If a piece of material is cut into three pieces the total area remains the same. The unit of measurement idea depends on children's recognition of the attribute to be measured as well as that the unit chosen influences the number assignment. Research has considered whether children can respond to both visual cues concerning attributes and numerical cues about unit measure. Carpenter found virtually all 6- to 7-year-old children responded as well to numerical cues as visual cues. Most children focused on a single dominant cue, either numerical or visual rather than considered them both together. Children seemed to have difficulty in coordinating numerical information with perceptual information when one type of cue was dominant or confusing. This suggests young children may not be able to coordinate what they know or observe about the attribute in question with what they know or observe about number assignment.

In a more general, diffuse but, nevertheless, powerful way as Walkerdine (1984) and Edwards and Mercer (1987) have noted the very knowledge base underpinning child development into which many primary school teachers have been socialized is derived from Piaget. In their pedagogical discourse, practices can often be traced from notions in Piaget's work, in particular, the empirical framework of stages of development, within an overall context of biological capacities. Walkerdine (1984) has provided examples both from current practice and from one of the most influential primary mathematics textbooks available, which communicate a belief that children can 'discover' number relationships, in this case place value, by physically grouping and carrying out operations on concrete objects. The textbook actively encourages teachers to locate place value as arising from and in relation to the properties of the mind of the child, which apparently 'emerge' spontaneously. By implication, then, place value is not taught, and will not be located in the system of representation or notation or existing practices of mathematical discourse.

It does seem reasonable to conclude from the evidence that young children of 6 to 7 years are still in the process of acquiring measurement concepts. This argues for the provision of well-planned activities which take account of children's current capabilities. The broader influence of Piagetian thought on practice, however, which leads to an unquestioning provision of concrete experience and a belief that somehow children's knowledge of number relationships will emerge spontaneously from their concrete operations is highly questionable.

This is not to underestimate the role of experience in practical work and, as noted earlier, there is some question whether this has been sufficiently provided through the primary years. The Cockcroft Report (1982) advocated practical activities should precede practice of skills and procedures and emphasized that instruction should include problem solving and applications to real life, as well as an interdisciplinary approach to mathematics. The report also advocated that mathematics instruction at all levels should include exposition by the teacher, with time spent by the teacher and children in verbal exchange concerning the subject of mathematics.

Mathematics as communication
The knowledge and values which young children draw upon, and which they exploit in their transactions with the social and physical world, however, are learned through and mediated by their interactions with other, and more experienced members of their culture. A crucial role in the transmission of culture to the child is played by language. For Vygotsky (see Kozulin, 1986) language or, for that matter, writing or number constituted a human sign system which served two major functions: firstly an interpersonal/communicative function and secondly, a means of cognitive representation. As suggested in the first section of this chapter, early mathematics is not only derived from social communicative contexts but is itself a form of discourse. Like language development, learning mathematics is a process of being supported by the adult into a particular form of discourse which carries its own development sequence, moving from an embeddedness in practical and social situations towards a more symbolic, self-contained and abstract system.

Well before they enter school children develop a rich working mathematical knowledge from everyday situations. The transcripts from the work of Gordon Wells in the *Language at Home and at School* project provide a rich source for conversations between pre-school children and their mothers. Examples abound of activities which give rise to counting and sharing, reference to time, money and simple fractional numbers, simple sorting tasks to a criterion, use of the language of measurement, position in space and on a line.

Wells (1985) identified as most effective a 'supportive' style of parental contribution to joint conversation. By contrast he described a 'teaching' style where the adult chose the topics and asked questions, giving the child, even if s/he knew the answer, a rather limited range of possible responses and the frequent experience of being evaluated as inadequate by adult standards. Corran

Carol Aubrey

and Walkerdine (1980) also found that pre-school children often engaged in tasks where numbers were involved. They suggested, similarly, that tasks fell into two distinct types: instrumental tasks in which the goal was related to the ongoing activity where, for instance, a mother might say, 'Bring me two eggs' when she was making a cake; and explicitly pedagogic tasks where the child might be asked to count buttons and stairs, and where the requirement was a display of knowledge.

Hughes (1986), examining the conversations between young children aged from 3 years 9 months to 4 years 3 months and their mothers, collected in a previous study (Tizard and Hughes, 1984), noted relatively few conversations where the mothers were explicitly using the language of arithmetic. He quoted the instance of a child and her mother singing the traditional song about current buns in a baker's shop, which describes the progressive reduction of five buns as they are sold. Here, and in another similar example related to a discussion of the number of cakes required for tea, the mother involved modelled for the child the use of fingers to represent the number of buns required. Hughes emphasized the point that fingers were being used as a concrete referent, thus playing a crucial role in linking the abstract and the concrete, both representing objects and serving as objects in their own right.

An understanding of the link between activity and natural language in the development of concepts of shape and space is vital too but, perhaps, not so clearly defined as in the learning of number. Through the pre-school years children experience many shapes, both man-made and natural, develop an awareness of colour, form and texture, and through their own physical mobility explore position in space. This experience lays the foundation for later description in more precise mathematical language of shape and space. Collecting, sorting and classifying three-dimensional shapes by attribute provides the impetus for learning new words. As shapes are subjected to finer discrimination ideas of congruence and similarity are required. Classification and discrimination depends upon the development of language and, in turn, this language is refined as mathematical experiences are extended.

The writer's own work has shown 4-year-old children bring into school an ability to sort and classify two- and three-dimensional shapes, build complex three-dimensional constructions, draw two-dimensional shapes and use common words to describe position in space and on a line. Children's descriptions of solid shapes and their faces showed an interesting mixture of everyday words and more formal vocabulary:

> its flat, its round . . . its pointy . . . its square . . . its an oblong . . . its a rectangle . . . its a triangle . . . its a circle.
>
> its like a wheel . . . like a tent . . . like a ball.

Such responses demonstrate the need for the teacher to listen, discuss and question individual children to assess existing experience and vocabulary and to enrich and extend this. Coxford (1978) outlined Van Hiele's theory of spatial development with reference to school geometry in terms of five levels: from Level I in which activities concentrate on individual figure recognition, production and naming, through to Level IV and V which is concerned with the development of deductive reasoning and theory construction without concrete representation. Our own children's responses which make reference to faces and to properties of solids indicate, as our research associate has pointed out, an awareness which verges on Level II.

Our children's three-dimensional constructions indicated an awareness of 'balance' or symmetry, which would need to be made more explicit by their teacher through discussion of such activities as model making and art work. Ideas of symmetry can be derived from pattern making, folded paintings and from reflections in mirrors and water. Through making and discussing three-dimensional shapes, through covering surfaces, drawing round and tracing faces of three-dimensional shapes, exploring space by fitting three-dimensional shapes together, children's understanding of geometry is extended, structured and supported throughout by explicit discussion and enhanced by mathematical language.

Mathematics as representation
As the previous section has indicated natural language has a fundamental role in supporting social communication and early mathematical representation. In the early years children are introduced to various activities which not only involve reciting of number names but include matching sets of objects and learning their number name and symbol.

In the course of daily living children gain much experience of number symbols — large numbers as well as small — and gradually they learn that the numbers they have learned orally in practical situations and pictorially in their story books have associated number symbols.

Lesh (1979) has suggested a number of modes of representation children use in addition to real-world situations and spoken symbols, which are pictures, written symbols and manipulative aids, all of which children are exposed to in the pre-school years. Post and Cramer (1989) have noted that mathematics is often used to represent the world in which we live and as such there must be a correspondence between some aspect of the represented world and the representing world, in the Hughes' (1986) case, fingers to represent cakes. The mapping between these two worlds is important at all levels of mathematics and is the essence of mathematical concept development in school-age children. Numbers and manipulative materials and later, tables, graphs and equations represent real world ideas and relationships. At a more advanced level these mathematical 'objects' themselves can be represented as formulae to serve both new problem-solving situations and as objects of investigation in their own right.

Pictorial and graphical representation is a most important aspect of mathematics and, in fact, graphical representation is a further development of mathematical communication. Through the primary years children learn how data can be organized, collected, recorded, tabulated and presented. Learning to use and interpret graphs, charts and diagrams of all sorts is vitally important. The action of recording mathematical information in pictorial form is usually the child's first introduction to graphical work. Direct recording with real objects, simple pictograms and the use of concrete material such as bricks or beads allows representation of, for instance, 'boys and girls on our table'. Relations and mapping between children's names and favourite foods or pets can be shown. At this stage there will be no framework and no baseline. Later count graphs with a baseline will be constructed using a base board or graph paper, as data is collected, for instance, on children who walk to school and those who travel by bus or car. This involves children in designing a collection sheet, collecting and recording data and the drawing of simple conclusions. At this stage the need for representation with uniform units arises and each set, or column will be labelled. Where days of the week or birthday months are used the sets concerned will be ordered and as numerical values as opposed to nominal values are introduced a number scale on the horizontal axis will be used. As the size of the count increases it will be necessary to label the vertical axis. At first, the spaces will be labelled, later the lines rather than spaces. The horizontal axis will continue to be labelled with either nominal or numerical values, ordered where necessary. Carroll, Venn and tree diagrams may be used to represent the result of classifications using two criteria, and towards the end of the early years period some children will be entering data into, and accessing information on a simple computer database and using it to find the answers to simple questions.

In important ways mathematics entails the internalization of mathematical symbols and systems for representing mathematical ideas, such as the base-10 notational system and Cartesian co-ordinate system, and supporting problem solving. As Kaput (1987) noted representation can be used to support personal thinking about mathematical ideas and to communicate them to others. Dienes (1960) believed children's active involvement in the process of learning mathematics should routinely involve the use of manipulative material. Learning place value and developing a full working understanding of our number system and notation used, is a fundamental aim for all primary-aged children. Although relevant to all areas of mathematics learning, the role of manipulative materials is particularly powerful in place value and notation. Dienes and Golding (1971) stressed the role of multi-embodiment in learning regrouping procedures for adding or subtracting two numbers (ten ones exchanged for one ten, ten tens for one hundred and so on). Hundreds, tens and units can be shown with multi-base blocks, graph paper models, an abacus, or bundles of sticks in elastic bands. Reviewing the research evidence, Moser (1986) has suggested that there may be long-term benefits from multi-embodiment if teachers are willing to teach generalization from one representation to another.

A range of issues is raised with respect to the match between the external representation being used and the mathematical concept it is intended to represent, its salience or relevance to the child, the relationship it has to the child's existing informal systems of representation, not to mention the motivational aspects associated with the use of a particular representation system. The writer's own work has shown 4-year-old children bring into school various levels of knowledge of formal mathematical symbols. In a sample of forty-eight 4-year olds, 25 per cent recognized ten or more numbers in a simple reading numerals task, 25 per cent recognized between five-nine numbers, 29 per cent recognized between two-four numbers and 21 per cent recognized one or none. No pattern was associated with the particular numbers being recognized. For writing numerals, where children were asked to put something on a piece of paper to represent different quantities of bricks (one-ten), all children were willing to offer some sort of representation for a mean of eight out of ten presentations, for instance, by drawing tally marks or drawing the blocks on the paper. Children recorded confidently the numbers they could recall and then swapped to invented representation when formal knowledge was exhausted. One child who wrote numbers up to four, added tally marks to number four to represent higher numbers. Another child who could write numbers up to five wrote 55 for ten, 45 for nine, 44 for eight and 321 for six. One child started drawing round the blocks but then switched to representing the blocks by circles. Other children used a mixture of tally marks and circles, spots and squiggles. One child lined up the blocks on the paper and drew a line exactly the same length to represent them. Nine of the children offered either a personal or formal system, or a mixture of the two for all the quantities presented. In fact all of the children offered some sort of representation for at least some of the presentations (see figure 5.1). Two of the children knew how to write all of the numbers up to ten, one knew how to write all the numbers except nine and 17 per cent could write at least some of the numbers. This certainly argues strongly for the need to move gradually through different stages of mathematical representation from personal to formal in situations where children recognize the interrelationships among ideas and can link their own informal representations to more formal systems. Hughes (1986) has described at length the difficulties children experience translating mathematical operations into written symbols.

By the time they come to school, however, long before they begin to deal with symbolic problems the writer's work has shown children have acquired competence in counting, simple addition and subtraction, social sharing and, in some cases, simple multiplication by continuous addition. Already they are able to demonstrate understanding of appropriate language for comparing and ordering objects, for position in space and on a line, and for selecting criteria appropriately to sort objects.

Their operations with addition and subtraction, social sharing and simple multiplication by continuous addition still for the most part required concrete representation and while concern for accuracy was not marked, their number operations were more effective with small numbers. Ginsburg (1977) has noted

Carol Aubrey

Figure 5.1: Children's representations of quantities of bricks

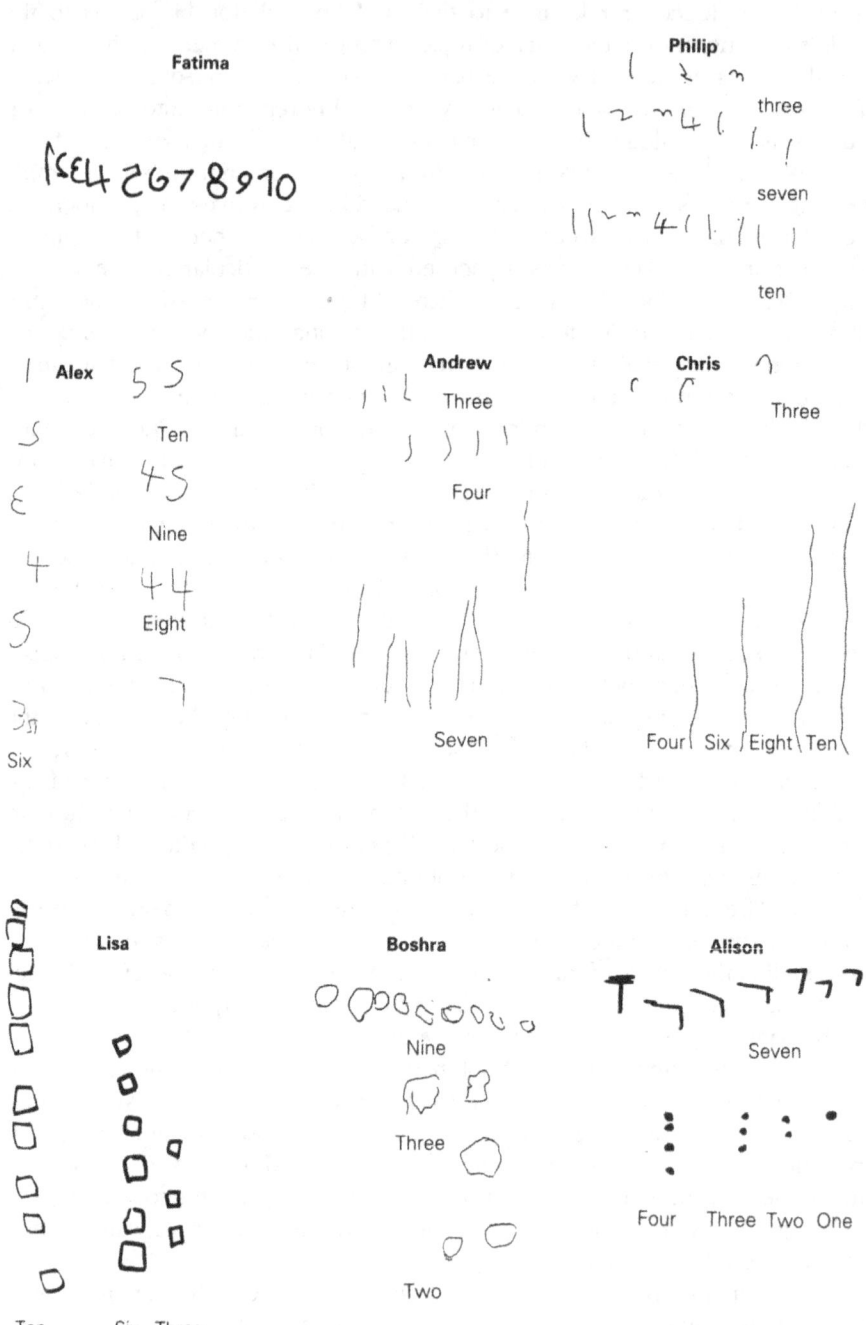

that children come to school with a strong sense of 'arithmetic' acquired from parents and older siblings in which counting plays an important role. However, in the writer's sample there was evidence still, in the case of some children, of use of an earlier acquired strategy, subitizing, where children rely on immediate perception of numerosity of small sets without counting, usually of not more than four or five items.

Carpenter, Fennema and Peterson (1987) have indicated that in their early invented solutions for addition and subtraction word problems children need direct and complete representation but gradually they develop in flexibility and abstractness, later using counting onwards and backwards strategies, and finally building up number facts to derive strategies. Steffe *et al* (1982) suggested that what is being counted gives an indication of the degree of children's understanding and abstraction. He identified three major types of 'items' which children count:

> perceptual unit items, which can be seen and touched as they are counted;
>
> motor unit items, where the touching or pointing movement itself is the object being counted and actual objects may not be present;
>
> abstract unit items, where the counting words themselves are being counted.

The research, for instance, of Baroody (1984) has suggested that number size does not account entirely for children's facility in counting. Double facts and their related subtraction facts, such as 2 + 2, 4 + 4, 6 – 3, 10 – 5, are easiest to learn. 'Zero' facts, such as 3 + 0, 5 – 0 are also very easy to learn. Successor/predecessor facts, for example, 3 + 1, 7 + 1 are easy too, and the writer's own work showed some 4-year-olds already developing an ability to say what came before, or after a presented number.

Some children will be using addition and subtraction facts to twenty by the end of their infant schooling. Here, too, use of memorized facts to derive solutions can be useful. Thornton (1978) has described frequently observed strategies, such as

> doubles plus one (or two): 5 + 7: 5 and 5 makes 10, so 2 more must be 12;
>
> bridging through ten: 8 + 5: 8 and 2 make 10, so 3 more must be 13;
>
> compensation: 5 + 7: if I take 1 away from 7, that makes 6 and if I give it to the 5, that makes 6, which altogether is 12;
>
> subtracting through ten: 14 – 5: if I take 4 away from 14 that leaves 10 and 1 more is 9;

nine is one less than ten: 9 + 7: 10 and 7 are 17, so one less than that is 16.

Children will not necessarily 'invent' all these strategies themselves which suggests that explicit teaching will be needed to extend the range children find for themselves. Steinberg (1985), however, showed that even after instruction children will not necessarily apply the strategy!

Research on the learning of multiplication and division has shown children find the repeated subtraction concept of division (Zweng, 1964), and 'equal addends' concept of multiplication less difficult at second grade, that is, 7 years of age (Hervey, 1966). Anghileri (1985) found the majority of primary school children, in fact, do not use the facts they have learned in their multiplication tables but prefer to use addition or to recite a number pattern such as 3, 6, 9, 12, 15, 18 . . . while tallying on their fingers or mentally. In fact for multiplication and division children appear to draw on the same set of derived facts as in addition and subtraction. Though, as in the solution of addition and subtraction problems, until they are able to recall the facts they will need to represent the process with concrete materials or with a number line.

During the infant years children will learn to double numbers up to 10 and by the age of 7 or 8 years may have immediate recall of the simplest tables, such as 2, 3, 4 and 5.

Mathematics as problem-solving
Young children, even pre-schoolers are able to solve a variety of addition and subtraction word problems. Research by Carpenter and Moser (1983) and later, by Carpenter, Fennema, Peterson and Carey (1988) has shown how analyses of addition and subtraction problems distinguish among different classes of problem on the basis of semantic characteristics, as well as on the basis of the ease with which they can be represented concretely. Evidence suggests young children note the semantic structure of problems and use different strategies according to the structure.

Different problem types (join, separate, combine and compare) lead to different methods of solution according to which quantity of the problem is unknown. Some 'separate' problems, which involve the action of removing a subset from a given set, and 'join' problems, where two sets are joined together can be solved by young children who still need representation (the use of fingers or the manipulation of objects). Other problems where the initial quantity is unknown cannot be solved at this stage since it is impossible for children to represent the action to the problem. Parallels have been drawn by Briars and Larkin (1984) with reading comprehension, where mathematical word problems are seen as a special kind of 'text' requiring the learner to bring to bear appropriate background knowledge or experience of quantities and relationships among known and unknown quantities. This relates to a previous section on mathematics as discourse and suggests, further, that children's success on such problems may depend, too, on their embeddedness in familiar, everyday practices and related discourse.

Again work by the writer has shown that 4-year-old children enter school able to manage problems at the simplest level of difficulty ('join' and 'separate' word problems in which the final resulting set is unknown). Other problems, such as separating problems in which the initial set is unknown and where the action cannot be represented are very difficult.

In fact investigation of all areas of young children's early mathematical strategies and competences suggests, as in language acquisition, a rule-governed approach is operating from the start. Ginsburg (1977) and Fuson (1988) have shown that even rote counting is a complex activity requiring implicit knowledge of a number of principles. Gelman and Gallistel (1978) suggested that the counting of young children involves five principles: the one-to-one principle which entails ticking off items in an array with one tick for each item; the stable-ordering principle in which number tags are repeated in stable order; the cardinal principle, where the last 'tag' represents the number of items in an array; the abstraction principle which allows any collection or array of items can be counted; and the order-irrelevance principle, which recognizes that the order of tagging is irrelevant. The writer's work with forty-eight 4-year-olds counting an array of four and six farm animals starting from the left, from the right and from the middle indicated that 81 per cent (thirty-nine) showing implicit knowledge of the above principles.

Evidence from children's counting errors suggests early understanding of the decade structure, that two-digit numbers comprise a tens and units value, with the repetition of the units sequence (one–nine) for every decade above twenty. The writer's own work in this area has demonstrated some tendency for children's counting to finish with numbers ending in nine or zero which would tend to confirm this early understanding of the decade structure. Of forty-eight 4-year-olds five stopped counting at the end of the unit sequence of nine, and eleven finished at the beginning of a decade (eight at 120, two at twenty and one at seventy).

The demonstration of such a range of early competences poses some challenge to the conventional reception class curriculum. Whilst they may not possess the formal conventions, reception-age children clearly enter school having acquired already much content of the mathematics curriculum. The range of invented strategies already in use suggests that teaching should aim to extend the range of strategies at their disposal rather than undermine it in the struggle to find a single, convergent and acceptable response. This means building on the alternative strategies that children themselves generate and using these to discuss and compare and consider in terms of their economy and accuracy. Perhaps most important is the need to provide opportunities to move through different stages of representation from personal to formal in familiar contexts where children can learn the interrelationships among ideas and link their own informal strategies to the more formal symbol system of mathematics.

Carol Aubrey

Classroom Practice and Mathematics

Existing Practice

The writer's own more recent work in reception classes (Aubrey, 1994) has suggested that teachers plan integrated topic work, stressing the importance of play, flexibility and choice, with opportunities provided for practical activities in areas, however, where it has been demonstrated that children already possess competence. The content and sequence of the curriculum used is derived from infant mathematics schemes which provide a rational analysis of subject knowledge. Less account is taken by class teachers of the nature and direction of young children's developing knowledge of mathematics gained in out-of-school problem-solving situations, and little evidence for its consideration in infant mathematics schemes can be found. This suggests that teachers, in fact, have little awareness of the richness and complexity of informal mathematical knowledge that children bring from out-of-school settings. An alternative explanation for the observed lack of teacher mathematical exposition and reliance on scheme work in British classrooms is lack of subject knowledge and knowledge of the way children learn mathematics. This is likely to be highlighted rather than relieved by the introduction of the National Curriculum.

Few studies in this country have considered the role of teachers' subject knowledge, their knowledge of young children's early mathematical competence in planning instruction or the extent to which they believe mathematics teaching should be organized to facilitate children's construction of knowledge. The study of Tizard *et al* (1988) of inner city infant schools showed the amount of mathematical knowledge with which children entered school was the strongest predictor of future progress and given the small amount of mathematics teaching observed during the first year of school this finding did not cause surprise. Only one in five of the infant teachers involved said academic progress was one of their main aims, and marked differences were found in what was taught. Written subtraction was introduced during the first year of schooling in one out of ten classrooms, whilst two had not introduced this even by the third year. Similarly with respect to money, for some the concept of 'giving change' was introduced in the first year, for others it was not introduced even in children's third year at school. Some reception teachers believed certain items were too difficult for children, others did not. A conclusion drawn from this study was that children's skills should have been assessed soon after entry to diagnose areas in which help might be needed. The writer's work in reception classes has shown vast differences in the content of the mathematics curriculum offered, with number work figuring most prominently for three of the four teachers observed. For occasions where supply teachers were called in this was overwhelmingly the case. Similar amounts of time were spent on shape and space and data handling, very little measurement work was observed (of one teacher only) and work using money was not seen at all. One instance, of one teacher teaching algebra at level 1 was observed.

From their intensive study of seven first school mathematics teachers, Desforges and Cockburn (1987) concluded that the level of success achieved by children seemed related to their familiarity with the task demands made. This familiarity was not passed on to teachers who did not find out about the degree of match between the tasks and children's attainments because they did not carry out any detailed diagnostic work. They suggested teachers do, in fact, hold elaborate views of children's learning and appropriate higher order skills. Teaching mathematics, however, is very difficult and management strategies militate against the development of children's thinking.

As yet few attempts have been made to access teacher and pupil knowledge through the analysis of classroom language, which provides the medium of instruction and, in the early stages, the medium through which children's own subject knowledge can be assessed. As mentioned earlier in the chapter, Cockcroft (1982) emphasized the value of time spent by the teacher and pupils in verbal exchange related to the the subject of mathematics and the role of exposition by the teacher at all levels. Forman and Cazden (1985), however, have noted the social relationship referred to as 'teaching' in psychological perspectives is the one-to-one relationship between an adult and a child. They see two separate but related issues with respect to school learning. First, there are problems posed for the teacher in carrying out direct teaching to a group of children; second, there are the questions raised for the teacher's more indirect planning for the social organization of all work-related talk in the classroom setting.

Wells (1985) noted too, that it is the one-to-one adult-child talk in the home which supports language development. In this setting the child is treated as a conversational partner, expressing reciprocity, negotiating shared meaning and extending the child's contributions. As he pointed out, however, this is not to say that the infant school should — or, in fact could — attempt to replicate the style of interaction that typifies effective practice in the home, which is informal, spontaneous and even, at times, haphazard. It would be neither feasible nor appropriate for a busy professional faced with the diverse needs of a class of, maybe twenty-thirty children to attempt this and the function of the school, in complementing the role of the home, has a goal of introducing the child to more formal ways of acquiring and using knowledge.

Talk at school, by contrast to home talk, is marked by lack of reciprocity, a high proportion of teacher utterances with a high level of questions, for which the teacher normally already possesses the answer. Children soon learn the 'rules' of 'teacher initiation-pupil response-teacher feedback/evaluation' (IRE) described by Sinclair and Coulthard (1975) and Willes (1983). Children learn to participate within these social transactions just as they learned to talk and think about everything else.

In the writer's recent work (in submission) teacher and pupil interactions were continuously recorded in four reception classes across children's first year at school. The emerging structure was one of coordinating segments and sub-segments which provided the 'warp' of lessons. Segments usually consisted of small group work and each had its own goals and actions. Analysis of lesson segments and sub-segments which carried implications for teacher and pupil actions, allowed access to recurrent patterns of teacher moves, or the 'weft' of lessons. Components comprised: introduction, presentation of new learning, links to known components, monitoring and assessing, pointing out conditions of use and comments on results or outcomes. Not all segments contained all elements and individual teachers had their own distinctive styles of working. The amount of time in which there were opportunities to engage in mathematical tasks varied as well as the number of children involved and the quality of experience provided. Teacher talk and support varied from the irrelevant and goal-free beset by management problems, through modelling, 'talk aloud' strategies with coaching and monitoring, to the more formal exposition with structured initiation-response-evaluation sequences. Rich teacher knowledge appeared to be reflected in the content and structure of lessons, in explicit and well-integrated instruction, varied representations with links to, or connections made with, pupils' existing skills and understanding. As shown by some recent research in elementary science teaching in the United States (Carlsen, 1991) marked differences in discourse style may be related to teachers' own confidence or competence in subject teaching. High teacher talk with many questions and talk about irrelevant matters may indicate low subject knowledge. Clearly a high level of questioning with evaluation of responses will lead to correspondingly less pupil talk, less investigaton and a growing awareness that mathematics subject knowledge is the gaining of approval for a correct response to a teacher question.

Leinhardt, Putnam, Stein and Baxter (1991) have attempted to identify points where teacher knowledge impacts on mathematics teaching. Their findings, based on comparisons of novice and expert teachers, suggest four aspects of the instructional process where teacher subject knowledge plays a crucial role: in the teachers' mental plans or 'agendas' which vary in detail according to depth of subject knowledge; their curriculum scripts, which transform teacher knowledge into accessible form during lessons; their explanations, which range from direct and didactic to indirect and discovery-based; and their representations which deal with analogies used to explain mathematics ideas and concrete materials used.

Towards Some Solutions?

The writer's own recent work has suggested some of the ways that mathematical knowledge is presented and understood by teachers and children in classroom contexts. This chapter has attempted to consider alternative frameworks for knowing and learning mathematics. Detailed descriptions have been provided of the young child's early construction of mathematics in the context of interactions with the physical and social world. As the section on mathematics from the point of view of the discipline has shown, the role of formal education involves more than the supporting of early competences and, anyway, of particular concern to the teacher is the child whose early experiences have not supported the development of early linguistic or mathematical skills. Knowledge of the young learner's early mathematical competence, however, does not necessarily provide a means for developing knowledge within the constraints of the typical primary school classroom.

Fennema, Carpenter and Peterson (1989) have begun to examine the kinds of knowledge teachers have, how this is influenced by new knowledge they acquire, how teachers use knowledge of children's mathematical problem-solving in their teaching, and how this knowledge might be related to children's actual knowledge and problem-solving. So far this work has focused on a small area of development in children's problem-solving in addition and subtraction and has involved teachers of 6-year-olds in their first school year.

This work rests on two assumptions; first that mathematical understanding should be fostered through the establishment of links between problem-solving and other mathematical skills, with problem-solving as the focus for teaching; second, that teaching should be built on existing knowledge children bring to instruction. Furthermore it is assumed, in line with Walkerdine (1984), that classroom practice is grounded in knowledge, thinking and beliefs about children's learning. Cognitively guided instruction provided teachers with knowledge about children's strategies for dealing with addition and subtraction word problems, emphasizing the need to base instruction on strategies used by individual pupils. The writers were able to demonstrate from their programme of workshops changed teacher beliefs and knowledge of children's mathematical learning with a corresponding change in instructional methods.

Steffe and Cobb (1988) attempted to change teachers' beliefs and practices through the introduction of materials designed to allow 7-year-old children to construct their own mathematical knowledge at a variety of levels and to facilitate whole class discussions, whilst at the same time seeking to avoid the separation of conceptual and procedural knowledge.

The last two studies illustrate some recent attempts to bring to bear on practice current understandings of children's learning mathematics in the early years by working with teachers to develop a knowledge base of learning and teaching mathematics. In reconsidering the questions posed at the beginning of the chapter, some tension emerges between what we know of the young learner constructing mathematics and what is possible within the constraints of classrooms. How should we respond? On the one hand, providing ongoing opportunities through the early years and beyond for children to construct mathematics is difficult and, on the other hand, the conventions of mathematics and the associated representational systems must be formally taught in meaningful contexts which take account of the learner's existing knowledge.

All three aspects of considering knowing and understanding mathematics have highlighted the importance of teacher's mathematical subject knowledge and children's growing competence to use and apply mathematics to their social and physical world. In both the home and the school language is the medium of instruction and, ultimately the goal of mathematics teaching is for children to be able to think and reason quantitatively and communicate these ideas as mathematically literate adults.

References

ANDERSON, N.H. and CUNEO, D.O. (1978) 'The height and width rule in children's judgments of quantity', *Journal of Experimental Psychology*, 107, pp. 335–78.
ANGHILERI, J. (1985) 'Young children's understanding of multiplication', paper presented at the annual meeting of the British Educational Research Association, Sheffield.
AUBREY, C. (1993) 'An investigation of the mathematical competencies which young children bring into school', *British Educational Research Journal*, 19, 1, pp. 19–27.
AUBREY, C. (1994) 'An investigation of children's knowledge of mathematics at school entry and the knowledge their teachers hold about teaching and learning mathematics, about young learners and mathematical subject knowledge', *British Educational Research Journal*.
AUBREY, C. 'Teacher and pupil interactions and the processes of mathematics instruction in four reception classrooms over children's first year in school', submitted to *British Educational Research Journal*.
BAROODY, J.A. (1984) 'Children's difficulties in subtraction. Some causes and questions', *Journal for Research in Mathematics Education*, 15, pp. 203–13.
BENNETT, N. *et al* (1984) *The Quality of Pupil Learning Experience*, London, Lawrence Erlbaum.
BRIARS, D.J. and LARKIN, J.H. (1984) 'An integrated model of skill in solving elementary word problems', *Cognition and Instruction*, 1, pp. 245–96.
CARLSEN, W.S. (1991) 'Subject-matter knowledge and science teaching: A pragmatic perspective', in BROPHY, J. (Ed) *Advances in Research on Teaching*, Vol. 2, pp. 115–44.
CARPENTER, T.P. (1976) 'Analysis and synthesis of existing research on measurement', in LESH, R.A. (Ed) *Number and Measurement*, papers from a research workshop. Columbus, OH, ERIC Clearing House for Science, Math and Environmental Education.
CARPENTER, T.P. and MOSER, J.M. (1983) 'The addition and subtraction concepts', in LESH, R. and LANDAU, M. (Eds) *Acquisition of Mathematics Concepts and Processes*, New York, Academic Press.
CARPENTER, T.P., FENNEMA, E. and PETERSON, P.L. (1987) 'Teachers' pedagogical content knowledge in mathematics', paper presented at the annual meeting of the American Educational Research Association, Washington, D.C.
CARPENTER, T.P., FENNEMA, E., PETERSON, P.L. and CAREY, D. (1988) 'Teachers' pedagogical content knowledge of students' problem solving in elementary arithmetic', *Journal of Research in Mathematics Education*, 19, 5, pp. 385–401.
COCKCROFT, W.H. (1982) *Mathematics Counts: The Report of the Commission of Inquiry into the Teaching of Mathematics in Schools*, under the chairmanship of Dr. W.H. Cockcroft, London, HMSO.
CORRAN, G. and WALKERDINE, V. (1980) 'Making it count: Children's acquisition of natural

numbers in speech', paper presented at the British Psychological Society Education Section Conference, Lancaster.

COXFORD, A. (1978) 'Research directions in geometry', in LESH, R. (Ed) *Recent Research Concerning the Development of Spatial and Geometric Concepts*, The Ohio State University, Eric Cleaning House for Science, Mathematics and Environmental Education.

DESFORGES, C. and COCKBURN, A. (1987) *Understanding the Mathematics Teacher*, London, Falmer Press.

DIENES, Z.P. (1960) *Building up Mathematics*, London, Hutchinson Educational Ltd.

DIENES, Z.P. and GOLDING, E.W. (1971) *Approach to Modern Mathematics*, New York, Herder and Herder.

EDWARDS, D. and MERCER, N. (1987) *Common Knowledge: The Development of Understanding in the Classroom*, London, Routledge.

FENNEMA, E., CARPENTER, T.A. and PETERSON, P.L. (1989) 'Learning mathematics with cognitively guided instruction', in BROPHY, J.E. (Ed) *Advances in Research on Teaching*, Vol. 1, Greenwich, CT, JAI Press, pp. 195–221.

FORMAN, E.A. and CAZDEN, C.B. (1985) 'Exploring Vygotskian perspectives, in education: The cognitive value of peer interaction', in WERTSCH, J.V. (Ed) *Culture, Communication and Cognition; Vygotskian Perspectives*, Cambridge, Cambridge University Press.

FUSON, K. (1988) *Children's Counting and Concepts of Number*, New York, Springer-Verlag.

GELMAN, R. and GALLISTEL, C.R. (1978) *The Child's Understanding of Number*, Cambridge, MA, Harvard University Press.

GINSBURG, H.P. (1977) 'The psychology of arithmetic thinking', *Journal of Children's Mathematical Behaviour*, 1, pp. 1–89.

HART, K. (1984) 'Which comes first — length, area, or volume?', *Arithmetic Teacher*, 31, 9, pp. 16–18 and pp. 26–7.

HMI (1978) *Primary Education in England: A Survey by H.M. Inspectors of Schools*, London, HMSO.

HMI (1991) *Mathematics Key Stages 1 and 3; A report by HM Inspectorate on the first year 1989–1990*, London, HMSO.

HERVEY, M. (1966) Children's response to two types of multiplication problem, *The Arithmetic Teacher*, April, pp. 288–291.

HUGHES, M. (1986) *Children and Number Difficulties in Learning Mathematics*, Oxford, Basil Blackwell.

KAPUT, J.J. (1987) 'Representation systems as mathematics', in JANVIER, C. (Ed) *Problems of Representation in the Teaching and Learning of Mathematics*, Hillsdale, NJ, Erlbaum, pp. 159–95.

KOZULIN, A. (Ed) (1986) *Thought and Language. Lev Vygotsky*. Cambridge, MA, The MIT Press.

LEINHARDT, G., PUTNAM, R.T., STEIN, M.K. and BAXTER, J. (1991) 'Where subject matter matters', *Advances in Research on Teaching*, Vol. 2, pp. 87–114.

LESH, R. (1979) 'Mathematical learning disabilities: Considerations for identification, diagnosis, and remediation', in LESH, R., MIERKIEWICZ, D. and KANTOWSKI, M.G. (Eds) *Applied Mathematical Problem Solving*, Columbus, OH, ERIC/SMEAR.

MOSER, J.M. (1986) 'Arithmetic operations on whole numbers: Addition and subtraction', in POST, T.R. (Ed) *Teaching Mathematics in Grades K-8. Research Based Methods*, Boston, MA, Allyn and Bacon, Inc.

PIAGET, J., INHELDER, B. and SZEMINSKA, A. (1960) *The Child's Conception of Geometry.* (E.A. Lunzer, Trans.) London, Routledge and Kegan Paul.
POST, T.R. and CRAMER, K.A. (1989) 'Knowledge, representation, and quantitative thinking', in REYNOLDS, M.C. (Ed) *Knowledge Base for the Beginning Teacher,* London, Pergamon Press.
SINCLAIR, J.M. and COULTHARD, R.M. (1975) *Towards an Analysis of Discourse: The English used by Teachers and Pupils,* London, Oxford University Press.
STEFFE, L.P. *et al* (1982) 'Children's arithmetical problem solving', in GINSBURG, H.P. (Ed) *The Development of Mathematical Thinking,* New York, Academic Press.
STEFFE, L.P. and COBB, P. (1988) *Construction of Mathematical Meanings and Strategies,* New York, Springer-Verlag.
STEINBERG, R. (1985) 'Instruction on derived facts strategies in addition and subtraction', *Journal for Research in Mathematics Education,* 16, 5, pp. 155–67.
THORNTON, C.A. (1978) 'Emphasizing thinking strategies in basic fact instruction', *Journal for Research in Mathematics Education,* 9, pp. 214–27.
TIZARD, B. and HUGHES, M. (1984) *Young Children Learning. Talking and Thinking at Home and at School,* London, Fontana.
TIZARD, B., BLATCHFORD, P., BURKE, J., FARQUHAR, C. and PLEWIS, I. (1988) *Young Children at School in the Inner City.* London, Lawrence Erlbaum Assoc.
WALKERDINE, V. (1984) 'Developmental psychology and the child-centred pedagogy: The insertion of Piaget into early education', in HENRIQUES, J. *et al* (Eds) *Changing the Subject. Psychology, Social Regulation and Subjectivity,* London, Methuen.
WELLS, G. (1979) *Influences of the Home on Language Development,* Bristol Working Papers in Language No. 1, University of Bristol, mimeo, pp. 29–51.
WELLS, G. (1985) *Language, Learning and Education,* Windsor, NFER-Nelson.
WILLES, M.J. (1983) *Children into Pupils: A Study of Language in Early Schooling,* London, Routledge and Kegan Paul.
ZWENG, M. (1964) 'Division problems and the concepts of rate', *The Arithmetic Teacher,* 11, pp. 547–56.

Chapter 6

The Challenge of Science

Rosemary Feasey

The introduction of the National Curriculum has brought into sharp focus the role of subject knowledge. Early years education demands that the teacher makes sense of the curriculum areas and the multidimensional experiences children bring from home into the school context. With respect to science the reality may be that the teacher's understanding of the nature of science and its associated concepts is not sufficient to sustain the complexity of accommodating the demands of the curriculum alongside the informal knowledge and understanding children bring to school.

The challenge for teachers of the National Curriculum is to provide access to science for all children. It requires that teachers recognize the needs of children and are able to translate the curriculum in such a manner that access is facilitated. There is, however, an intimate relationship between the teacher's personal subject knowledge and the ability to deliver the science curriculum. Teachers will define the curriculum and match it to children's needs on the basis of their own subject expertise. In terms of the science curriculum this creates problems. For many years it has been recognized that insufficient subject knowledge in science has led to low teacher confidence and expertise.

Although the National Curriculum has provided a much-needed framework for science throughout the primary years, the framework is being provided for practice which is ill-defined, by teachers who have little or no scientific knowledge and understanding. It is intended that this chapter will not place the burden of blame on teachers but will indicate that the development of a knowledge base of science and of children's scientific thinking is essential, both for individual teachers and the profession as a whole.

Alexander, Rose and Woodhead (1992) make a timely reference to 'curricular expertise' in the primary school:

> We use the phrase 'curricular expertise' to mean the subject knowledge, the understanding of how children learn, and the the skills needed to teach subjects successfully. Effective teaching depends on the successful combination of these understandings and skills. Opinion

is divided about the the relative importance of the teacher's subject knowledge, but few now dispute that it is important. Our view is that subject knowledge is a critical factor at every point in the teaching process: in planning, assessing and diagnosing, task setting, questioning, explaining and giving feedback. (p. 25)

If a high level of confidence and subject expertise is required to teach science effectively then expectations that teachers will be able to deliver a content-driven National Curriculum are unrealistic. Over the past thirty years primary teachers have found difficulty in responding to a range of initiatives in science teaching. How much the imposition of the National Curriculum can do to raise the standard of practice in science teaching is open to debate, given teachers' existing knowledge base. In considering the nature of science and the development of scientific concepts, skills and ideas, it is important to recognize the complexity of scientific activity. To help unravel this complexity we need ways of describing this activity. In order to provide a view of science and of science education we need to describe the parts in order to understand better the whole. To simplify understanding of the living world in biology, for instance, we use taxonomies to organize the animal kingdom into more manageable compartments. Similarly the biological and physical aspects of science as a whole can be classified in an attempt to bring some order to a complex area. There are three aspects to consider. These are knowledge and understanding, processes and skills.

Aspects of science

SKILLS		PROCESSES
using equipment		observing
measurement		hypothesizing
constructing tables		interpreting
making graphs		inferring
		drawing conclusions

KNOWLEDGE AND UNDERSTANDING

Life and living processes
Materials and their properties
Physical processes

These should not be considered as competing (although in primary science they are often viewed as such), but complementary aspects.

These aspects are, in fact, no more than ways of looking at scientific activity. Nor are they the only ones, but they are ways which have been popular over the past decade and, hence, have influenced the whole of the primary science curriculum. Just as each aspect of scientific activity is related to the others, so each aspect has its own related, component parts which help to define the whole.

Over the years teachers have been exposed to different views placing different emphases on these three aspects of scientific activity, and, according to their own perspective and scientific knowledge have responded in different ways. In order to appreciate the impact this has had on classroom practice we need to consider each of the three aspects in order to appreciate how teachers may have interpreted them and the possible effect this has had on classroom practice (see Gott, 1991).

1 **Knowledge and understanding** of science encompasses the different content areas. It is organized in terms of the current grouping of concepts in terms of biology, chemistry and physics.

2 **Scientific skills** revolve around the development through practice of children's skills in using measuring instruments of various kinds, recording in tables, displaying on graphs.

3 **Scientific processes** in combination provide the means of testing ideas by scientific methods. These comprise:
observing — using the senses, where appropriate, to find out about an object or event,
predicting — suggesting what may happen,
hypothesizing — suggesting what will happen on the basis of reason,
interpreting — linking patterns and noting relationships,
inferring — drawing conclusions from evidence.

The use of such skills and processes is not unique to science. The application of measurement skills may be a feature of mathematical as much as scientific investigations, for instance. Similarly we make predictions everyday of our lives in a whole variety of situations. The combination of these skills and processes and the ideas and generalizations which result from this process provide a developing understanding of the physical and biological world which is defined as school science.

As noted earlier, different emphases have been placed on these three aspects of science over the years. It is equally important, however, to appreciate the personal interpretations placed on such views of science in order to consider the effect on science teaching. Given that so many teachers lacked confidence in science it is not surprising that many chose to make use of those aspects which they understood or with which they felt sympathy. The consequence of this was that some teachers adopted the then, dominant approach wholesale, appreciating and developing each of its components in relation to the others, whilst many other teachers incorporated in their teaching only those components in which they felt most confident, often selecting some (but not all) of the components from one or more aspects of science.

The first aspect **subject knowledge and understanding** has, to a large extent, been marginalized in practice. One can only suggest reasons for this. High on the list must be low teacher knowledge and confidence in terms of developing children's scientific concepts. Many teachers, quite naturally, have had a reluctance to place themselves in a position which could expose their inadequate personal subject knowledge in science.

Another factor which helps to explain a reluctance on the part of teachers to teach science concepts in the early years has been the influence of Piaget's work on teachers' pedagogical discourse and practices which has been developed more fully by Carol Aubrey in chapter 5. Egan (1988) has referred to teachers' utilization of the framework of stages of development as 'most influential in education in a restrictive way'. He has argued that 'most of the inferences one sees in education from his (Piaget's) learning/development theory concern what children cannot do' (p. 21).

Alexander *et al* (1992) echoed this sentiment in their suggestion that the following of Piagetian notions of developmental stages had depressed expectations and 'discouraged teacher intervention'. No where is this more apparent than in early years science.

In many respects early years science has worked on a deficit model, that is, it has operated on assumptions about what children *cannot* do. This has been the case particularly with respect to children's ability to learn scientific facts and develop understanding of concepts. This view of children's learning, allied to teachers' own low level of subject knowledge, has resulted in scientific subject knowledge receiving least attention from teachers. To make sense of the content of the science curriculum requires a more considerable science knowledge base than many teachers possess.

The second aspect of science, or **skills** aspect has been more readily adopted by teachers. The acceptance of this aspect of science related to teachers' recognition of what has been regarded as familiar, most easily translated into or closest to, existing classroom practice.

Although observation was included under the process aspect of science, teachers have frequently regarded observation as part of their skills approach to science. Its inclusion in this context is misplaced, however. Observation is conceptually based. Its development, in connection with exploration of scientific phenomena, is associated with a widening and deepening understanding of the biological and physical world. Putting on 'science spectacles', that is, appreciating the distinctive features of scientific observation is essential. Certainly teachers can assist in the development of scientific observation by increasing children's skill, for example, in using a hand lens or a microscope, but what children make of their observations, the ideas which emerge from the process, is dependent on their development of scientific concepts.

The focus on observation offered teachers an approach to science with which they could feel comfortable and confident. It is, therefore, no surprise to find that much science of the early years has revolved around observation. 'Observation using all the senses' has been the definition associated with this approach. It has given rise to activities in which children have been asked to touch, feel, listen, smell and taste. A plethora of activities in published schemes and science text books have validated this approach as science. Research evidence from the *Exploration of Science* project (Foulds, Gott and Feasey, 1992) has indicated that observation has become a central component of early years science. Further analysis of activities which were defined by teachers as scientific observation turned out, in fact, to be art- or language-related. The lack of any link in these so-called observation activities to science knowledge and understanding meant that the observation was serving other areas of the curriculum. This tended to be due to the individual teacher's inability to select relevant knowledge and understanding and, thus, recognize the scientific outcomes from the activity.

It is significant that the emergence of observation, however misconstrued, has become a central feature of a skills approach to science. Measurement as a skill, however, does not appear to have been as highly valued. This conclusion is supported by evidence, from the same study, which has suggested a lack of standard measuring equipment available in early years classrooms. Once again this *may* be associated with teachers' acceptance of a Piagetian view of the development in children's measurement concepts. A consequence of this for classroom practice may be that children can remain for too long in the realms of measuring with hand spans and other, arbitrary units. There is also some evidence to suggest a lack of demand for the use of measurement in science unless it relates to such topics as, for instance, 'Ourselves' and concerns body measurement. In science children should be encouraged and, indeed, challenged to use mathematical skills in reading and using measurement instruments of various kinds, as well as to apply measurement within scientific measurement.

The skills approach as interpreted, in summary, allowed teachers success without making demands on them of trying to make sense of, and develop scientific ideas relating to, for instance, forces, energy transfer, using light or processes of life. The consequence of this was that teachers offered observation as a skill in a sterile manner, instead of using scientific observation as a means to develop science knowledge and understanding.

Where teachers focused on the third aspect, the **processes** of science, the same study suggested they divided into two groups. The first group seemed to conceive the process approach in terms of activities where children were encouraged to engage in developing each of the associated components outlined earlier in the chapter separately. Activities, for example, were planned for children to predict what would happen first, and then try to find out whether their prediction was correct. Such activities frequently served mathematics rather than science, for instance, predicting the distance a toy car would travel and then testing the prediction. Science processes were, thus, compartmentalized and selected for inclusion in classroom activities on the basis of the teacher's confidence and understanding.

The second group of teachers defined processes in terms of fair testing, attempting to incorporate all of the components of this aspect of science in a problem solving approach. Fair tests became central to this interpretation of science but evidence from the *Exploration of Science* project (Foulds, Gott and Feasey, 1992) indicated that invariably what took place was a series of truncated investigations. Children were encouraged to be decision-makers and to carry out fair tests in a practical manner but failed to appreciate the central role of 'evidence'. They were invited to create fair tests but were provided with little support in relating their data to the original question or to the believability of the evidence.

The nature of evidence, the need to collect data and analyze it in terms of the level of confidence that can be placed in it was a component frequently missing from teachers' understanding of this approach. The reason may rest with teachers' inability to challenge pupils to use their existing ideas to make sense of data and test their ideas against evidence.

This requires teacher appreciation of both scientific knowledge and understanding and the purpose of measurement for generating numerical data in investigations.

Both approaches to the process view are equally narrow in perspective since each lacks the integration and development of pupils' own knowledge and understanding in science. The development of the processes aspect of science has been validated by the goal, or intention that primary science should be practical and activity-based or 'hands on'. But what such activities have gained in terms of offering children practical experience, they have lacked in terms of their linking of the 'doing' to the development of understanding and a sense of coherence and progression.

The inability of teachers to accommodate the process aspect of science with scientific knowledge and understanding has provided ammunition for critics of primary science education. The processes outlined earlier are ways of thinking, they are cognitive processes which may be applied to other areas of the curriculum and, indeed, to everyday situations outside the school context. The process approach, or rather an overemphasis on this aspect of science, may offer children practice in making sense of new phenomena and events and considering whether their ideas fit the evidence but unless these are scientific ideas the activity will be indistinguishable from other areas of the curriculum.

What have been the repercussions in terms of practice from the overemphasis on particular aspects of science?

1. Some teachers have been teaching what they genuinely have considered as science but, in fact, has been mathematics or language masquerading as science.
2. Some teachers have extracted components at random from the different aspects of science, including 'bits' of skills, some knowledge and understanding and fair testing which has resulted in lack of coherence and many areas of science being underdeveloped.
3. Another group contained those teachers whose views of science could

be described as unidimensional who, for whatever reason, disregarded two of the three aspects of science described. Their approach might be described as well-defined and cohesive in terms of the aspect espoused but not, however, balanced.

4   A final group of teachers comprised those who were able to recognize that a composite approach was one best-suited to science teaching. Such teachers were able to choose components from each of the three aspects, as appropriate, for a series of science-based tasks. Their view of science was a balanced one, appreciating how the different elements fitted together.

Science practice is also shaped by teachers' philosophy towards early years education. The impact of teachers' beliefs about early years education should not be underestimated. In many respects it has led to the lowering of credibility of science for young children which, as noted earlier in the chapter, has resulted in a view held by some that little identifiable science occurs at this level.

The influence of the Plowden Report (1967) and its espousal of Piagetian theory is still felt today in early years classrooms. Phrases such as 'child-centred' and 'allowing children to experience their environment' are probably the most used and abused phrases in the lexicon of science teaching. They have lost much in translation, having been attached to so many different contexts they are almost meaningless. Contrary to popular belief the report did not endorse uncritically 'discovery learning' and caution in its application was advised. The treatment of science teaching in the report, however, could well be summarized by this term.

The view of science through observation characterized as 'using all the senses' has been referred to already. All humans do this, from the new-born to the elderly. This is how the species survives. Are we to say that every time we observe something, feel the texture of a piece of clothing, taste a food that we are being scientific? What tacit understanding *do* teachers have of such phrases? Perhaps it is precisely the lack of definition which allows early years educators to feel comfortable. Such loose definitions of the science curriculum are dangerous. They may be used to validate almost any kind of practice and diminish the role of science in the early years.

There may also arise from this philosophy, a reluctance by the teacher to impose ideas, strategies or facts, in other words to *teach* children. Many teachers still rely on a 'discovery' approach assuming that pupils will find out by experiencing the world and without teacher intervention. Browne (1991) asked the question,

> Why have we been willing to leave science to luck whilst maintaining that other areas of the curriculum, such as literacy and maths require higher teacher input? (p. 20)

In the 1960s and 1970s a child-centred 'dogma' and low teacher subject knowledge resulted in a view that intervention strategies in science were not appropriate for the early years. At the same time as the Plowden Report was being prepared the Nuffield Junior Science Project was in progress. This project, the first, and most influential curriculum innovation in primary science in the 1960s, endorsed the view that children should engage in self-appointed tasks across the curriculum, aimed at developing observing, questioning, exploring, interpreting findings and communicating these.

Within this climate topic work became the mainstay of most primary schools and science was translated into language, maths and art activities by teachers who felt more comfortable with these areas of the curriculum than with science. As the skills-process aspects of science teaching became accessible teachers embraced them because they served to validate teaching which was experiential and activity-based.

Alexander *et al* (1992) in discussing progressive and informal approaches in education indicated that a minority of classrooms in Leeds,

> exhibited wholeheartedly 'exploratory characteristics'. However, elsewhere they were ignored — or most damagingly in our view, adopted as so much rhetoric to sustain practice which in visual terms might look attractive and busy but which lacked any serious educational rationale. (p. 9)

In many respects the observations made about primary schools in Leeds would be equally true for much of the practice in primary science. Evidence from a range of sources, for example, HMI (1978) has, for many years, criticized the low level of science offered in schools, and led to its being described as resembling 'busy work'. Recent research by the *Exploration of Science* project (Foulds, Gott and Feasey, 1992) into teacher perceptions towards science investigations confirms the lack of clarity in thinking many have had in this area of the curriculum.

> In Key Stage 1 science is seen as activity based and a vehicle for achieving a wide range of learning outcomes but the outcomes themselves are poorly defined.

The result has been a 'context driven' science curriculum derived from early years, child-centred pedagogy. This has been translated into practical activities which are, for want of better terms, 'experiential' or play. This is not to devalue the role of either of these activities with respect to children's learning but the lack of focus and recognition of the role of scientific knowledge within these activities renders them useless in terms of developing science. Science *can* be developed from play and 'experience' but only when the teacher has defined the scientific purpose in terms of the conceptual knowledge involved which, in turn, determines the outcome. Learning is then identified with using children's existing ideas to make sense of the activities and testing these against the results of the activity.

Within the early years an important dimension of any learning situation is the knowledge and understanding that children bring with them to the classroom. Egan (1988) stated that

> we are treating our young children as fools. (p. 18)

in that we do not offer them sufficient challenge. This has been due not only to lack of subject knowledge but also to the gulf between rhetoric and practice with respect to accessing what children know and matching the activity to this understanding. Alexander *et al* (1992) noted that recent research into children's learning has emphasized young children's immense cognitive and linguistic competence. Harlen (1985) has long espoused the view that children will develop ideas about their world from their earliest years. She has suggested that

> The teacher's role in helping children to develop ideas has several aspects of which we shall consider the following:
> - gaining access to children's ideas
> - deciding the next steps which can be attempted
> - taking action to help the development
> - knowing when to stop. (p. 74)

We ignore the informal ideas which children bring from home at our peril. Many of our children are subjected to activities with little cognitive challenge, for instance, about the colour and texture of objects, or the parts of the body which children have known since they were 2-years-old. Indeed the first round of Standard Assessment Tasks (SATs) (1991) for science provided a classic example, where children were asked to name the parts of the body and teachers were invited to accept such answers as head and legs. All but a small percentage of children have had this knowledge for a number of years.

Whilst one would not question the validity of eliciting children's ideas the fact remains that in order to be able to recognize and develop children's ideas in a useful manner the teacher requires personal knowledge on a number of levels:

- knowledge and understanding of science concepts
- an ability to elicit children's ideas
- the ability to recognize those ideas for what they are, part concepts, misconceptions, no idea at all
- the ability to facilitate children in the process of making sense of their own ideas
- the ability to recognize and match activities which provide a suitable route in the development of an idea.

Rosemary Feasey

There appear to be a number of dynamic forces at work in the shaping of early years science teaching:

- personal knowledge and understanding of scientific concepts
- personal beliefs about teaching science
- personal knowledge about the development of young children's scientific concepts.

This is captured in the view expressed by Alexander *et al* (1992)

> Our view is that subject knowledge is a critical factor at every point in the teaching process, in planning, assessing and diagnosing, task setting, questioning, explaining and giving feedback. (p. 25)

How artfully the teaching process is carried out will depend, to a large extent, on the personal knowledge and understanding of the teacher. The following is a suggested model for planning in science and an indication of how the need to use subject knowledge imposes itself at different stages.

Knowledge and understanding, processes and skills have, in this chapter, been viewed as aspects of one perspective. During a child's school career the teacher would endeavour to develop the different aspects of the perspective in order to provide a complete coverage:

Knowledge and understanding	Sound, light	Forces	**Living things**	Materials
Skills	**Using equipment**	Measurement	Tables	Graphs
Processes	Plan	Predict	**Observe**	Interpret

This table provides a framework for planning science which allows the teacher to make decisions about which component to focus on according to the needs of the child and the curriculum.

The combination and order in which components are developed would be determined by a class or school's scheme of work. In order to accomplish this teachers would need to move from a context- to a task-based approach towards science. The approach demands that teachers identify the purpose of the task, the scientific knowledge involved and the outcome(s) entailed and then choose the type of task which is appropriate to the successful delivery of the outcome. This task-based approach substitutes for the less coherent approach which seeks to identify a context and then find activities that appear to relate to this context, or the topic chosen.

The Challenge of Science

Below is an example of how the teacher might choose purposes relating to the development of knowledge and understanding about an aspect of living things, for instance, classification of insects, through observation using and developing a skill in handling specific equipment.

Knowledge and understanding	Sound, light	Forces	**Living things**	Materials
Skills	**Use of Equipment**	Measurement	Tables	Graphs
Processes	Plan	Predict	**Observe**	Interpret

The question then becomes: what kind of tasks can assist the delivery of the purposes identified by the teacher? Within primary science we can identify a menu of tasks which provide the means within the classroom for the development of the different aspects of science. The tasks can be classified as:

- observation
- skills
- illustrative
- research
- explorations (try it and see)
- investigations

Observation tasks enable:

> pupils to look at objects or events in a 'scientific way'. (Gott and Duggan, 1992)

Science provides a context which demands that the observer makes sense of an object or phenomenon in terms of previous scientific experience and knowledge. *Observation* tasks require that teachers develop children's:

- scientific knowledge
- appropriate use of their senses
- ability to use and choose equipment to enhance observation
- ability to note similarities and differences
- ability to focus on salient points or events.

Skills work usually develops the use of aspects such as producing graphs or learning to use a thermometer. The most useful context for teaching children the skill of reading a thermometer or constructing a graph is when the child needs to apply measurement within a science investigation. One of the most common problems in carrying out science investigations is the inability of children to apply measurement skills to school science. Often children develop skills in isolation or in inappropriate contexts. Typically it is the teacher who decides when and for what reason measurement skills are used, rather than placing children in a situation which demands that they make the decision as to which skills to bring into play.

Illustrative activities are invariably those which involve children in carrying out a set of recipe-like instructions. The intention of these activities is to lead children through a task to a defined outcome, which it is intended will lead to the understanding of a specific concept or the practising of a specific skill. A consequence of the prescriptive nature of such tasks is that they preclude children from being involved in the decision-making process. An additional problem associated with such instruction-based activities is that they are unsuitable to those children whose ability is above or below the level of the instructions in terms of reading, mathematics or science attainment. Despite the inherent problems of this type of activity it is most powerful in terms of children's learning when used to teach or develop understanding of a concept. Illustrative tasks should not be confused with investigations, since there is little or no scope in the former for children to be involved in the decision-making process which is central to investigative work.

Research activities by their very nature do not lend themselves to 'hands on' tasks. Facts such as the distance of the Sun from the Earth or how snails breathe require children to be able to research information, using a range of resources from books to videos. There are also times when the teacher should be seen as a resource and feel free to impart certain knowledge and understanding to children. Alexander *et al* (1992) raised the issue of the teacher as a source of knowledge and commented on the 'persistent and damaging belief that pupils should never be told things, only asked questions' (p. 31).

Try it and see types of task are generally known as exploration. Such tasks might be teacher-organized or defined by children as work with materials and objects. Here children are attempting to make sense, usually of an object which they manipulate. The interaction with the object should be viewed in terms of children's having a construct and testing whether it is correct. In the light of their interaction the original idea might be changed, reinforced or lead to a new set of ideas they may plan to explore. To the observer a child's exploration might appear unstructured, as an *ad hoc* series of actions. Commonly, however, the child has a particular idea which is being tested in a deliberate and structured manner. In many ways this type of working is, indeed, a natural precursor to the development of more formal investigations.

Investigation is a term now more clearly defined than it has been at any other period in the history of primary science. Until the advent of the National Curriculum the word 'investigation' referred to a wide range of activities which closely resembled the *Oxford Dictionary* (Swannell, 1986) definition 'to find out'. This literal interpretation appears to have been widely used to apply to activities where children were given a practical activity to carry out. In the National Curriculum the term 'investigation' is used in connection with developing concepts, processes and skills in a way which enables children through the planning and the carrying out of a fair test to find the solution to a problem, or the answer to a question.

The knowledge base in investigations has a number of levels. At one level is procedural knowledge which relates the use of a component part of the skills aspect of science such as using a ruler to measure to a process such as recognizing the need for a fair test in an overall strategy which will help towards a solution. Scientific ideas and concepts come into play in recognizing the problem or appreciating the nature of the question, and in the interpretation and understanding of the evidence produced to reach a conclusion. Overarching conceptual and procedural knowledge is the development of an ability to deploy them together in investigations. For the teacher this entails developing the two in tandem whilst appreciating that the needs of children may necessitate the emphasis on a particular one.

These tasks, as noted, provide the basic menu from which teachers can make an appropriate choice to match the development of the intended outcome. Early years science, at present, may run the risk of being narrow in the focus of tasks, using mainly observation and exploration-type activities. The combination of such a narrow range of activities with outcomes which are ill-defined in terms of scientific concepts is unlikely to fulfil the requirements of the National Curriculum.

In order to provide adequate coverage across knowledge and understanding, skills and processes, the range of activities needs to be broadened to include illustrative, skills, research-based activities and more investigations. This is crucial since it is mandatory that at least 50 per cent of all activities should fall into the category of Attainment Target 1 (scientific investigation). It would be naive, however, to suggest that all teachers have to do is increase the range of activities and be specific about the intended science outcome. The whole process is more complex and may demand from individual teachers a shift towards more structure and precision with the acknowledgment of the need for strategic teacher intervention. Such a model of planning is suggested below. It depends on the successful interaction of the following:

- teachers' personal knowledge and understanding of scientific concepts
- an understanding of the relationship among the different components of science to each other in order to develop the whole
- the ability to elicit and make sense of the knowledge and understanding children bring to science.

The *Exploration of Science* project (Foulds, Gott and Feasey, 1992) suggests it is important that teachers are able to recognize what they expect to learn or develop from the activity. The outcome might include children's knowing that magnets have a pull and suggest questions about magnets to which children might try to find an answer. Without specified outcomes it is less likely that children's learning will be taken forward. The suggestions that such a strategy

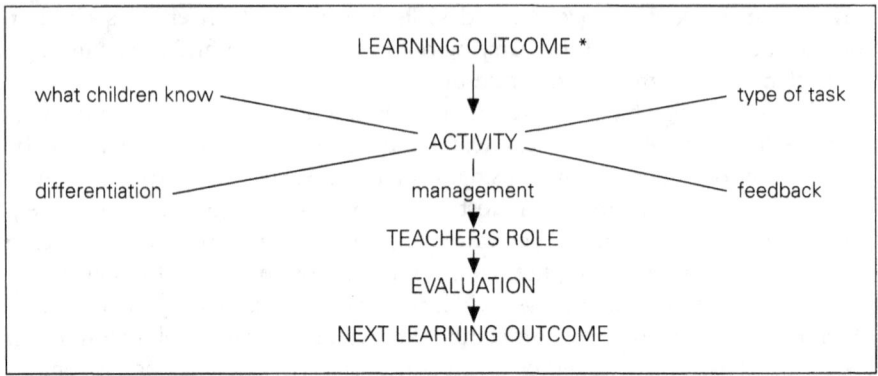

* The term outcome is used instead of objective in order to focus attention on what children are to learn as a result of the teaching.

might be too prescriptive misses the point. Teachers confident in scientific knowledge will be flexible enough to manage an activity which develops at a tangent to the original outcome. They will be able to recognize and accommodate new outcomes. For less confident teachers the outcome at least provides a focus which they can develop rather than allowing the floundering with an activity the purposes of which they are unsure.

The **activity** type will be dictated by the learning outcome. Decisions are multiple and complex and are frequently made in parallel rather than in the linear fashion the diagram might suggest. The decision about the type of activity to be carried out should be determined by, for instance, such factors as the need to elicit children's particular scientific ideas or the need to cater for children who are still at the exploration stage, rather than at the stage where they might be able to handle a simple investigation. One aspect of the activity which is frequently overlooked at this stage is decision-making related to the nature of feedback. This is an essential component of the activity and it is where the teacher can access the development of children's ideas, and through discussion, help the crystalization of ideas. The more confident the teacher is in terms of personal knowledge in science, the more effective questioning strategies and, hence, feedback sessions are likely to be.

The **teacher's role** should be fluid, constantly changing to suit the circumstances. In the planning stages, however, the role should be scrutinized and decisions taken not only about the type of role to adopt but about how the role is likely to be most effectively executed. The nature of the activity might dictate that children are autonomous, the teacher interacting with the group only when it is time for them to give feedback on their activity. Equally where appropriate, formal teaching should not be eschewed. It should also be recognized, however, that teaching is appropriate for only a limited set of learning outcomes.

Having specified outcomes at an early stage of the planning process the **evaluation** decisions focus on the strategies for accessing any developments

The Challenge of Science

in children's scientific ideas. Having decided, for example, that children should understand that magnets can pull objects this will influence the next outcome, for example, that children are able to classify those materials which can be pulled by the magnet.

Topics relating to magnets need to be broken down into small steps and organized in a logical manner where a general progression can be identified. This is for the teacher's benefit as it offers a structure and a support. It does not necessarily entail a linear treatment. A teacher might opt to invite children to find out as much as they can about magnets on an activity table. The general planning strategy, however, remains valid for both.

What is evident from this model is that a number of propositions emerge in terms of the requirements for effective delivery of science in the early years:

- the need for a higher level of personal subject knowledge in science
- an awareness of the nature of science
- an appreciation of the range of activities and their functions in order to deliver the science curriculum
- the need to use the above to define learning outcomes which take into account children's existing knowledge and understanding

The interrelationship among teacher knowledge of science, early years pedagogy and children's ideas is complex. Without a firm understanding of subject knowledge in science the teacher is less likely to be able to incorporate the other two elements successfully.

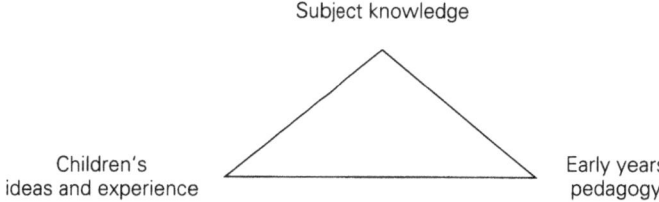

The year 1989 saw the initiation of the first cohort of children into the National Curriculum at the age of 5 years. The year 2002 will see some of those children entering teacher education. One might presume that their science would be more adequate in terms of knowledge and understanding than those students entering teacher education at present. That is dependent, however, on teachers being able to make sense of the National Curriculum for science. The evidence suggests that we still have a long way to go.

References

ALEXANDER, R., ROSE, J. and WOODHEAD, C. (1992) *Curriculum Organisation and Classroom Practice in Primary Schools — A Discussion Paper*, London, HMSO.

BROWNE, N. (1991) *Science and Technology in the Early Years*, Milton Keynes, Open University Press.
DES (1967) *Children and their Primary Schools*, London, HMSO.
EGAN, K. (1988) *Teaching as Story Telling*, London, Routledge.
FOULDS, K., GOTT, R. and FEASEY, R. (Exploration of Science Project) (1992) *Investigative Work in Science, A Report Commissioned by the National Curriculum Council*, York, NCC.
GOTT, R. (1991) *The Stratification of Knowledge and Understanding in School Science*, Internal Working Paper Number 2, Exploration of Science Project, University of Durham.
GOTT, R. and DUGGAN, S. (1992) *Why Investigations?*, Internal Working Paper, Exploration of Science Project, University of Durham.
HARLEN, W. (1985) *Primary Science Taking the Plunge*, London, Heinemann.
HARLEN, W. (1992) *The Teaching of Science*, London, Fulton.
HMI (1978) *Primary Education in England. A Survey by H.M. Inspectors of Schools*, London, HMSO.
HODGSON, B. and SCANLON, E. (Eds) (1985) *Approaching Primary Science*, London, Harper and Row with the Open University.
SWANNELL, J. (1986) *The New Little Oxford Dictionary*, London, Oxford University Press.

Chapter 7

Teaching History in the Infant Classroom

Deirdre Pettitt

Introduction

Since the introduction of *History in the National Curriculum* (DES, 1991) the teaching of history has been extended to infant schools by mandate. Before that, history teaching was often found in the infant classroom, but was not always implemented in any systematic way. *Primary Education in England* (DES, 1978) reported that there were only a few schools in which children were able to develop historical concepts and skills. History was more often an established part of the curriculum for older than younger primary school children. Between 1982 and 1986 further surveys were made by HMI. It was reported:

> The standards of work achieved in history, whether taught separately or as part of topic work, were very disappointing. In only one in five infant schools or departments and one in three junior schools and departments were standards judged to be satisfactory or better. (DES, 1990, pp. 2 and 3)

Clearly, from the attention given to it, HMI believed that history should be part of the infant curriculum. Equally clearly they took the view that it did not receive the attention it deserved. One reason for this was identified as the lack of curriculum leadership and curriculum policy. Currently, with the introduction of the National Curriculum matters have improved (DES, 1992). Curriculum leaders in the humanities have been appointed, in-service courses have been run and another complaint of HMI, namely the weakness of history tacked on to topics, is being addressed. However, teachers, including curriculum leaders, are at the sharp end having to translate history in a way which is suitable for young children. Few teachers have studied history at their own level. Even when they have they, too, must consider how it can be introduced to their pupils.

Not a great deal is known about how young children cope with historical concepts. Teachers themselves are adding to that knowledge as they teach. What can be added to that experiential knowledge has been documented, fairly exhaustively, by Cooper (1992). Much of the work she reports relates to children in the later years of primary school. However, she concludes:

> Bruner (1963, p. 22) believed that 'the more elementary a course, and the younger its students, the more serious must be its pedagogical aim of forming the intellectual powers of those whom it serves.... We teach a subject, not to produce little living libraries, but to consider matters as a historian does, to take part in the process of knowledge'. Bruner was aware, however, that much work was needed to provide detailed structure of the humanities and that this has been postponed in the past, on the mistaken grounds that it is too difficult. (p. 33)

This suggests that in order to consider how children cope with historical concepts teachers must also consider matters as a historian does. Marwich (1970) proposed that the fundamental justification for historical study has two aspects. Firstly, it is fundamental in the sense that it meets a need of society (or a person living in that society) to know itself through its relationship with the past. Secondly, it is fundamental in a poetic sense in that there is a basic instinct in all individuals, a curiosity and a sense of wonder about the past which wishes to break down barriers about time and mortality to extend the limits of consciousness beyond the span of a single life. What a historian does, which distinguishes him/her from, say, the social scientist is that he works at all times within the dimensions of time.

> history is the necessary recollection of past activities of men (and women) and societies which makes it possible for the individual and the society to orientate themselves amid the bewildering currents of human diversity. (Marwick, 1970, p. 17)

Piaget (1969) suggested that in our attempt to determine the role of time in human experience generally, and in particular with children, we invariably discover that temporal ideas are linked to memories. They are linked as well to the grasp that a series of events occurs in temporal order and that between these events there are intervals whose duration must be appreciated. Memory is the construction of our own personal history which we construct and reconstruct in the same way as we construct history in a broader sense.

Since history is concerned with change and continuity over time it would be reasonable to assume historical reasoning requires some temporal framework and that some relationship exists between children's thinking about history and about time. In a useful review of this field Thornton and Vukelick (1988) suggested that children's understanding of time and of historical concepts is developmental and gradual. Young children may recite dates and some time terms which have little real meaning for them. The past-present dichotomy, however, is well within the grasp of 4-year-olds and most children of 5–6 years can be introduced to the cyclical nature of events by starting with those in their immediate life.

Time understanding will be one major consideration, then, which informs the way historical concepts are introduced (Vukelick, 1984) and time language used properly may simplify or bring persons and events in the past into historical focus. Historical concepts and historical time language should be taught within history just as time measurement and duration of time are taught within mathematics, acknowledging that there will be some overlap. Whilst we need a clearer understanding of the way young children learn history (Thornton, 1987) if we take a developmental view we may conclude that different concepts have importance at different stages and whilst some concepts have been mastered others are being added, with early naive concepts generating new meaning later in life. The complexity of concepts about time, however, cannot be over-looked. Adults, for instance, have difficulty getting any idea about the length of time this planet has existed because human history occupies such a small period of this time.

Small children have similar difficulties on a smaller scale. They may not know when their birthdays occur or ask if it is time to go home at 11.00 a.m. The subjective nature of time as well as the more objective ordering of temporal events is not easy to comprehend. The words today, tomorrow, yesterday, days of the week and months of the year are mysteries which only experience will solve. It should be remembered that it is expected that these words will be learned and used to meet Level 2 Attainment Targets in the mathematics curriculum (DES, 1988 *Mathematics for Ages 5 to 16*). So, children's experience will include these words and the related concepts in the infant school. In so far as history itself is concerned there is much else to build on. Children know about bed-time and tea-time. They may connect days of the week and clock time to favourite television programmes. They know that they have a history. They were babies, their siblings were born, they went to playgroup or nursery and they came to school, for example. Their grandparents and parents may have reminisced. (My own son was particularly fascinated that older people always seemed to talk about prices when they got together 'half a crown (*sic*) for an apple!')

History contains many other abstract concepts such as the nature of evidence and using imagination in an informed way. These will be discussed in more detail in the next sections. They will be drawn from the National Curriculum document because there we have what historians consider to be crucial. It is interesting to consider that when the working party drew up its first report (*History for Ages 5–16*, DES, 1990) it was in the position of having to explore, without a lot to go on, what history might look like at Key Stage 1. Whatever the merits of its recommendations, its authors were mainly historians eminent in the field giving serious attention to this problem. (It is well worth while for teachers to go back to this document, which is more extensive than the

Non-Statutory Guidance, not to swallow it whole but to compare their experience with the thinking of these people.) Evidently, the working party felt that we have been 'mistaken' in thinking some concepts too difficult.

Outside of the confines of history itself we have some confirmation about children's ability to deal with issues previously thought to be too hard. Donaldson (1978) pointed out that children can think logically and cope with abstraction in situations which make sense to them. Hughes (1989) admits that 'developmental psychologists now regard the young child as being intellectually more competent than was previously thought' and that 'most young children start school with considerable intellectual capacities'. It may be surmised, therefore that these 'intellectual capacities' can be used in history. Teachers can hardly be blamed if they believed what developmental psychologists 'previously thought' which may have led to underestimation and a weak inclusion of history in the curriculum. It is, of course, important not to underestimate the power of young children's capacity to think and reason. It is equally important not to teach history in such a way as to turn children off a fascinating subject because it does not make sense to them. Teachers have to know or come to know about the subject and have it make sense to their pupils. However, they also have to teach the rest of the curriculum. Can the place of history be justified in an overcrowded and 'impossible job' (Alexander *et al*, 1992)?

Whether or not teachers are historians by training they have had to implement history in the curriculum. Many have done a sterling job, have come to know what children can do and have found the subject suitable and interesting. However, there are signs that the infant curriculum may be narrowed as it is feared that its broad nature can cause a fall in standards of literacy and numeracy. It is agreed that children need to leave the infant years with these basic skills. However, reading and writing and mathematics need a context and a reason for learning. History is a subject where reading and writing of all kinds illuminate the subject and where the subject provides meaningful situations for reading and writing. No doubt similar cases can be made for other foundation subjects but the argument here is for the retention of a broad curriculum. It can be argued further that it would be a great pity to lose the opportunity teachers have seized, of introducing children to socially-valued knowledge. A move to a more narrowly-conceived and decontextualized curriculum in the name of improving basic skills may be regarded as misguided. The possibility of basic skills themselves suffering from such a move is also there. That the curriculum is overcrowded is clearly the case. It may of course be overloaded more by the pressure to move children quickly up levels of attainment than by the breadth of its content. Perhaps teachers should fight for a broad curriculum, properly taught, and against pushing children through it too quickly.

Be that as it may, history is a subject which lends itself to some of the most positive aspects of infant practice. Much of the history curriculum at Key Stage 1 is process-oriented. Processes such as understanding the difference between fact and fantasy exemplify the gradual accretion of concepts through

Teaching History in the Infant Classroom

many experiences. It seems therefore that history is worth defending and keeping in the infant curriculum.

The rest of this chapter is devoted to the subject knowledge of teachers and the historical content at Key Stage 1. These two facets have not been dealt with as though they are separate. They are not. Teachers are not encyclopaedias, nor should they be. Historical knowledge will often be as new to teachers as to children. Teachers, however, have the skill and experience to identify knowledge and to add to it the principles which such knowledge must embody.

Knowing the Subject

It was suggested in the introduction that even if teachers are historians they may have some difficulty in translating what they know for young children. Historians may have tended to get very involved in the specific periods of history they have studied and non-specialists may feel daunted about teaching something they have not considered for years. It is probably necessary for all teachers to think about the basic principles and ways of thinking inherent in the subject. A start is to look critically at *History in the National Curriculum* (DES, 1991). In this we find:

> 2.6 The history Attainment Targets do not prescribe items of historical content. These are to be found in the Programmes of Study. Pupils make use of historical content from the Programmes of Study to show they have attained one or more of the levels of knowledge, understanding and skills laid down in the Statements of Attainment.
>
> 2.7 The same level of attainment can be demonstrated through different types of historical content... (p. B2)

In the Programmes of Study there is one history study unit at Key Stage 1, encompassing levels 1–3. (It should be remembered, too, that Key Stage 2 overlaps Key Stage 1 as it covers levels 2–5.) At Key Stage 1 no specific periods of history or topics are prescribed. Instead, children are expected to be introduced to content which enables them to develop 'an awareness of the past' and to learn 'from a range of historical sources'. The content has to include opportunities to investigate changes in their own and their families' lives, changes in the lives of British people since World War II and 'the way of life of people in a period beyond living memory' (*ibid*). In so far as content is concerned, therefore, there is a lot of choice at Key Stage I. Teachers are not expected to cover every change, for example in the lives of people since World War II, but to select examples which typify changes. The Attainment Targets are: AT 1, Knowledge and Understanding of History; AT 2, Interpretations of History; and AT 3, The Use of Historical Sources.

Deirdre Pettitt

Apologies are made for the inclusion of what is very familiar to teachers but the very openness of this curriculum illustrates the need for teachers to have the knowledge to select appropriate content. At Key Stage 1 content has to be selected which will enable children to begin to 'describe and explain historical change' (AT 1), 'acquire evidence from historical sources and form judgments about their reliability and value' (AT 2) and 'understand interpretations of history' (*ibid*). Selection of content is crucial. Aspects of historical content related to matters of undisputed fact must be accurate. But content also has to be selected with at least two principles in mind. It should lend itself to the introduction of the important strands of history identified in the Attainment Targets and it has to make sense to children. The Programmes of Study state, sensibly, that progress is made 'from familiar situations to those more distant in time and place' (*ibid*).

Teachers, therefore, need to feel secure in their own minds that they themselves can explain or have some idea about how to explain historical change, are aware of the problematic nature of evidence and are critical about interpretations of history. This is a tall order, particularly for the non-specialist but, as suggested, familiarization with *History in the National Curriculum* (DES, 1991) including the Non-Statutory Guidance is a sensible start as are in-service courses. It may be that teachers, even allowing for the constraints of time, have found that beginning to think about the processes and principles of history have led them to wanting to know more. They may have begun to ask questions about their own taken-for-granted assumptions. They may also begin to question certain non-statutory items in history documents (*ibid*).

Most teachers, even if they are historians, will need to read up on any period of the past they intend to select. They will need to be familiar with landmark national and local events and the social history of the time. They will need accurate sources, powerful examples and typical artefacts. (Sources will be discussed in the next section.) In addition they will have to consider the contrasts, anomalies and interpretations inherent in their content in order to introduce young children to history with integrity. It has to be recorded that some of the non-statutory examples at Key Stage 1 do not seem to meet this objective very well. For example, 'to suggest reasons why people in the past acted as they did' (AT 1 Level 2, DES, 1991) does not seem well served by the example 'Explain why the Britons fought against the Romans'. It requires only a slight knowledge of history to know that the Roman occupation of Britain took place over hundreds of years. A simplistic answer such as 'to protect their wives and families' is problematic. Over that period many Britons probably saw the Roman occupation as a way of life to which they were accustomed.

Teachers, after a little thought might also reject the example 'Re-tell the story of the Gunpowder Plot' as suitable to meet Attainment Target 1, Level 1a) 'place in a sequence events in a story about the past' (*ibid*). This would be for two reasons. One is that the actual story of the Gunpowder Plot, as opposed to a celebration for which reasons have been blurred over time, is hardly the stuff for Level 1. The other is that sequencing a story about the past has hundreds of more suitable examples. To some extent the non-statutory examples do not seem to match up with the aims and objectives of the Programmes of Study. Teachers, seriously engaged in promoting the young child as historian — a not impossible aim — might see part of their subject knowledge and their knowledge about children learning being used to devise schemes of work which provide better examples than those suggested for Key Stage 1.

Sources for Subject Knowledge and for Teaching History

Sources for teachers and children are taken together because they are complementary. Teachers as well as children can learn from the same books and other material. What teachers need to know is where to look for and how to use and interpret historical sources. Of course, these are many and varied and only a few pointers can be offered in this section. It is sensible for teachers to share their knowledge with colleagues. Historical resources can be built up over time and be accessible to all with careful planning and efficient storage and referencing. Much equipment and indeed advice can be obtained from LEA sources and from museums.

It may be thought that the lives of children and their families will not need resourcing because the children themselves will provide information. Teachers will, of course, talk with children and their parents but there is a good deal they can do to help draw out experiences. They will be aware of the need for sensitivity. The undisturbed nuclear family can be a rarity and neutral time lines are preferable to family trees. Teachers will also make use of the experiences of minority groups. Undoubtedly, the reference to changes in the lives of British people in *History in the National Curriculum* (DES, 1991) includes those whose families derive from different countries and cultures. However, there is much else which can be researched. The history of the school itself — the older it is the more records there will be — can be established. If it is new it is still the case that its site has a history. When was it built and why? Moving out from the building, the environment — the road, the town, village, suburb or city have history which can be used selectively but which is part of the lives of children. Selection will depend upon whether the children need to study that which relates to the very recent past and therefore childrens' direct experience or whether it related to living memory or the more distant past. Information can be gathered from local people, school and other archives, local authorities, teachers' centres, museums and libraries. In a project on a housing estate the local Parks and Gardens Department may be an invaluable resource. Unexpected sources like this are often revealed by talking with colleagues, parents and governors.

Written Resources — Factual

A major source of historical information is always books and other written material of which the most obvious are history textbooks, books written by historians for adults and historical diaries. Apart from history which teachers might read at their own level there are books intended for school use: for infants, juniors or secondary-school children. All of these may be useful to teachers and some to young children. Books too difficult for young children to read and search out information may have useful pictures. Whether or not they are suitable for direct use in the infant classroom, all books available in school need to be carefully selected. In general it seems that these books are of higher quality if they are written by an author not a committee. Those written more recently tend to avoid overgeneralization such as, for primary schools, amazing and unconnected collections of 'homes through the ages'. Older books are useful if not too dated or if they contain information which does not change up to the date of publication such as the history of toys. Books which children will use should contain pages for contents, bibliographies and if possible glossaries. All books need to be checked as far as possible for accuracy and compared with other books on the same topic by teachers and when appropriate by children. Books will provide information about artefacts as well as events. If children are to be asked to identify the uses of artefacts and put them in chronological order teachers must at least be able to help with these tasks.

Other historical written material includes facsimile newspapers, census returns, old school exercise books, the schools' own records, recipe books and the like. Items such as these are beginning to be available commercially as are commercial schemes for history in the infant and junior school. Some are very good but need scrutiny to see if they will indeed embody the principles and processes of the subject as outlined above.

Stories and Myths

Stories which are written for children, whether they are true or fiction but which are set in the past, are an invaluable resource and some particular stories will be discussed under content. 'Storying', that is telling ourselves stories, has been described as a 'primary act of mind' (Hardy, 1977). We all tend to make sense of our experiences by telling ourselves stories which connect the new to the known (Wells, 1986). We tell others about our activities in a narrative mode. Storying is a way of thinking and communicating which is common to all human beings. Therefore a story is something which makes sense to children. Egan (1985) argues that reading fairy stories introduces children, very early on, to powerful concepts. He points to 'binary opposites' inherent in these stories such as power and powerlessness, rich and poor, and good and evil. So, even before there appears to be a direct connection with the history curriculum, historical ideas are brought to children's attention. The language of stories: once upon a time, long ago, when I was a little girl develops ideas about chronology. When a story is set in the 'real' past, either about actual events or in a definable era, children are helped to:

make that imaginative leap into the past which genuine understanding of history demands. It carries conviction of reality in relation to the past. It does both these things by putting historical information into three dimensions, by personalizing events and making vivid the setting. (Little, 1989, p. 46)

There are many stories for young children about growing, about grandparents and about change in family life. There are fewer which are set in the more distant past or which might illuminate what it was like to live even a couple of decades ago. Here teachers' own power as story tellers comes into play. It is not usually necessary to invent a story — many are available for older children — but to retell and make the stories accessible to infants.

Artefacts

The use of artefacts — from which teachers also learn — provides the essential experiences of using all the senses. Children need to see, touch, hear, smell and taste the past. Using smell, hearing and taste may be more difficult to provide than seeing and touching. However, consider the characteristic smell of old books or the smell of candles and oil lamps (used with care of course). Sounds can be simulated. What would one hear in the street before the invention of the motor car? Real sounds might include old clocks and old 78 rpm records. Tasting involves using the old recipes.

An invaluable and inexpensive resource are family photographs brought in by children or accumulated in the school. They are most valuable if they can be dated with some degree of accuracy and show not only clothes, but toys, cars, furniture, houses and other items some of which change and, equally important of course, some which do not. (The interesting thing about irons is perhaps not how much they have changed but how the basic shape is quite constant.) Schools can also collect picture postcards which have historical connections to be discussed with children. These can often be obtained from museums. Pictures by famous artists from the past will be needed for the art curriculum. They are also food for historical discussion of old fashioned clothes, activities and dwellings. They can often be obtained from discarded calendars which has the advantage that they are large, unlike postcards and photographs. Of course, photographs and pictures are not as good as real objects in the classroom or seen and which nowadays, can often be handled, on an historical visit. It is taken for granted that teachers will use any nearby place for such visits. When they do their own familiarizing this visit will contribute to their own historical knowledge. They may have been before, but it is amazing how having to teach and explain sharpens up one's own learning.

Similarly artefacts in the classroom can tax teachers' knowledge but often they can tax 'the experts'. The major problem is that it is not that easy to get hold of suitable things although, once again, museums and LEAs normally have loan collections. Teachers also find that parents are amazingly generous when it comes to loaning both photographs and precious objects of all kinds. The problem here is to take care of them. Some are so rare they can only be showed to the class and then sent home. Permission has to be gained for others to be handled but those that could be damaged can be sealed into plastic bags. This applies especially to coins and other small, collectable items.

The final and important source to be mentioned, although there are many others, is people. Oral history can be supplied by parents, school staff including dinner ladies, cooks and secretaries as well as by amateur historians and museum staff on visits. Teachers themselves are historical to children (which may be disconcerting to a young teacher). When teachers themselves recount their experiences and reinforce them by photographs and artefacts they may find that they consider for the first time how changes in their own life and attitudes were shaped by events. Reflection on all sources of historical knowledge are learning experiences for teachers as well as for children. However, all historical resources are used, not randomly but in relation to the selected content.

Selecting Content

It has been suggested that the selection of content has to be grounded in whether or not it will introduce children to the principles and processes outlined above and will engage children because it makes sense to their developing concepts of history. That is they can make connections between their experience (starting with what they know on entering school and extending to what they have learned since at school and outside of it) and what is to be presented to them. Nevertheless, it would be foolish to suggest that content is not, to some extent, driven by what is available. Indeed, content should be influenced, rightly, by the immediate environment and spiral out from that. It is sensible and appropriate to use the history of the place where children are to study a period beyond living memory, for example. Similarly, what a local museum or historic house or remains have to offer might suggest the period before living memory to be chosen.

It is also the case that there is often more material available on, say, the Victorians than decades since that period. However, it may well be worth the effort to seek out less obvious periods for study or more unusual changes in furniture, clothes or household appliances. The excitement for teachers and children of finding out — in effect researching — something a little offbeat may be worth the hard work involved. Moreover, an eye needs to be kept on the more prescriptive curriculum at Key Stage 2, by liaison with the junior school or colleagues. It is undoubtedly possible to do 'The Normans' again with profit. However, bearing in mind that 'the same level of attainment can be demonstrated through different types of historical content' (DES, 1991) different content in the two key stages might be more attractive and interesting to children.

As content is likely to be so various no attempt will be made to be specific in this discussion. Instead suggestions will be made about the sort of content appropriate to levels of attainment in both topics and ongoing teaching. The history study unit at Key Stage 1 is stated to be a two-year programme. Depending on the experience of children it might be appropriate to plan history teaching within broadly-based topics for the reception class. If this plan were adopted it would be possible to envisage a topic in each of years 1 and 2 which were both mainly subject-based with history as the major focus. Before elaborating on this suggestion the notion of 'ongoing teaching' needs explanation.

Ongoing Teaching of History

Reference back to the Attainment Targets and Programmes of Study for Key Stage 1 (*ibid*) indicates that many of the Attainment Targets contain concepts which are built up gradually over time. In addition, apart from AT 3 — The Use of Historical Sources — there are skills and concepts which are not specific to history although they can be linked to history by the teacher. Familiarity with the requirement of the history curriculum will enable teachers to make such links during their other work although not, it must be emphasized, at the cost of dragging them in at inappropriate times. Some of these concepts can be examined.

AT 1 Level 1a) states 'Place in sequence events in a story about the past' (*ibid*). Teachers are likely to be asking children to sequence stories orally and in writing as part of the English curriculum. Oral story telling is not the easiest thing in the world for children to do at Level 1 but such stories are normally and naturally set in the past. So, outside of a history topic, children will move towards this Attainment Target. The peculiarity of the example given for this Attainment Target has already been discussed. There seems to be every reason why young children should understand that the recent past *is* history. In ongoing teaching teachers will point out that the stories they read to children took place 'A long time ago' or 'When Victoria was queen'.

AT 2 Level 1 states 'Understand that stories may be about real people or fictional characters' (*ibid*).

This is perhaps a controversial item. Mutterings about Father Christmas surface although children may keep the secret for adults' benefit longer than we might like to suppose. However, experience with children indicates that this understanding is a long and patchy process. Stories are also patchy. An historical novel can be set in an accurate representation of the past but have fictional characters. Myths may not have happened but are expressions of the truth. However, children will have many, many stories read to them and will read stories for themselves. They will ask: 'Is it true? Is it real? Did it happen?' To meet the Attainment Target, although it is dubious whether many infants would really be clear about the distinction, teachers will select a great many different genres of story to read with children. As part of their intention to introduce children to a wide range of fact and fiction in the English curriculum they will be doing this in any case. However when the moments arise they can discuss 'real and fictional' characters but this would not be solely during a history session or topic.

AT 2 Level 2 states 'Show an awareness that different stories about the past can give different versions of what happened' (*ibid*).

The example here is also easier to think of than to set up. ('Detect differences in two adults' accounts of the same past event'.) Teachers are ingenious and it may be possible. However, reading to and with children can be returned to for help in leading up to this attainment. There are several splendid story books for young children which introduce the idea that different accounts can be given of the same event. *Fourteen Rats and a Ratcatcher* (Cole, 1976) tells the same story from the point of view of the rats and an old woman and her cat. *The True Story of the Three Little Pigs* by A Wolf (Scieszka, 1989) speaks for itself. *Satchelmouse and the Dolls House* (Barber and Munoz, 1987) finds its heroine transported by magic into a Victorian doll's house, not as the daughter of the house but as the maid of all work.

More generally teachers can use 'the age old power of the story to teach as it entertains' (Little, 1989), sometimes with history in mind. As suggested earlier, with the youngest children the vocabulary of today, yesterday, long ago, when I was little and, of course, once upon a time can be introduced. A charming story about change is *Once There Were Giants* (Waddell and Dale, 1989) where the baby on the first page grows up and is the mother (and therefore a giant) on the last. As noted earlier, it is necessary to search carefully for books set in the past or about the past but more are being published. *The Model Village* (Fisk, 1991), *Old Bear* (Hissey, 1990) and *The Toymaker* (Waddell and Milne, 1991) spring to mind. It has been emphasized that one important way to help children to get a sense of the past is through stories which are authentic and well written. Often they can be used to support and illuminate a history-based topic but if excellent in their own right they are essential to ongoing teaching.

Other ongoing teaching occurs in mathematics where the language of time is also essential. Again there will be specific mathematics sessions but teachers also use every suitable opportunity to reinforce ideas about chronology through the days of the week, the date, the time, birthdays and discussions about relative age of children and their siblings. There are also those occasions where children bring items of interest to school which may be of historic interest. There is a curriculum to be covered but time for discussion of such items can be found. Similarly events such as a royal birth or wedding can be discussed and real princesses compared with story book princesses.

History Topics

One of the problems for infant teachers designing the curriculum is how to fit all of the curriculum into the time available. Integrated topics are often suggested as a means to this end. However, I have suggested elsewhere that integration does not mean that every topic covers every area of the curriculum (Palmer and Pettitt, 1993). To attempt to do this may lead to much loss of the principles and ways of thinking in each subject. History and geography in particular have come under heavy fire from successive HMI reports as getting lost in topics which are too broadly-based (DES, 1978). The rationale underpinning the suggestions which follow is therefore that any topic should include only those subjects which have a definite connection with each other. Following Alexander *et al* (1992) topics can be divided into those which are broadly-based (but having a rational connection of subjects) and subject-focused topics. The latter would have one subject — or possibly two, such as history and geography in an environmental project — as the major focus. Those subjects which could not be included sensibly would be taught separately. It has also been suggested (*ibid*) that topics for infants are often too long. A termly or even a half-termly topic can drag on and become more and more diffuse and unrelated to the National Curriculum. With these points in mind, a few suggestions will be made about where history can be situated in the curriculum for Key Stage 1 and what it might consist of.

Reception Classes

In the reception class, given the two-year programme in *History in the National Curriculum* (DES, 1991) the curriculum is leading up to Level 1. As suggested a good deal of teaching will not be specific to history but will be linked to it in ongoing teaching. The reception class seems to be the one above all where topics are broadly-based. Normally reception class topics are centred on the children's own lives and experiences. (Although it has to be said that calling a topic 'Ourselves' covers such a multitude of possibilities that this label might be best avoided.) The obvious and valuable topic, broadly-based but looking towards Level 1 in history is about the change and growth which the children have experienced. 'Change over time' may be another odd title as it is hard to know what change does not occur over time. However, many exciting topics can focus on birthdays, babies, growing, moving from playgroup to nursery to school, what I liked and was like when I was little, where I was born and so on. The focus is perhaps 'Who am I?' as children's lives have a chronology which they can explore and compare with each other. Photographs of children as they grow can often be obtained and, of course, they are fascinated by teachers' photographs of themselves as babies. Pictures of babies from different countries also intrigue and, of course, if a real baby can come in. . . .

Deirdre Pettitt

Other topics might be on toys or on traditional tales which can lead to discussion about 'real characters' and will naturally include language about the past. In the reception class, whatever the topic, the basis will be the development of oral language leading, not too abruptly, to reading and writing. Depending on the experience of the children a danger to be avoided is to bring in ideas, which children can deal with but which they might get more out of later on. For example charming timelines can be seen in reception classes of baby clothes pinned on a line dating from Victorian times to the present day. If the children get a lot out of this well and good. If it goes over their heads this nice idea might be better reserved to Year 1.

Year 1 and Year 2

The history curriculum spirals out from the children's direct experience to further back in time. It may be possible to plan a history focused topic in each of these years. In year 1 this might keep to history within living memory and in year 2 to further back in time. Choice of topic is wide and as suggested would depend on resources which could be obtained. In either year this choice could be to take an era, a dipstick into the past or a famous person or event. An era for year 1 might be the 1970s and for year 2 the 1940s. (The latter is not yet beyond living memory but the Second World War even from a domestic and remembered point of view may be more suitable for the oldest infants.) For year 2 the Vikings or the Romans might be suitable but as suggested, Key Stage 2 planning needs to be taken into account as well as the warning given about reception topics. Will children get more out of this sort of topic later on? However, if one of these is chosen it is sensible to narrow the focus. For example, a focus on domestic life of the Romans in Britain: their food, baths and central heating. Local connections are probably essential but young children are often very disappointed by a long walk followed by a few rather uninteresting looking walls.

Dipsticks into the past can focus on domestic life looking at play, or household articles or transport. Famous persons and events are again most valuable where there are local connections: Captain Cook in the north-east or Elizabeth Fry in Norfolk, for example. There is so much to choose from and to explore with children. However, although it has been argued that their capacity to learn about history is vast it is still necessary to provide them with the links with their own experience which help them to make sense of their activities.

Suggestions that have been made for years 1 and 2 have been taken together. In planning the curriculum teachers will take into account what has been done before and what will follow. In this planning it is sensible to vary selection. That is if a famous person seems appropriate to year 1 then a different kind of content should be selected for year 2.

The need for an extended piece of work — a history focused topic — is partly because the subject demands it. It is also the case, however, that it is hardly possible to assess what children have learned in relation to the Attainment Targets if an extended piece of work is not included in the curriculum. Assessment of bits and pieces of history tagged on to broadly-based topics is very difficult. When planning a history focused topic, assessment can be built in.

Conclusion

It is a bit much to expect teachers to become enthusiastic about every subject in the curriculum. However, history is so much part of our lives, so much a part of our cultural heritage that it seems at least likely that learning more history with children can be rewarding for both teachers and for children and bring a fresh dimension to those teachers who are historians already. What subject knowledge teachers need to teach any area of the curriculum is a serious question. One cannot presume to teach from ignorance. However, teaching history is not a matter of being able to answer an examination question about facts. Indeed many historians might be hard put to it, for example, to list the Kings and Queens of England, much less the dates of their reigns. It is a matter, as suggested in the introduction, of being aware of the basic principles of the subject and being prepared to try to apply these to the content selected for children. This is possible and many teachers have begun to feel more confident about their ability to introduce children to a subject which affects how we make decisions as adults.

References

ALEXANDER, R., ROSE, J. and WOODHEAD, C. (1992) *Curriculum Organisation and Classroom Practice in Primary Schools: A Discussion Paper*, London, HMSO.
AMES, L.B. (1946) 'The development of the sense of time in the young child', *Journal of Genetic Psychology*, 68, pp. 97–125.
BARBER, R. and MUNOZ, C. (1987) *Satchelmouse and the Doll's House*, London, Walker Books.
BARTON, G. (Ed) *The Cool Web*, Trowbridge and Esher, Bodley Head.
BRADLEY, N.C. (1948) 'The growth of the knowledge of time in children of school age', *British Journal of Psychology*, 38, pp. 67–78.
COLE, T. (1976) *Fourteen Rats and a Rat Catcher*, Reprinted 1977, 1980, 1983, 1986, London, Penguin (Puffin Books).
COOPER, H. (1992) *The Teaching of History*, London, David Fulton.
DES (1978) *Primary Education in England*, London, HMSO.
DES (1988) *Mathematics for Ages 5 to 16*, London, HMSO.
DES (1989) *Aspects of Primary Education: The Teaching of History and Geography*, London, HMSO.
DES (1990) *History for Ages 5–16: Proposals of the Secretary of State for Education and Science*, London, HMSO.

DES (1991) *History in the National Curriculum*, London, HMSO.
DES (1992) *Standards in Education 1990–1991: The Annual Report of HM Senior Chief Inspector of Schools*, London, HMSO.
DESFORGES, A. and DESFORGES, C.W. (1980), 'Number based strategies in sharing in young children', *Educational Studies*, 6, 2, pp. 97–109.
DONALDSON, M. (1978) *Children's Minds*, London, Fontana.
EGAN, K. (1985) *Teaching as Story Telling*, London, Ontario, Althouse Press.
FERREIRO, E. and TEBEROSKY, A. (1982) *Literacy Before Schooling*, Portsmouth, Heinemann.
FISK, N. (1991) *The Model Village*, London, Walker Books.
GELMAN, R. and GALLISTEL, C.R. (1978) *The Child's Understanding of Number*, Cambridge, MA, Harvard University Press.
HARDY, B. (1977) 'Narrative as a primary act of mind', in MEEK, M. and WARLOW, A.
HISSEY, J. (1990) *Old Bear*, London, Arrow Books.
HUGHES, M. (1989) 'The child as learner: The contrasting views of developmental psychology and early education', in DESFORGES, C.W. (Ed) *Early Childhood Education*, BJEP Monograph Series No. 4, Edinburgh, Scottish Academic Press.
LITTLE, V., (1989) 'Imagination and history', in CAMPBELL, J. and LITTLE, V. (Eds) *Humanities in the Primary School*, London, Falmer Press.
LOVELL, K. (1966) *The Growth of Basic Mathematical and Scientific Concepts in Children* (5th edn), Sevenoaks, Hodder and Stoughton.
MARWICK, A. (1970) *The Nature of History*, London, Macmillan.
NCC (1991) *History, Non-Statutory Guidance*, York, NCC.
PALMER, J. and PETTITT, D. (1993) *Topic Work in the Early Years: Organising the Curriculum for 4–8 year olds in School*, London, Routledge.
PIAGET, J. (1969) *The Child's Conception of Time*, trans. by POMERANS, A.J., London, Routledge and Kegan Paul.
SCIESZKA, J. (1989) *The True Story of the Three Little Pigs By A. Wolf*, London, Penguin (Puffin Books).
THORNTON, S.J. (1987) 'What can children learn from history?', *Childhood Education*, 63, pp. 247–51.
THORNTON, S.J. and VUKELICK, R. (1988) 'Effects of children's understanding of time concepts on historical understanding', *Theory and Research in Social Education*, XVI, 1, pp. 69–86.
VUKELICK, R. (1984) 'Time language for interpreting history collections to children', *Museum Studies Journal*, 4, 1, pp. 43–50.
WADDELL, M. and DALE, P. (1989) *Once There Were Giants*, London, Walker Books.
WADDELL, M. and MILNE, T. (1991) *The Toymaker*, London, Walker Books.
WELLS, G. (1986) *The Meaning Makers: Children Learning Language and Using Language to Learn*, Portsmouth, Heinemann Educational.

Chapter 8

A Sense of Place: Geography/ Environmental Education in the Early Years

Joy Palmer

The principal aim of this chapter is to incorporate a discussion of children's early learning about the natural/physical environment and their development of a sense of place within the context of teaching and learning in the curriculum areas of geography and environmental education. Implications for the planning and organization of the early years curriculum in these areas will also be considered, as will the critical importance of designing appropriate learning tasks.

It is perhaps difficult, if not impossible, to pursue any discussion of learning experiences without reference to content; and since environmental education and geography are inextricably linked in the early years curriculum, a brief overview of these areas and their interrelationships will provide a focus for elaboration of the teacher's task.

From the outset it must be emphasized that whilst National Curriculum documentation for Key Stage 1 is referred to, discussion incorporates general principles of teaching and learning applicable to all 'early years' children of school age, that is, in the first three years of school.

The National Curriculum Order for Geography (DES, 1991) interpreted in *Non-Statutory Guidance* (NCC, 1991), provides a much needed rationale for teaching and learning in the subject, and addresses a number of fundamental criticisms which have been directed at teaching and learning in geography, notably the lack of attention that has been paid to the distinctive contribution that geography can make to children's learning, and the traditional limitations of study in this area:

> in most schools there was a tendency for geography to lose its distinctive contribution and become a vehicle for practising skills related to language and art . . . in contrast the mathematical and scientific potential of geographical skills . . . was only occasionally exploited . . .

> ... work related to other places in the British Isles and the world was limited. The almost total absence of a national and world dimension to the work in many cases highlighted the need for schools to consider a broader perspective. (DES, 1989, p. 12)

The National Curriculum for geography (unlike history) has no content-specific study units. Teachers are free to design their own topics, bearing in mind the programmes of study, attainment targets and statements of attainment. Within the programme of study for Key Stage 1 (as with all stages), physical, human and environmental geography are referred to as *themes*. As a whole, the Order outlines five sections, corresponding to attainment targets, which describe what should be taught. These are

- Geographical skills —
  Places and Themes
- places
- physical geography
- human geography
- environmental geography

Planning and implementation of schemes of work and topics need to take account of each of these five elements. It must also take account of crucial links with other areas of the curriculum. In particular, the cross-curricular theme of environmental education is interwoven with elements of geographical learning, and has been singled out for closer scrutiny in this chapter.

Within the overall framework of the National Curriculum, environmental education is one of a number of cross-curricular themes which permeate the curriculum as a whole. As such, it shares with other themes:

> ... the ability to foster discussion of questions of values and belief, they add to knowledge and understanding and they rely on practical activities, decision-making and the interrelationship of the individual and the community. (NCC, 1990a, p. 4)

It is recognized that cross-curricular themes have a substantial body of knowledge and understanding in their own right, whilst incorporating this 'values/belief' dimension. The aims, components and suggested content of environmental education are published in *Curriculum Guidance* 7 (NCC, 1990b). As an officially recognized cross-curricular element of the National Curriculum, it must be regarded as part of the entitlement of every school-aged pupil. It is not a statutory subject in its own right, but must be viewed as being complementary to, arising out of, and permeating all of the core and foundation subjects. No single approach to the organization of the curriculum or teaching methodology for environmental education is recommended. Perhaps the combination of a variety of approaches is appropriate. In the early years of schooling,

Geography/Environmental Education in the Early Years

teaching through a series of subject-based or general topics lasting for various periods of time, combined with teaching through National Curriculum subject areas is probably the best arrangement. Topics may be subject-based, incorporating elements of environmental education, or the actual focus of a topic could be an issue deriving from the content of the theme. In this way, there is ample scope for cross-linking the content of geography and environmental education within suitable starting points for integrated development. Seven key areas of knowledge and understanding of the environment that should be covered in the curriculum are:

- climate
- soils, rocks and minerals
- water
- materials and resources, including energy
- plants and animals
- people and their communities
- buildings, industrialisation and waste.

Interpretation of these into topics and learning tasks is a matter for individual schools and teachers to pursue. What is certain is the need to incorporate within such plans the three essential interrelated components of environmental education, namely:

- education *about* the environment (that is, basic knowledge and understanding of the environment);
- education *for* the environment (concerned with values, attitudes and positive action for the environment);
- education *in* or *through* the environment (that is, using the environment as a resource with emphasis on enquiry and investigation and pupils' first-hand experiences).

These three components are inextricably linked, and are thus essential to planning of educational programmes and tasks at all levels, including whole school curriculum plans and specific programmes of work/activities for individuals and class groups. Part of the planning process should take account of the need to help learners understand the interrelationships that exist among the three elements.

An alternative or complementary way of interpreting this structure is to suggest that every child has a basic entitlement in environmental education, incorporating two strands which interrelate with other areas of curriculum. These are:

1 *Knowledge and Understanding*
   (a) knowledge about the environment at a variety of levels, ranging from local to global;

(b) knowledge and understanding of environmental issues at a variety of levels, ranging from local to global, to include understanding of the different influences, both natural and human, on the issues;

(c) knowledge of alternative attitudes and approaches to environmental issues and the value systems underlying such attitudes and approaches.

2 *Skills*

(a) finding out about the environment, either directly through the environment or by using secondary resources;

(b) communicating:
  (i) knowledge about the environment
  (ii) both the pupils' own and alternative attitudes to environmental issues, to include justification for the attitudes or approaches advanced;

(c) participation
  (i) as part of group decision-making
  (ii) as part of making a personal response.

The success of incorporating worthwhile programmes of environmental education into the school curriculum is thus dependent upon the inclusion of these two strands within the overarching, three-fold framework outlined above *and*, taking account of meaningful integration with other subject areas through carefully structured cross-curricular tasks. Figure 8.1 provides a diagramatic representation of this framework for planning.

A further analysis of the essential content of geography will help to illuminate the common ground between these two curriculum areas. The fundamental skills of graphicacy (mapwork) and fieldwork incorporate the 'essence' of environmental education which is learning from first hand, practical 'field' experiences. These skills cannot be taught in isolation, but need to be related to content of other dimensions of the subject of geography, in many instances overlapping and incorporating the seven topics of environmental education. Geographical education requires a knowledge and understanding of places, in the local area, a contrasting locality in the UK, and a locality beyond the UK. Once again, this is totally in line with the 'essence' of environmental education which is to incorporate learning in, through and about the environment, using both the immediate locality and places further afield. When young learners set about learning physical geography (weather and climate; rivers, river basins, seas and oceans; landforms; animals, plants and soil) they are inevitably learning *about* the environment overlapping with the topics of climate; soil, rocks and minerals; water; and plants and animals. A similar pattern is seen for learning about human geography (population and settlements; communications and movements; and economic activities). These are interlinked with the environmental education content areas of people and their communities and buildings, industrialization, waste. Finally, elements of environmental geography

Figure 8.1: A framework for planning

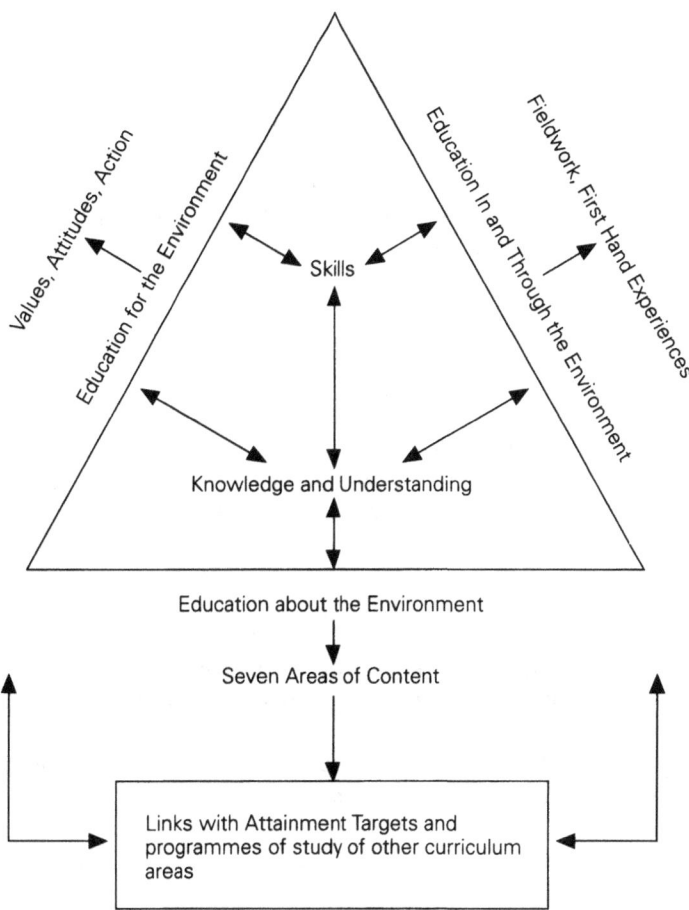

are very closely linked with the theme of environmental education. These highlight a critical dimension of geography teaching, that which is concerned with values, beliefs and issues. Environmental elements of the subject include the use and misuse of natural resources; the quality and vulnerability of different environments; and the possibilities for protecting and managing environments. This not only incorporates the dimension of learning *about* the environment, but also the critical third component of environmental education, that of learning *for* the environment, concerned with values, attitudes and positive action.

Thus a picture unfolds of geography as a subject which has a distinct integrity and identifiable content of its own, whilst maintaining meaningful, rather than contrived, links with a cross-curricular theme. The juxtaposition of these two areas of knowledge, understanding and skills on the curriculum map raises a number of issues relating to the development of children's subject knowledge and the organization of teaching and learning in these areas. An attempt will be made to tease out a number of these key issues in early years geography/environmental teaching highlighted by the requirements of the National Curriculum, and then to relate these to some thoughts on a young child's development of spatial knowledge and cognition. Issues raised are in no particular order of priority. Neither do they form a comprehensive list. They do, however, provide a focus for further staffroom discussion on the design and implementation of policies and programmes of work. A suggested agenda might include:

- the use of *first hand experiences* in the *local environment* — the essential starting point for development. This will capitalize upon the children's spontaneous experiences and previously acquired knowledge of the world around them, whilst developing this understanding through careful structured, progressive activities.
- the need to go *beyond the locality*, to challenge parochialism and develop children's awareness and understanding of places further afield.
- a focus in teaching and learning on the concepts of space and place i.e. on the nature and dynamics of *places*, spatial relationships in the environment, the *human* dimension and *environmental* impacts and *issues*. This focus incorporates the all important dimension of *attitude* development and the question of making informed value judgments about places.
- the central role of fieldwork and the *process and skills of enquiry* in teaching and learning. These are an integral part of any successful topics/schemes of work and progressive attainment in fieldwork and environmental enquiry skills should be recognized as a essential component of geography teaching.
- the *context* of geography and environmental learning. That is, the relationship with and interconnectedness of these areas to other aspects of the curriculum — links should not only be recognized and respected but planned for. Geography and environmental education can clearly be *supportive* of learning in other areas . . . and can provide the unifying element in an integrated topic. Furthermore they can make a *distinctive* contribution to children's learning — particularly in the area of spatial knowledge. Both of these roles — the supportive and the distinctive — cannot be left to chance and must be planned for.

Let us move away from this rather abstract analysis to consider the development of 'a sense of place' in action thus illustrating a number of these issues. In the 'red' classroom at Ashwood School, a group of 5- and 6-year-olds are discussing their drawings . . . their teacher has asked them to draw around familiar objects on a plain piece of paper. Such objects include an eraser, building cube, coin, spoon, pencil, drinking glass and a leaf. Having drawn around them, the children have then coloured them in and are playing 'guessing games' to try and identify what their friends have drawn. A great deal of discussion is generated by this task — guided when appropriate by the teacher who poses such questions as 'do your drawings really look like the thing you have drawn round?' 'what has stayed the same?' (size, shape) 'What has changed ... why can't you recognize it any more?' (colour, texture, specific detail etc.) This task represents an important stage in the development of these pupils' skills of mapwork, particularly relating to the element of perspective. The formalities of direction and scale are not involved, but as the drawings and relative positions of the objects are discussed, and then linked together with lines, they are located in space — both on paper and in the children's minds — a crucial mapwork concept. These activities were gradually extended over the period of two school terms — familiarizing children with the idea that a map is a representation of space occupied by objects depicted in plan form and of the spatial relationship between them. Work progressed with tasks designed to compare plans of objects with oblique views, and the introduction of the concepts of scale and symbolic representation. At all times, the teacher built upon the spontaneous reactions and everyday experiences of the children — capitalizing on their existing awareness of such concepts without formal understanding. When introducing the idea of scale, for example, much discussion took place concerning the contents of the reception classroom next door and scaled down versions of reality with which the learners were very familiar ... 'Why is the dolls' hospital smaller than a real one?' 'Why can't we have a real railway bridge for the train to pass over?' Such discussion not only developed an understanding of the mathematical concept, but promoted valuable geographical understanding and the acquisition of related vocabulary. The formality of scale developed from the 'drawing around objects' exercise when certain objects were selected that would not fit on to the piece of paper. Similarly, the use of keys and symbolic representation were formally introduced. When friends could not identify objects, the teacher steered thinking towards the need to be able to 'read' or interpret plans and maps as well as to construct them. Classroom models were assembled, and reassembled ... objects arranged in sequence and order ... routes around the room devised and marked out on the floor, linking together aspects of the physical environment in space ... all very worthwhile activities which afforded practice in recording locations, extending geographical vocabulary ('opposite', 'in front of', 'by the side of' 'next to', etc.) and understanding spatial relationships.

Children in this classroom were encouraged to draw pictorial, spontaneous maps of everyday places and journeys (for example, 'my street', 'my walk to the shops' 'the park') without restrictions of mapwork formality. Imaginative picture mapping was also encouraged, deriving from carefully selected stories of people going on journeys and living in 'colourful' places. The classroom walls carried not only the children's own representations, but a wide range of pictorial and printed plans and maps, including ones of the local area, the school site, the streets of the town and the world. It certainly was not expected that their complex symbolism and details of scale and relief would be understood completely, rather that they would contribute to the development of the children's awareness of the elements of mapwork.

In these ways, the teacher concerned successfully approached the teaching and learning of mapwork skills and elements (perspective, position and orientation, scale, map content and symbols) as a crucial aspect of geographical and environmental understanding which needs to be addressed in its own right. In this classroom it was rightly perceived as a discernible core of subject knowledge to be developed for its own sake whilst linking it when appropriate to other curriculum areas (notably mathematics, English, art and PE). Not only does this example show how the understandings and skills of geography (in this case, graphicacy) can contribute to the general intellectual development of children in the early years, it also shows how their development can arise out of traditional good practice and everyday experiences of the infant classroom, capitalizing upon what the young learners already know and bring to their tasks.

Inevitably, young children *do* know a great deal about their immediate surroundings. They come to school with some sense of place, and its related elements. Whilst every individual will obtain detail of environmental information from indirect sources (descriptions by others, the media, maps, books etc.), the chief source of a child's knowledge and understanding of his/her environment is direct experience of it. Such experience does not commence at the reception class door. Surprisingly little research evidence illuminates the development of environmental cognition, by which is meant the development of knowledge which comes with increasing experience of an environment and the development of a child's ability to learn about his/her environment. Methodologies are perhaps problematic for, as Evans (1980) points out, the central methodological issue of all environmental research is the problem of 'how to externalize the individual's mental map of the environment'. A useful discussion of research and methodologies on environmental cognition is provided by Spencer, Blades and Morsley (1989) who suggest that most approaches to the problem articulated by Evans rely on 'laboratory' methods to assess the individual's knowledge. They group these according to whether individuals have to rely on recall of a previously experienced environment (for example, giving a verbal description of a place) or recognition of an environment (for example, selecting photographs of places that they know). One focus of research is this area which has probably received more attention than others is the child's development of understanding of the location of objects and self in space, and again, attention is drawn to Spencer, Blades and Morsley (*ibid*) for a fuller overview and analysis of work in this area which is so closely linked in classroom practice to the development of mapwork skills. It has already been suggested that spontaneous mapping is to be encouraged from the moment a child enters school. Such early maps are likely to be pictorial and egocentric. As demonstrated by Piaget and others (1956, 1960), by the age of about 4

Geography/Environmental Education in the Early Years

years, children are beginning to understand the locations of objects which surround them in relation to one another, or in a topological sense. Topological cognitive maps (Catling, 1978) will be drawn, which are pictorial, with representations of places linked together without formalities such as scale and orientation. Progression from these involves the making of more accurate connections between objects. Pathways, for example, may be drawn through the pictorial plan of the park, and buildings may be linked by streets. Direction, orientation and scale will still be absent or inaccurate. Gradually, a 'projective' representation of objects evolves from the topological, wherein objects such as trees and buildings are represented in two rather than three dimensions. Children at this stage, identified by some research as being around the age of 7 (Boardman, 1983), will draw that which more closely resembles a 'map' as we know it, with attention paid to the more formal details of direction, orientation, scale and symbolic representation, although accuracy will still be lacking. The teacher's task involves the design and monitoring of a range of activities that will assist in this progression towards formality and accuracy. A variety of learning tasks will need to focus on each of the formal elements of mapwork, building upon the learners' existing spacial awareness that has developed as a result of everyday interactions with the environment.

The above example has focused upon children's immediate and everyday experiences of the world and their understanding of 'personal' space. Thus a second case study has been selected to address the issue of challenging parochialism and responding to the need to incorporate teaching and learning about distant lands in the early years curriculum. Once again, the crucial aim of this teaching is to help children make sense of their existing understanding and to build upon this in a progressive and constructive way.

In classroom 2 of Wayside School 6-year-olds mingle with giant hissing cockroaches, millipedes some staggering twelve centimetres long and giant African land snails. These exotic animals form part of a collection of non-native invertebrate creatures maintained by the school for use in scientific (and other) studies. The children are totally captivated by the sheer size of these specimens compared to their counterparts in the UK. Discussion and imaginative writing generate a wide range of relevant vocabulary, creative thinking and spontaneous suggestions for further investigations. Detailed observation parallels measuring, experimentation, illustration and recording tasks. Movement, feeding, breathing, reproduction, life cycles and habits are observed, investigated and recorded in appropriate ways, covering a wide range of scientific, mathematical and cross-curricular skills (including observation, problem-solving and communication). From the immediate and the observable, the teaching skilfully steers questioning and investigation into the area of the native background of these creatures . . .

'Why don't we have snails this size in our country . . . ?'
'In which countries would you find such creatures in the wild?'

Joy Palmer

> 'What do they eat? . . . where do they live?'
> 'What is the weather like in their native lands?'
> 'Do they live in forests, or open lands?' . . . etc.

Many questions were generated by the children as were answers . . . some of which were far more accurate than others. Gradually the topic evolved into a sub-theme of 'Invertebrates of the Tropical Forest' and a rather exciting and successful series of lessons ensued in which geographical/environmental knowledge and understanding emerged as a very discernible and worthwhile core. Planning and organization ensured that this focus covered a range of specific issues, incorporating knowledge, understanding and skills from the curriculum areas of both geography and environmental education.

Space does not allow for full details of content and planning. Key attainment targets covered in geography were AT2 — Knowledge and Understanding of Places; and AT5 — Environmental Geography, though all attainment targets were covered to some extent, through the use of maps (AT1), investigations into weather and the invertebrates themselves (AT3) and human population and activities of the forests (AT4). Content ranged across all of the seven 'topics' of environmental education and incorporated a great deal of learning about the forest environment, and indeed *for* it. Issues of conservation were at the forefront of discussion. Young as these learners were, they demonstrated very genuine concern for the need to preserve the world's timber resource and appreciation of the different ways of life of rain forest communities.

This particular topic was undoubtedly successful for a variety of reasons. The teacher appreciated at the outset the need to find out as much as possible about the children's existing background knowledge of the distant lands which were to be studied, that this might be built upon or indeed *challenged* in a constructive way. Children have an ever-increasing incidental contact with places around the world, largely through the media and also through holidays, stories and personal contacts. As a result, 'mental maps' or images of distant lands are constructed, which to an extent may be blurred or even false. Television, video films and books are extremely powerful influences on a young child's mind, often imparting partial or indeed biased information, resulting in a mental map that is far from complete or accurate. Bale (1987) provides a discussion of the blurred knowledge contained within children's 'world inside their heads', drawing attention to various research findings on both quantity and quality of information which children possess of places beyond their immediate environment (and it must be emphasized that 'distant land' to a 5-year-old does not necessarily mean a place several thousand miles away. To the child of the London east end, the Scottish croft or the Derbyshire village is as remote as the paths of Outer Mongolian yaks). Research on the development of children's concepts of city, region and country shows confusion. Piché (1981) interviewed 5–8-year-olds on their understanding of 'place' in the world from most local to most distant places. Five-year-olds commonly described a building, district, city and country as all being the same kind of place, for the reason that one could go there.

As well as factual errors in knowledge, research demonstrates the problems of stereotyping and ethnocentricity that result from media inputs.

It has long been suggested (Tajfel and Jahoda, 1966) that children absorb from the media and social discourse, attitudes and prejudices about other nations and peoples well before they learn accurate factual information about them. Furthermore, information available to the young child will be selectively sought, received and remembered, in ways that are supportive of pre-existing (pre-judged) categories (Tajfel, 1981).

Fyson (1984) reports conducted word-association tests with children of primary school age. Results showed that the words most commonly associated with 'Africa' were 'lions', 'heat', 'snakes', 'elephants', 'trees', 'tigers', 'palm trees' and 'black people'; conjuring up images of the exotic, colour and perhaps excitement of Africa — far removed from many of the realities of everyday life there today in the shape of poverty and cities.

Crucial issues to bear in mind when approaching and planning the study of distant lands with young children are thus stereotyping, bias and often incomplete or erroneous subject knowledge which may be brought to the classroom. Perhaps it should also be pointed out that the situation may not be helped by a teacher's genuine ignorance of particular facts or biased viewpoint about a place, perhaps arising from a particular media coverage or a holiday in an atypical part of the land. The teacher's task is thus a complex and difficult one — yes indeed it is to build upon the existing knowledge base of the children, yet bearing in mind the problems and limitations of this as identified. In an ideal world, by providing appropriate accurate information and experience, leading to an appreciation of environmental conditions which are different from our own, and building up a more coherent and complete picture of the place being studied, then the confused infant will emerge into an adult with accurate and unbiased views of people and places. Unfortunately, the world of the school classroom is not that ideal! Yet awareness of the issues must go some way towards planning work which avoids or corrects stereotyping and racialist overtones wherever possible. When teaching about distant places teachers should avoid possible pitfalls such as:

- portraying an outdated or stereotyped image of places and people (for example, modern life for the Inuit, as they prefer to be called, may involve working for the oil industry and living in houses rather than hunting and living in temporary shelters such as igloos);
- giving a limited view of a country, (for example, that Sri Lanka only produces tea);
- using biased material about a country, (for example, material which portrays only the attractions of living, working, or travelling in a country). (NCC, 1991)

Of critical importance is the need to relate distant lands learning to reference points in the children's own lives. If tasks are in some way linked to the pupils' own locality or personal experiences then firstly they will identify far more easily with the topic, place or people under consideration, and secondly, they will be helped to develop an understanding of the interdependence of the modern world. Relevance may also help in the elimination of bias and stereotyping — if learners can feel a part of the 'total world' and appreciate the importance of links between nations, then they may be less likely to view distant people as alien or remote from present-day reality and world issues.

Another key reason for the success of the topic at Wayside School is that the teacher recognized this need for relevance. The distant lands dimension developed out of suitable reference points in the children's own lives, in this case, invertebrate animals which could be compared with their native counterparts. In general, there can be no better starting point than that which is 'real' and exciting to young children; and animals, plants, food and weather are perhaps four of the most highly motivating and worthwhile connections between nations of the world which can be developed. The first three at least provide tremendous scope for using real objects as the point of contact between the children and the land of its origin. One single object, for example, the stick insect, rubber plant or artichoke, could stimulate considerable motivation and generate a complete sub-topic on its natural environment. Alternatively, a collection of artefacts/souvenirs, maps, photographs etc., could be established about the land to be studied.

The two examples used in this chapter have been selected for their very different emphases — immediate spatial awareness and approaching distant lands teaching — each with its contribution to discussion. A key question in practice is, of course, achieving balance and progression within the geography/environmental curriculum as a whole. Organization and planning issues will need take account of whole school and class curriculum plans as well as details of specific schemes and topics. Key general questions for discussion and resolution will include:

- the balance between geography based topics, environmental education and other areas of the curriculum, with statements on how cross-curricular themes are successfully to permeate the curriculum as a whole;
- approaches to the inclusion of geography and environmental education in the curriculum, i.e. whether by topic work or by supplementary teaching of specific content, skills and issues in their own right;
- the amount of time to be allocated to geography-based topics and environmental work and when they are to be tackled;
- criteria for selection of places to be studied and for ensuring a balance of local and distant environments;
- methods of teaching and appropriateness of tasks, ensuring adequate fieldwork/first hand experiences;

- arrangements for assessment, record-keeping and evaluation of schemes/topics/school programmes;
- availability and organization of appropriate resources.

For children in the first three years in school, topic work will no doubt seem the most appropriate method of organizing learning experiences. Topics should be planned so that they draw and build upon knowledge, skills and concepts acquired in previous topics, relate in a meaningful way with other curriculum areas, and take account of links between the geography attainment targets. For the youngest learners (reception, year 1) the focus could well be the children themselves, so that their own life experiences and knowledge thus acquired may be capitalized upon. There is endless scope for work on the immediate environment and community, gradually building upon knowledge and skills acquired in a structured and progressive way ... gradually moving 'outwards' into study of distant and contrasting places. For example, a progression from a topic on 'Myself' to 'What I like to eat' allows for the introduction of content on a variety of distant places, through the link of imported foods. No doubt a variety of teaching methods and wide range of tasks will be incorporated in any single topic — with great emphasis on the enquiry/fieldwork approach. Once again this links with progression in content. No child in school is too young to take part in a variety of learning tasks outside the classroom, in the school grounds and immediate neighbourhood. Any work of this kind cannot fail to extend the world with which the children are familiar, adding to and extending their subject knowledge and application. By year 2 children should have opportunities to visit and investigate 'distant' or contrasting environments. Such arrangements may be as straightforward as visits to the countryside or coast for inner city dwellers. It is here that the early skills of comparing and contrasting ... and of appreciating environmental and socio-economic differences will be acquired, so closely linked to the development of attitudes and values.

It may be concluded that children's early learning in geography and environmental education can provide those meaningful links which go a long way towards drawing together the curriculum as a whole whilst providing a distinctive contribution of knowledge, understanding and skills in its own right. Such learning must aim to help young children make sense of their surroundings and of the wider world. As such it must take account of formative influences associated with the development of a sense of 'place' and the origins of environmental awareness. Implications for the planning and organization of the early years curriculum include the provision of learning contexts which take account of children's experiences in the natural world and their existing knowledge of it. Few would question the importance of helping children in their task of constructing personal meaning to their sense of 'place'. Hopefully, this task will result not just in factual knowledge of locations in the world ... but also in the ability to understand and interpret, to question and debate, to respect, value and to care about the environment.

References

Bale, J. (1987) *Geography in the Primary School*, London, Routledge and Kegan Paul.
Boardman, D. (1983) *Graphicacy and Geography Teaching*, London, Croom Helm.
Catling, S. (1978) 'Cognitive mapping exercises as a primary geographical experience', *Teaching Geography*, 3, pp. 120–3.
DES (1989) *Aspects of The Primary Curriculum: The Teaching and Learning of History and Geography*, London, HMSO.
DES (1991) *Geography In The National Curriculum*, London, HMSO.
Evans, G.W. (1980) 'Environmental cognition', *Psychological Bulletin*, 88, pp. 259–87.
Fyson, A. (1984) *The Development Puzzle*, CWDE, Sevenoaks, Hodder and Stoughton.
NCC (1990a) *Curriculum Guidance 3, The Whole Curriculum*, York, NCC.
NCC (1990b) *Curriculum Guidance 7, Environmental Education*, York, NCC.
NCC (1991) *Geography, Non-Statutory Guidance*, York, NCC.
Piaget, J. and Inhelder, B. (1956) *The Child's Conception of Space*, London, Routledge and Kegan Paul.
Piaget, J., Inhelder, B. and Szeminska, A. (1960) *The Child's Conception of Geometry*, London, Routledge and Kegan Paul.
Piche, D. (1981) 'The spontaneous geography of the urban child', in Herbert, D.T. and Johnson, R.J. (Eds) *Geography And the Urban Environment: Progress In Research and Applications*, Vol. 4, Chichester, John Wiley.
Spencer, C., Blades, M. and Morsley, K. (1989) *The Child In the Physical Environment*, Chichester, John Wiley and Sons.
Tajfel, H. (1981) *Human Groups and Social Categories*, Cambridge, Cambridge University Press.
Tajfel, H. and Jahoda, G. (1966) 'Development in children of concepts and attitudes about their own and other countries', *Proceedings of the 18th International Congress of Psychology*, Moscow.

Chapter 9

'I Can't Teach Music — So We Just Sing'

Coral Davies

The nervousness with which many non-specialist teachers approach the music education of young children seems to have its roots in the traditional view of the music curriculum as training in performance techniques and musical literacy based upon a complex system of notation etc.

There is a wealth of curriculum materials for music which demonstrate that such a view is inappropriate, and which provides ample resources for developing approaches which allow children to engage with sound as an expressive medium from their earliest years in school.

But teachers who were beginning to feel confident in organizing explorations in sound may have had their apprehension rekindled by the apparent overemphasis in the National Curriculum for Music (NCC, 1992) on understanding and knowledge, particularly since these are embodied in Attainment Target 2 Attainment and might be in danger of becoming separate from the activity of music-making itself.

In focusing upon songs and singing, I argue that, far from being apologetic about it, teachers who feed their children with a repertoire of songs can be confident that they are laying vital foundations of the children's musical knowledge and understanding.

As well as using words, children singing nursery songs are working with musical rhythms, phrase structures and tunes, in short, with the language of music. It appears from research, by, for example, McKernon (1979), Gardner *et al* (1981), Dowling (1984 and 1988) and Davidson (1985), that learning to sing a song does not just involve imitating like a parrot, nor is it simply a matter of memorizing what the adult does. By looking at song acquisition in ways akin to research into language acquisition, researchers are finding that children appear to develop cognitive schemata governing song-production through which they filter their attempts to sing standard (pre-existing) songs. Studies have particularly focused upon melody acquisition but it seems likely that a similar process is at work in the production of rhythms.

Children's earliest musical sounds are indistinguishable from speech babbling, but by the second year, the two aspects of vocal play have begun to diverge, and observers have traced the development of vocalizations that are clearly recognizable as songs. These first songs do not usually include words, though parts of words may occur in a string of nonsense syllables or as the beginning of a song which then continues on a single syllable (Moog, 1976).

Children's earliest songs bear no resemblance to the music of others; but children in their second year begin to sing songs which resemble those sung to them. In these attempts, words are the earliest feature, then something of the rhythm begins to appear, with attempts to produce pitch coming later. Many observers have noted that young singers follow the overall direction of the melody but do not match the intervals accurately. Shuter (1968) commented:

> it is interesting that it was the general melodic shape rather than the longest or most prominent notes that was learned first. This suggests that learning proceeds from an initial apprehension of a tune as a whole, with more definite perception of the parts taking place later. (p. 68)

Gardner *et al* (1981) have also described the process of the child mastering the outline, or 'first draft' of a song, by the age of 3 or so. They trace the further development, 'from first draft to mastery', in their report of a study in which a song was taught to a group of $4^1/_2$-year-olds. Initially the children grasped the words, and the rhythm and phrase boundaries were carried by the words. At first, they only managed the contour of the melody, never accurately reproducing the pitch values (still the 'first draft'). But during the year of the study ($4^1/_2$ to $5^1/_2$ years) 'an impressive degree of key stability emerged, resulting in more accurate reproduction of the intervals and melodic content and the children became able to imitate the standard song' (p. 310).

Davidson (1985) has begun to identify some of the rules which very young children seem to work to when processing melodies. He has classified four levels of 'contour scheme'. At first, children's melodies are framed within an overall contour of three notes, descending. At Level 2, the overall contour widens to four notes, with some filling in between the two extremes; then the contour expands to five, and, at Level 4, to six and seven notes. The restrictions are not because children's vocal apparatus does not allow them to sing wider intervals. In their free vocal play, children may explore over a range of pitches; so the narrow range of their earliest attempts to sing standard songs seems to be a response to the need to temper their free expression with developing ideas of the restrictions in the song forms of their culture.

Davidson (*ibid*) gives an illustration from a child of 24 months singing her version of the Alphabet Song. In the target song, the first phrase (see Example 1a) goes up, then down. But the child has not yet got that melodic contour in her scheme of things. She only has one contour scheme, the falling third, which she sings at 'B — C' (Example 1b). She then returns to her starting note, and makes another descending third at 'E m', and stops.

Example 1a: Target song

A B C D E F G

Example 1b: 2-year-old's version

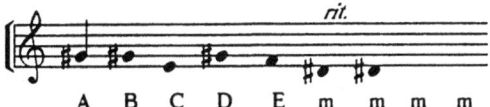

A B C D E m m m m

The precise nature of children's early melodic schemes is debated by other researchers. For example, Michel (1973) found that, in their second year, his children had six basic melodic sequences in their repertoire; some of these are similar to those identified by Davidson (1985), but others seem to indicate more advanced understanding. But what this work demonstrates is that children, even at the earliest stages of making a song, are constructing relationships between musical sounds; their early musical utterances make sense as structures, but in children's, rather than adult's, terms.

Davidson (*ibid*) looked at children learning to sing standard songs. Dowling (1984) has shown other kinds of schemata in operation when children invent their own songs, in his study of patterns of repetition and contrast in musical phrases; and has argued that 'children achieve ... schematic control over the songs they sing ... not by simply copying the cultural models, but rather by developing ... mental representations in response to their musical environment' (p. 157).

Both Davidson and Dowling have noted that children overuse musical 'rules' as they discover them, which parallels children's use of, for example, 'buyed' and 'goed' as they acquire the rules governing past tense in English.

So it seems that, in acquiring a musical language, children filter their songs through their current mental representation of how a song goes, and they overlearn procedures. They also make novel utterances, which seem to be evidence for the existence of mental representations and against the idea of simple imitation.

Even after children have begun to imitate standard songs successfully, they continue to invent their own, 'spontaneous' pieces. Observers have noted that the incidence of these increases between the ages of 2 and 3, and peaks around 3 to 4. Moog (1976) described 'narrative songs' in which 'any words are sung so long as they seem to tell a story', and what he called 'pot pourri songs', where children made up new pieces 'by putting together pieces of songs they already knew. Words, melodies and rhythms are mixed up, altered,

Coral Davies

taken apart and put together again in a different way, and then filtered in between stretches of original ideas' (p. 115). Example 2 is a narrative song by Sarah, aged (3 years 5 months).

Example 2: Sarah (3 years 5 months)

122

Sarah begins with an echo of the song these children knew as 'I hear thunder' (perhaps 'umbrellas' suggested this, or vice versa). The song continues with Sarah's own ideas. There is some organization, in the repetitions of music and words; the three-note rising pattern at 'for the rain' and its repetitions at 'last night' are particularly striking, as if she is practising this figure as a cadence to end her phrases. Construction becomes looser as the piece continues, but repetition is still a feature; and it is perhaps not insignificant that she again sings the rising three-note figure as her final cadence ('then I played'). Even at this age, it seems, Sarah has some idea of important aspects of a song.

The researchers referred to earlier suggest that such song play dies out as children enter school, and seemed to consider it mainly as an aid to learning how to sing standard songs. But it need not disappear, and with composing enshrined in the National Curriculum for music, perhaps it should not do so.

But work in composing at Key Stage 1 has tended to focus on the exploration of sounds, including vocal, but more especially instrumental and environmental sounds, rather than song-making. Thus Paynter (1970), who with Addison (1967) and others pioneered the development of composing in schools, outlined the approach to the task:

In the infant school, creative experiment in music will in the main be a matter of developing interest in the variety of sounds available; of encouraging discrimination between sounds, both in pitch and timbre; and of beginning, in various simple ways, to improvise music of mood or atmosphere for drama or to heighten the characters and events in a story. (p. 30)

Addison (1967) in *Children Make Music* included a whole chapter on song-making by young children, but the emphasis upon exploring sounds and using instruments is found in much of the music curriculum material related to young children and is reflected in Mills' account of music in the primary school (1991). So it comes as no surprise to find a similar emphasis in the National Curriculum for music. Composing at Key Stage 1 is defined as 'investigate, choose and combine sounds to produce simple compositions'. The programme of study includes taking part in 'simple vocal and instrumental improvisations', which can, of course, encompass making up songs; but the overall impression in the composing strand is of 'exploring sounds', in which 'tell a story in sound' seems to be a familiar centre-piece.

Children's developing subject knowledge can be traced in their work with instruments; Glynne-Jones (1974) made a study along Piagetian lines of children aged 8+ years, while a recent report by Bamberger (1991) traces 'the mind behind the musical ear' in relation to one child's exploration with instruments. But my own work (Davies, 1992) has focused upon the invented songs of children aged 5 to 7 years, to see how the musical language acquisition traced by others in pre-school children continues in children's early years in school. The thirty-two children in my sample produced various kinds of songs, of which I shall consider three kinds here.

There are many examples of story-songs, which appear to be continuations of what Sarah was doing in example 2. Some of these use very restricted melodic contours (see example 3), but some are much more tuneful, though still discursive in character (example 4). Adults do not normally sing such songs to children; the singers have formed their own idea of what a song is.

Example 3: Melanie (6 years 10 months)

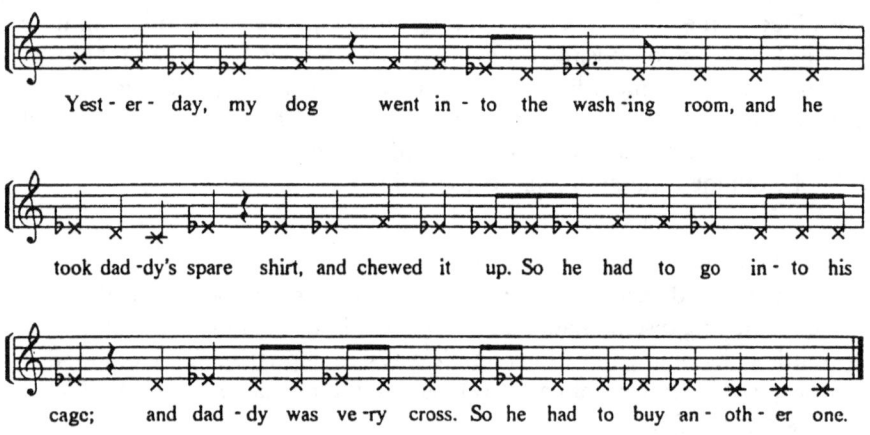

Example 4: Zoe (6 years 8 months)

'I Can't Teach Music — So We Just Sing'

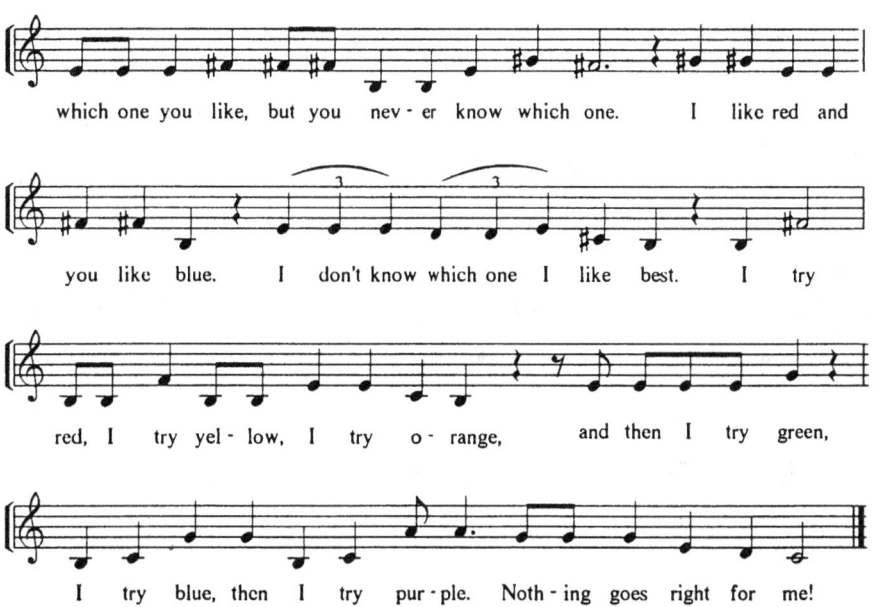

There is also evidence, in a second type of song, that children have perceived that the songs which they have been taught (i.e. the songs of their culture) have restrictions, being cast usually in four lines, perhaps with some repetition of words and/or tune. There are many examples of such 'frame songs' in my sample. Like the story-songs, they may use very restricted melodic contours, as in example 5.

Example 5: Caroline (5 years 9 months)

But others are more tuneful, satisfying small statements capturing an aspect of the children's feeling lives, as in example 6.

Coral Davies

Example 6: Ruth (6 years)

Patterns of repetition and contrast, such as we can see in example 6, show that children have absorbed an important aspect of simple song forms. Children also seem to have definite ideas about how songs begin and end. Children who do not pitch intervals accurately tend not to use adult endings, but rather to fall to the final note, which may be repeated, an ending which they share with music of some non-western, non-tonal, cultures. Example 3 gives an illustration of this.

While their final notes descend, their opening notes frequently rise, giving an aspiring, progressive feel to the beginning. The rising opening and falling ending are common in nursery songs (as, for example, in 'Twinkle, Twinkle Little Star'), so it seems that children have absorbed these into their ideas of how a song goes to use them in novel pieces of their own.

Reference was made earlier to children overlearning or over-using procedures in language and in music. A striking instance of such overlearning can be seen in the many frame songs which used the formula of which 'Here We Go Round the Mulberry Bush' is an example.

    (a)   (b)
        Here we go round the mulberry bush
    (b)   (b)
        The mulberry bush, the mulberry bush,
    (a)   (b)
        Here we go round the mulberry bush
    (c)
        On a cold and frosty morning

The pattern of this piece can be represented as ab, bb, ab, c. Children frequently adopted this four-line frame and its phrase pattern with repetition and contrast, changing the words and the melodic contour each time. The resulting pieces were not very original; but abstracting a form from known songs and using it in this way seems to be important, in that it provides a framework within which children can explore and reinforce their understanding of some basic features of song-making.

Originality seems not to be a concern with children anyway. For example, several children sang the same opening three lines

> Jamie's going to Leicester,
> Leicester, Leicester,
> Jamie's going to Leicester

but each added a different final line and said that he/she had made a new song. In this, children's work in the classroom seems to parallel their treatment of traditional rhymes in the playground. The Opies (1959) have drawn attention to the fact that children, like adult folk singers, are preservers of tradition, being economical with their invention of new material but at the same time being very ready to make minor alterations and to claim that they have made up a new rhyme. The idea of what makes a new song, what composing is, may be different for the young child to what it is for the teacher. Some of the children in my sample sometimes sang pre-existing songs to 'lah' and said they had made them up. They can abstract the tune from the words, but for them this is a new entity, and they often did not recognize that they had borrowed in this way.

As well as the story-songs and frame songs (which might also tell a story but which I have discussed as a separate category because they seem to indicate a difference in musical understanding), children might also engage in free vocal play, usually to 'lah', making complex musical structures, developing musical ideas in pieces which suggest a sophisticated use of musical language. Such a piece is example 7.

Such songs are not easy to capture in classrooms. Children responding to my invitation to make a song were more likely to sing a story-song (or 'sing their news') or to produce the restricted frame song which seemed to be associated with an increased awareness of the shared, social aspects of song-making. These songs of the third type, which one might almost call the secret songs of children, were generally produced spontaneously at ends of sessions, or in the playground or corridor. Only about 30 per cent of the children sang such songs in my hearing; perhaps other children did something similar in their play?

Coral Davies

Example 7: Caroline (6 years and 3 months)

The singer of example 7 could not sing standard songs in tune at all, nor match a note sung by her teacher; nor could she recognize 'up' and 'down' or 'high' and 'low' in relation to pitch, even after we had played many games with these concepts. She seemed, in conventional terms, to be quite unmusical, yet, when she felt free to explore according to her musical imagination, she produced this and other similarly complex and satisfying songs. Yet other children who could sing well in tune and were beginning to be able to talk about aspects of melody and rhythm, might, like the singer of example 3, produce only the most restricted story and frame songs.

This raises interesting questions about the development of children's musical understanding.

The sequence of musical development outlined by Swanwick and Tillman (1986), with illustrations from children's compositions, identifies modes of working with, and perceiving, music. Swanwick (1992) has used these as the basis of his account of 'the variety of knowledge, skills and understanding' in relation to music in his critique of the National Curriculum proposals.

According to Swanwick's and Tillman's sequence, children first respond to musical materials and their sensory character and are concerned with manipulation in an attempt to secure mastery over them. At the second level, children become more aware of the expressive character of music; while a developing concern for structural relationships marks the third level. Eventually children become aware of their own and other people's music in the context of the tradition of their culture and become able to reflect upon music's value to themselves and others. Swanwick associates these four aspects of musical encounter with the Key Stages of the National Curriculum. Thus, in

'I Can't Teach Music — So We Just Sing'

Key Stage 1 'students should be able to recognise and identify different musical materials and use these . . . to express an atmosphere or dramatic sequence' (compare the emphasis on exploration of sounds and mood already noted for this level). At Key Stage 2, 'students should be able to distinguish and discriminate melodic and rhythmic devices found in songs and instrumental pieces and use these expressively'; while at Key Stage 3, 'students should be able to draw attention to, and exploit repetitions and contrasting musical ideas . . .' (p. 16–17).

Swanwick considers that 'Expressive character and structure lie at the heart of musical *language*. They are qualitatively different from the perception and manipulation of sound materials'. So he sees progress through the four levels involving qualitative, fundamental transformations in knowledge. Each level is also characterised by a swing from personal, self-centred expression, to a sharing in the cultural, social use of music.

The children in my sample, at Key Stage 1, are at the age where we would, according to Swanwick's model, expect them to be making personal, expressive statements (the story songs, perhaps) then moving into the vernacular, learning what a song is in their culture (the restricted frame songs and the formula).

But the 'secret' songs of my third type do not so easily fit into this sequence and raise important questions, reminding us of the difficulty of making neat models of development and activity in the arts. Swanwick says that the third level (beyond the vernacular mode) is characterized by a concern for structure, and by imaginative speculating with musical ideas. Example 7 seems to belong here. But among the children in my sample, such songs, which seem to indicate a high level of musical understanding, might occur *before* they have learnt to sing in tune, or acquired a musical vernacular.

This prompts discussion of what we mean by musical knowledge. Swanwick (1992) is clearly referring to reflective, analytical, knowledge; he uses terms such as 'recognize and identify' for KS1, and 'distinguish and discriminate' for KS2. It seems that, by 'fundamental transformations' from one level of understanding to another, Swanwick means changes such as Piaget outlined, between intuitive, pre-conceptual knowledge and operational knowledge.

My singers do not appear to have this latter knowledge. Several things suggest such a conclusion, but I shall mention just two of them. Firstly, when children tried to take deliberate control, or to repeat their songs, they became much less fluent and successful musically. This is seen if we compare the first version of Mary's song (example 8) with what she produced when I asked if she could repeat it (example 9).

What Mary does keep, in her second version, is the four-line frame, as if this is becoming established as her idea of what a song is; but the free-ranging melody, and the contrast between the rising opening of the first three phrases and the falling contour which marks the final phrase, important in the effect of the musical whole, have been lost.

Coral Davies

This was the first of Mary's songs which she had tried to repeat. Earlier, when I had invited her to do so, she said, 'I can't sing it again, I just made it up'. It seems that, while memory obviously plays an important part, being able to repeat a song also depends upon cognitive development, for example in realizing that the spontaneous expression can be considered and recalled as an entity.

Example 8: Mary (6 years 3 months)

Example 9: Mary (6 years 3 months)

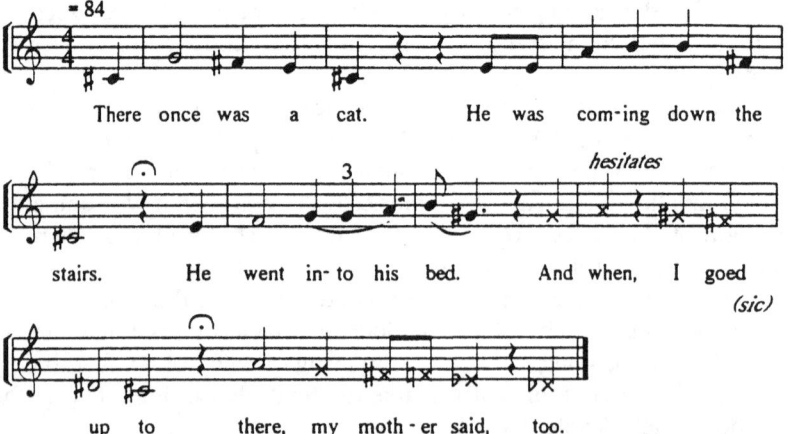

A second reason why I conclude that children do not have verbal, conceptual knowledge of their songs is quite simply that they cannot talk about things which they do in the music itself, nor do they pick up, and act upon, suggestions as to how things might be done. For example, when I asked a singer, who had just sung a piece using a pre-existing tune, if she 'recognized' any of it, if it was borrowed from anywhere, she nodded and, said 'There was *one note* that I recognized, but the rest was new.'

So these children's knowledge seemed to be intuitive, pre-verbal. What, then, is its significance?

Gardner, who with his Project Zero team at Harvard University has contributed interesting and challenging work in relation to artistic development, made the startling suggestion that children do not need to develop intellectual understanding in order to function as artists, that the major symbolic developments needed to participate in the arts are in place by the age of 7 or 8 (Gardner, 1973). Full discussion of this provocative idea is outside the scope of this chapter but it is worth noting that, while knowing *about* music requires the kind of knowledge outlined in Swanwick's sequence, the essence of musical expression, the fundamental requirement for participating in music, may be intuitive and is certainly non-verbal. Adult composers speak of musical 'inspiration' which seems to spring unbidden from their subconscious, and is hardly under their conscious control (Sessions 1941), though adult composers may have conceptual and technical skills with which to manipulate this inspiration.

There are important aspects of knowing in music, as distinct from knowing about music, which can only be experienced through the act of 'musicking' itself and which are fundamental to the exercise of musical imagination. It seems from the examples presented here (and many more like them in my sample), that children and their teachers can be participants in this expression without the formal training which is all too readily associated with education in music.

Composing is now enshrined in the National Curriculum for Music, from Key Stage 1 onwards. I have not attempted to outline a programme for teaching young children to compose songs. The teacher's role seems to be to teach children a repertoire of standard songs and to encourage and give authority to their song-play. I have attempted to show that children use these songs, and the experience of singing them, to construct their musical language and to make their own expressive statements. Knowledge about music comes after, and must take account of this early, intuitive understanding, (or the lack of it).

Teachers, too, have acquired a musical language in this way; and, in singing with their pupils, are providing a fundamental basis for the development of musicality.

References

ADDISON, A.R. (1967) *Children Make Music*, Edinburgh, Holmes McDougall.
BAMBERGER, J. (1991) *The Mind Behind the Musical Ear*, Cambridge, MA, Harvard University Press.

DAVIDSON, L. (1985) 'Tonal structures of children's early songs', *Music Perception*, 2, 3, pp. 361–74.

DAVIES, C.V. (1992) 'Listen to my song: A study of songs invented by children aged 5 to 7 years', *British Journal of Music Education*, 9, 1, pp. 19–48.

DOWLING, K. (1984) 'Development of musical schemata in children's spontaneous singing', in CROZIER, W.R. and CHAPMAN, A.J. (Eds) *Cognitive Processes in the Perception of Art*, Amsterdam, Elsevier.

DOWLING, K. (1988) 'Tonal structure and children's early learning of music', in SLOBODA, J. (Ed) *Generative Processes in Music*, Oxford, Clarendon Press.

GARDNER, H. (1973) *The Arts and Human Development*, New York, John Wiley and Sons.

GARDNER, H., DAVIDSON, L. and McKERNON, P. (1981) 'The acquisition of song: A developmental approach', *Documentary Report of the Ann Arbor Symposium on The Applications of Psychology to the Teaching and Learning of Music*, VA.

GLYNNE-JONES, M. (1974) *Music*, London, Macmillan.

McKERNON, P. (1979) 'The development of first songs in young children', in GARDNER, H. and WOLF, D. (Eds) *Early Symbolisation*, San Francisco, CA, Jossey-Bass.

MICHEL, P. (1973) 'The optimum development of musical abilities in the first years of life', *Psychology of Music*, 1, 2, pp. 14–20.

MILLS, J. (1991) *Music in the Primary School.* Cambridge, Cambridge University Press.

MOOG, H. (1976) *The Musical Experience of the Pre-school Child*, English translation by CLARKE, C., London, Schott.

NCC (1992) *Music in the National Curriculum: A Report to the Secretary of State for Education and Science on the Statutory Consultation for Attainment Targets and Programmes of Study in Music*, York, NCC.

OPIE, I. and OPIE, P. (1959) *The Lore and Language of Schoolchildren*, Oxford, London University Press.

PAYNTER, J. (1970) 'Creative music in the classroom', unpublished DPhil thesis, University of York.

SESSIONS, R. (1941) 'The composer and his message', in CENTENO, A. (Ed) *The Intent of the Artist*, Princeton, NJ, University Press.

SHUTER, R. (1968) *The Psychology of Musical Ability*, London, Methuen.

SWANWICK, K. (1992) *Music Education and the National Curriculum*, London, Tufnell Press.

SWANWICK, K. and TILLMAN, J. (1986) 'The sequence of musical development', *British Journal of Music Education*, 3, 3, pp. 305–39.

Au audio-cassette of the children's songs featured here may be obtained from the author at University of Durham, School of Education, Leazes Road, Durham, DH1 1TA. Please write for details.

Chapter 10

Teachers' Understanding of Children's Drawing

Jennifer Buckham

> The capacity for representation of experience using visual means emerges naturally in the course of development, and visual materials offer a particularly satisfying mode of expression to many young children. As a consequence the visual arts are a powerful means for helping children to organize experience of both fantasy and reality. Through them children can come to know themselves and their world more fully. (Smith, 1982)

> Our teaching of art to children will surely be more successful, firstly, if we understand the motives children have for making drawings and secondly, if we understand the major factors that influence the nature of their drawings. (Wilson and Wilson, 1980)

With the introduction of art into the National Curriculum in England and Wales, teachers' understanding of children's learning in art has been highlighted as an area with important implications for teaching. Non-statutory guidance for art suggests that 'teachers need to be sensitive to the needs of each pupil in her/his use of a particular mode of expression and representation, but must also adopt a positive role to ensure that the quality of learning offers challenge and enrichment' (DES, 1992, pp. 9–10). Such a role would require teachers to take an active interest in each individual child's artistic learning, being aware of its nature, progress and development and their own contributions towards it.

Part of the contribution will be in the practical provision of materials and especially resources, in the demonstration of processes and use of equipment as well as in the allocation of time and space for children's work and for dialogue and discussion to take place. Another part will involve being sensitive to children's developmental needs and enabling them to respond to, and draw on, an appropriate variety of direct and indirect experiences that will help them 'know themselves and their world more fully'. Yet another part will involve seriously attending to what children are doing or have done in their artwork, talking to them about their ideas, supporting them and responding to their achievements. 'Talk about quality and intention forms an essential part of the dialogue between pupil and teacher, and such discussion informs and promotes the teaching, learning and assessment process' (*ibid*, p. 55).

Understanding children's drawings, whether they are spontaneously made or as a result of a carefully planned lesson, emerges as an area primary school teachers sometimes find difficult. Finding out about the events or objects represented in a piece of work and establishing its context, determining the way it has been made and exploring the formal and expressive means it employs, is an important part of making an objective assessment of its aesthetic, intellectual and emotional significance, and valuing its achievement. Careful observation, sensitive discrimination and discussion are crucial in this process. It is with this in mind that this chapter will consider a range of children's drawings and discuss some important aspects of teachers' knowledge and understanding in this area of children's artistic learning. This knowledge and understanding will have a direct bearing on what is observed and how it may be interpreted (Atkinson, 1991; Golomb, 1992; Matthews, 1988 and 1992; Smith, 1983 and 1992; Wilson, 1992; Winner, 1982; Wolf and Perry, 1988).

The chapter is in three parts. The first part will focus on a drawing episode in a nursery setting, and the discussion of that drawing activity will be explored further in the second section looking at a range of work from 4–7-year-olds. The third part will look at some aspects of the drawing 'repertoire' of an individual child so that the initial discussion may be put into the broader context of continuity and change in drawing during the primary phase.

Jasvir: Monster Drawings (illustrations 1a-1f)

With a video-record, it is possible to look more deeply into the nature of the engagement that led to these pieces and what they might represent for the child concerned. This episode is of particular value as it lasted some seventeen minutes and records Jasvir (aged 4 years) talking out loud at each stage of his drawing, making his intentions, decisions and knowledge of his world accessible.

Jasvir carried out two drawings before the recorded monster drawings (1b and 1c). A student teacher had introduced a small drawing area into a nursery during teaching practice and for two consecutive afternoon sessions, she stayed at the drawing table so that she could observe the children's activities. On the first afternoon Jasvir spent only a very short time at the table and drew a snowman figure (1a) and then a monster figure using very similar drawing configurations. The following afternoon after a story session that included stories featuring monsters, he joined four other children who had already been at the drawing table for some time and announced that he was going to draw another monster. He drew enthusiastically, chuckling and grimacing at his drawing, talking to himself and to the student about it. 'It gobbles people up', he announced to her between exclamations of 'look!' and 'look at him now!'

Illustration 1 (Jasvir 4.0.)

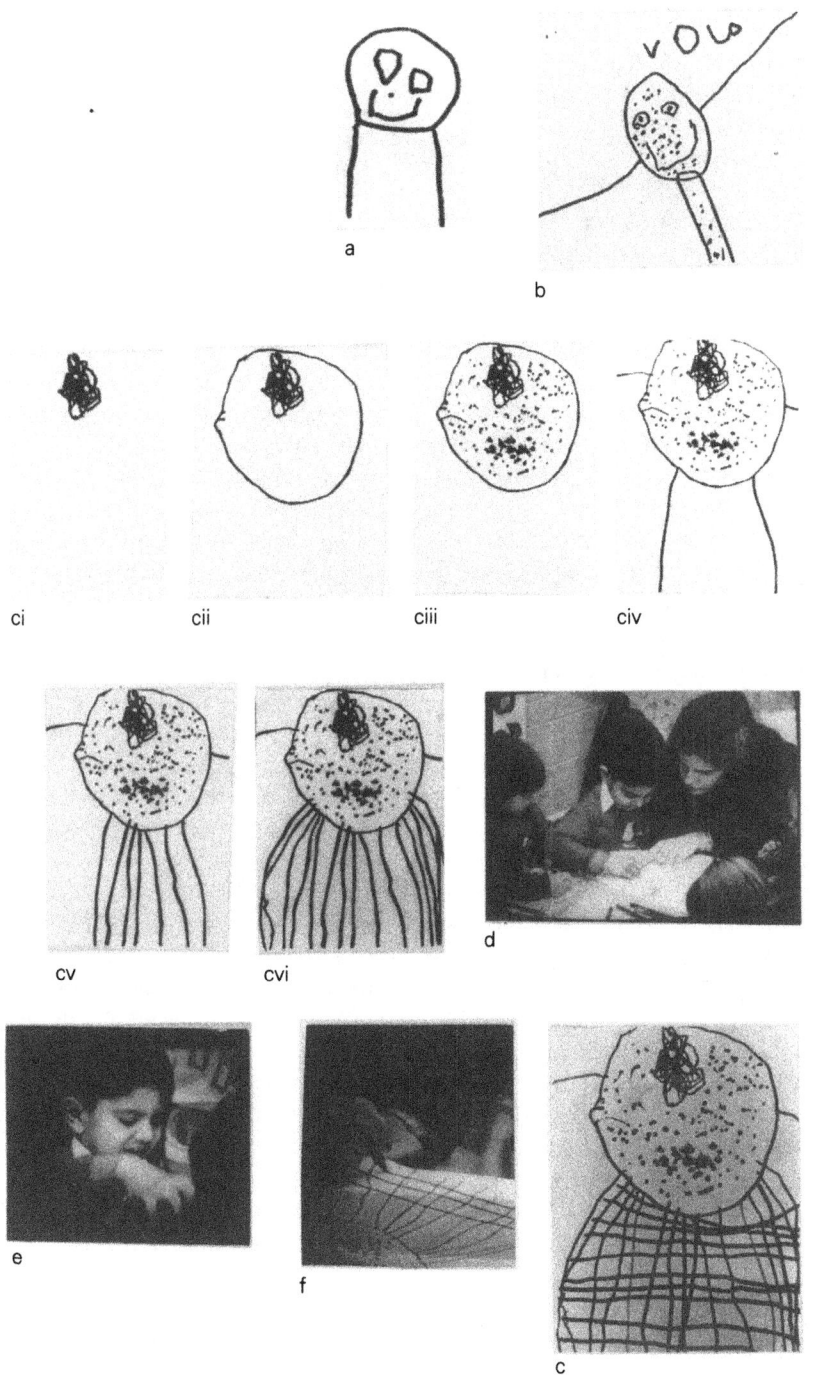

as he added dots to the surface of his drawing (1b). He wrote 'dirty monster' above the drawing and pointed to each of the four letter symbols as he read it back to himself. As he handed over his drawing when he had finished he warned the student to be careful that she didn't get her hands dirty. She looked surprised and he explained that the monster lived in the mud and was 'all dirty'.

Her smiles and gestures, as well as other children's interested glances and the general atmosphere around the table appeared to encourage his increasingly confident stance. The children around the table were drawing intently but glancing at each other's drawings and also watching the student carefully. (One child said she was drawing a 'nice' monster, another was already engaged in drawing rows of letter forms, yet another was 'mapping' the route to Santa's Grotto, recently set up in the corner of the nursery. Another child was making an elaborate design, rotating her paper systematically and also making patterns on her hand.) Meanwhile Jasvir had taken a fresh paper and announced to no-one in particular what he was drawing. 'It's a hairy monster... a nasty one' he said as he drew a tangle of red lines near the top of his paper (1ci). Surveying it with a mixture of satisfaction and mock horror he took a purple pen and accidentally dropped it on his paper. He looked startled at the mark it made, pulled a face, and promptly used it as the starting point for a large circle which he described carefully around the tangled lines in the upper half of his paper (1cii). As in his previous drawing he placed dots very carefully over this enclosed area (1ciii). A child nearby watched as he did this and decided to add dots to her drawing. She did so using a stabbing action with her marker and made a loud noise. Within five seconds Jasvir, without looking up, changed to a stabbing action with his marker also making a loud noise and much larger splashy, spidery marks (a cluster in the lower part of the enclosed shape, 1ciii). He then looked up at the student and pointing to his drawing said excitedly 'Look, now he's smashing the windows!'.

After this he drew two yellow lines downwards from the edge of the circular shape and a green line from each of its sides (1civ). While he was doing this he was saying to himself 'look at him now... he gobbles everybody up'. He then added five purple lines between the yellow lines he had already made (1cv) and held up his drawing for all to see, saying with obvious satisfaction 'look how many legs he's got!' The student suggested that they could count and see how many there were, which they did. She did not indicate that she in fact thought he had finished his drawing and did not suggest labelling it in any way as she did not wish to prompt him. She was surprised when he immediately continued drawing, saying to himself 'Now I'm making *all* the legs'. He had only stopped briefly to watch the girl next to him making rows of letter forms with a blue pen. When this girl heard what he had said she promptly drew a blue line for a leg on his paper. He was systematically adding pairs of red lines to both sides of his drawing and incorporated her contribution into his scheme without any comment. When he had finished there were fifteen legs altogether (1cvi). Again he showed it to the student (1d) and she and the other children reacted with interest and surprise. He suggested counting the legs again and the girl next to him whispered confidentially to her friend that she had also drawn one of them.[1]

Jasvir listened while the student described the content of his drawing to another child, all the while grinning and looking carefully at his drawing. He pointed to the red tangled lines at the top and said to himself 'Look! now ... *angry* ... grrr' and growled as he made a movement up and down with his clawed fingers (1e). At this point it appeared that the drawing might be finished but as soon as the black marker pen was free, Jasvir seized it and made carefully and deliberately spaced horizontal lines across the legs until he reached the bottom edge of the circular shape (1f). He waited impatiently while the student talked to another child and then excitedly told her 'He's in the jail –look at him now!' She asked him why and Jasvir replied 'because he's been a naughty boy' and added 'smashing everybody's windows'. As she replied to this response, he added a final vertical line in the middle of the legs and a horizontal one crossing it and then picked up the drawing, paraded it across the table and handed it to the student.

Discussion

This episode reveals drawing as a powerful medium for this 4-year-old to engage in making sense of his world, through events combining fantasy and reality. He has already listened and entered into stories where the possibilities of situations have emerged, been explored and resolved in many different ways. Through drawing he has constructed his own world, inhabited by a hairy monster, whose actions have resulted from the interaction between Jasvir's intentions and the visual and aural feedback of the drawing process. To these actions he has made a deliberate response, both graphic and moral. The whole process appeared intensely satisfying, and this must be partly due to the confirmation he received from the student and other children nearby.

This episode also reveals the nature of drawing as a system for symbolizing objects and events and it is very important to view this episode from the child's point of view, bearing in mind that 'at every phase in development, the symbolic systems used by the child are legitimate and powerful systems capable of capturing the kind of information the child feels is essential' (Matthews, 1992; Willats, 1992). Jasvir's drawings reflect the young child's capacity to spontaneously generate a whole range of graphic features, including circular enclosures, small circular shapes and dots, straight, curved and tangled lines. In combination they are capable of representing both objects and events, and expressing feelings and emotions. There is great flexibility of use in these features. The lines may represent limbs extended from a body (1c) or denote the outside boundary of a body (1a) or combine both in the same drawing (1b). The dotted marks can stand for mud or spots. The action of making the marks can represent an event such as the smashing of windows, and the marks can in turn conjure up an idea of danger or movement through the resulting configuration of spiky forms; gesture and perception are intricately combined here.

Gestural representation (Wolf and Perry, 1988) is one of the earliest systems that children employ to symbolize certain movements and events. A 2-year-old jumped his graphite stick in a zig-zag pattern up a page, making a trail of dots and said he was drawing a monkey being chased up a tree. Older children continue to make use of gestural representation when they show speed through a series of zoom lines following a moving object. An example of this is shown in the PE picture 8a, where a child has thrown a ball at the teacher and the line of its path is shown as a long curling spiral. As young children gain increasing control over a range of materials, they are able to determine and anticipate the effects that they make. Jasvir's tangle of red lines (1ci) was made with careful deliberation to denote part of the hairy monster, and express something of its being horrible. At the end of the sequence when he was staring at the drawing and said 'angry', he was pointing to this spot, showing the affective power of that particular configuration. Matthews concludes that 'it is at this level that graphic structure acquires not only its representational potential but also its emotional values, and this is the origin of aesthetic sensibility' (Matthews, 1992). Jasvir's association of 'angry' with the form of his tangly lines corresponds to what may be perceived as correspondences between certain elements of design, such as arrangement, shape or colour, and particular moods or feelings (Arnheim, 1974; Blank, Massey, Gardner and Winner, 1984; Gombrich, 1977 and 1982; Winner, 1982). Art derives its unique power from the fact that emotional content may be embodied in its *formal* qualities as well as represented in its imagery and 'because of the interplay between thought and feeling in form and content, it is possible in the arts to symbolize the complex blend of objective and expressive qualities in the experience of real life' (Smith, 1982).

There are strong arguments suggesting that young children (and mature artists) have particularly heightened 'physiognomic' perception (Werner and Kaplan, 1963; see also Gombrich, 1982) and this is important to understand in relation to Jasvir's drawing. Nancy Smith, who has related this aspect of perception most cogently to children's drawings and paintings, explains why it is sometimes difficult for adults to understand particular characteristics of children's drawings based on physiognomic perception; 'the objective contours of shapes may be ignored and objects may be rendered in simple circles or lines; spatial relationships are simplified and based on topological concepts; movement is often a feature of correspondence' (Smith, 1982 and 1992).

These points are of crucial importance for reading young children's drawings. Children as young as two may, particularly on request, draw a circle to represent an entire person or animal. Even younger children may use a single vertical line (Golomb, 1992; Wolf and Perry, 1988). In the case of Jasvir's hairy monster, the circular enclosure can be said to stand for the mass and volume of the monster's head and body combined, and not a simplified version of its outline or profile. In the same way, using descriptions based on topological geometry, the lines that are attached to the circular enclosure indicate that legs and arms are extended from the body but the single drawn line does not correspond proportionally to the actual length of arm or leg, nor does it show thickness, the actual angle of its attachment to the body, or even its exact position. Children have been shown to have a preference for certain arrangements of lines and shapes (such as parallel lines and right-angled orientation of shapes) so it is important for adults to understand both how the shapes and lines in a drawing are arranged and also what they stand for (Matthews, 1991; Willats, 1985 and 1992).

Because Jasvir's drawing is centred on the creation of the monster itself and not a particular *view* of it, this allows him to place the horizontal lines across the legs, thus creating a new type of enclosed structure in a grid-like pattern to represent being in jail. The horizontal lines counterbalance the effect of movement that the repetition of the leg lines sets up, and also the sense of weight that is suggested by this more solid shape anchors the monster firmly on the page. He also chose the black marker to make these final lines, giving them additional visual weight. Young children's drawings are often, by the nature of their production, full of movement and visual rhythm. As children make arrangements, where, for example, repetition sets up a particular effect of movement, it is helpful to talk to them about the fact that this is happening. The same applies when movement may have been contained, as in this example at the end, where the monster is effectively secured both visually and in the 'story'.

The student in this episode responded to both Jasvir's suggestions that the monster's legs should be counted. Young children are quick to sense the importance that is attached to counting. However, the literal number of items in a given drawing may be less significant than their visual impact as 'many', or the appropriate number to balance an arrangement, or fit into a shape. In Jasvir's hairy monster drawing, the pattern in the coordination of the design is noticeable. So, for example, after counting the legs, the way the colours were grouped (and balanced) may also have been explored. Drawing children's attention to features in their own work enables them to recognize them more fully, and in turn be more sensitively alert to corresponding features in the environment (Athey, 1981 and 1990). The grid-like arrangement in the lower part of the hairy monster offered an opportunity for such recognition and for identifying similar shapes in the environment including the new grids being put up to protect the nursery windows. As described earlier, after telling the student that the monster was in jail for being a naughty boy, Jasvir also said the monster had been smashing everybody's windows. He then paused to look at his drawing and added the two final crossed lines, as if drawing a window. The student's question encouraged Jasvir's explanation and the second part of his explanation in turn appears to have prompted this further visual configuration. The student's interactions and interest throughout this episode were important and hearing her describe his drawing to another child appeared to have a significantly encouraging effect on Jasvir's reflectiveness at that stage of the drawing.

Jasvir's drawing emerges as the product of an activity, sustained throughout by his imagination. This drawing activity would be completely undervalued by equating imagination with the young child's 'capacity to form images rather than the capacity to think' (Egan, 1992). It is only by close observation of the drawing activity itself and the talk that accompanies it that reveals the range of his thinking. It is also the sort of thinking that includes playfulness in the suggestion that the student might get her hands dirty touching his drawing or in the claw-like gesture representing the monster's movement or the vocalization of the monster's angry mood. When we take these symbolizing activities of young children for granted, we are also taking a powerful means for their understanding for granted, understanding that needs time to emerge and a supportive environment where it will be observed and valued. Goodman's (1969) reminder that the cognitive 'does not exclude the sensory or the emotive, that what we know through art is felt in our bones and nerves and muscles as well as grasped by our minds, that all the sensitivity and responsiveness of the organism participates in the invention and interpretation of symbols' is actually very appropriate in the context of this drawing episode.

Young Children Drawing (illustrations 2, 3 and 4)

In the case of Jasvir's monster drawing, a complex interplay of factors influenced the final form of his image. This section discusses some further examples of the factors that influence children's drawing and explores the contexts in which these drawings were made. Frequently the contexts that 'motivate children to operate at their most sophisticated level' (Pidgeon, 1992) involve the sensitive support of an adult (as in 2a, 2g, 3j, 4a-4f). There are also examples presented where a powerful experience has prompted the spontaneous and independent exploration of an image that has led to new levels of achievement. This may reflect the stimulating environment in which children are working (as in 2c) or a particular set of personally significant experiences (as in 2e, 3b, 3c, 3g). These examples also signal how rewarding it may be for teachers to closely observe children's drawing activities (2c) and to attend the range of drawing that accompanies children's writing activities (2d, 2e, 3a, 3b, 3e-g).

Daniel (aged 4 years 3 months) made his drawing (2a) at the end of a session where he had worked closely with a student and had used sharp scissors for the first time. He was excited by this experience and among other things, he had used them for cutting lengths of wool and for fringing the edge of a paper. He explained his drawing (2a) to the student observing him. It shows the student (centre) and his sister (right) both crying because they have 'cut their skirts'. Daniel (left) is laughing. This particular fusion of fantasy and reality has driven him to generate new ways of differentiating the human

Illustration 2 (4 and 5 year olds)

a Daniel 4.3
b,c Lee 4.8
d Isabel 4.9
e Isabel 4.9
f Isabel 5.1
g Carl 4.11

a

ci

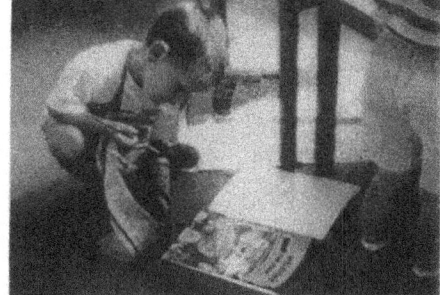

b

c

d

e

f

g

Illustration 3 (5 and 6 year olds)

a,b Joanna
c   Neill
d   Ricky
e,f,g Greg
h,j Penny

a

b

c

d

e

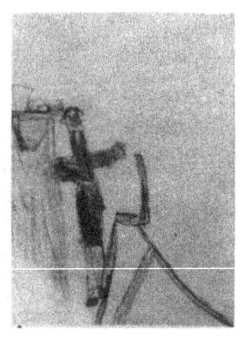

f

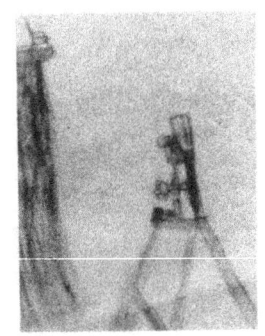

g

h

j

Illustration 4 (5 and 6 year olds)

a,b Caroline
c,d David
e,f Zoë

a

b

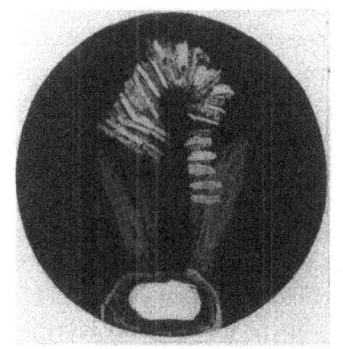

c

d

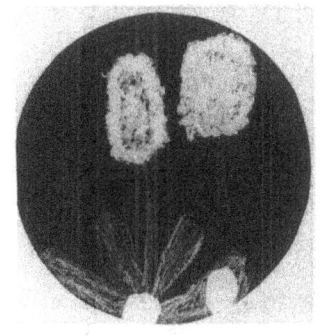

e

f

figure in his drawing repertoire. The basic units of figure construction are embellished with additional detail to indicate gender and denote events in his storying. Lines are drawn beside the legs to represent Daniel's trousers and a skirt has been constructed for the student using a triangular shape. Hair is also differentiated and indicated around the heads of the figures. The student's and his sister's face have marks drawn to represent crying. The zig-zag horizontal lines drawn across the female figures suggest the skirt cutting action. This drawing was noticeably more elaborate in structure and meaning than Daniel's previous ones, and reflects not only his lively imagination but the situation in which he was working. He was able to move through a series of activities at his own pace, exploring his newly-found interest in cutting and with the support and encouragement of an adult in the immediate environment. His drawing was an important part in this learning process, allowing him to construct alternative realities and explore the experience in a different dimension.

Lee (aged 4 years 8 months) was also excited by an event in his school environment. The children had constructed a skeleton from a book that had been brought in to the nursery and several children had chosen to draw it at the painting table. After drawing one skeleton image, Lee made a second one (2c). This image was very thoughtfully and deliberately constructed and in the lower part of the drawing Lee included the line with two small circles, to indicate a skateboard. He had carefully left a space below the figure for this to be included. Observations of his subsequent actions revealed his independence and ability to seek out more information to add to his image. Without any prompting he moved from the painting table and looked for the skeleton book in another part of the classroom. He consulted it before making several additional marks and indicating some new objects in his picture. (Illustration 2ci shows a reconstruction of the stage he reached before consulting the book.) A burst of short marks (left) indicate a spider, a configuration with vertical spiky lines on top (right), is a ghost tree, and a thick diagonal mark at the junction of the skeleton's head and body represents a bat. The body area was also filled with horizontal lines and then covered over.

It is necessary to consider the nature of what is happening here because teachers need to understand the role of the surrounding cultural environment (including comic and picture books) in children's artistic learning (Gardner, 1980; McFee and Degge, 1992; Wilson and Wilson, 1980; Wilson, Hurwitz and Wilson, 1987; Wilson and Litveogt, 1992). This is probably more powerfully significant than many teachers may realize and requires sensitivity and alertness to recognize ways in which children may draw on elements to incorporate in their work as well as to know how and when to introduce suitable models to children and for what purposes (Hughes, 1989). In making his painted drawing, Lee showed his awareness of the image in the picture book. He demonstrated a good visual memory, an ability to evaluate his work and make changes to it. He recalled an image he had seen (only briefly) and recreated it using his own drawing system. He continued to use this system even when he referred directly to the book and drew the extra details. What he did, however, adopt was the relative scale and position of these features as they appeared in the book and this gave his drawing a sense of environment it may not have had otherwise. The match between his drawing and the book illustration shows that he is observant in two ways, both of which could have led to discussion. First of all he has conveyed, most economically, the main visual features of the book illustration in his own drawing. Secondly he has conveyed, and I would suggest just as importantly, something of the expressive character of the picture; he evokes the sense of humour and movement of this zany grinning skeleton on a skateboard, as it hurtles through the night.

Looking at the school in which he was working, it appears that his independence, concentration and considerable painting skills had been fostered by careful organization and support in the classroom. Encouraging children to be visually aware and sensitive to their environment also characterized the school in general and the nursery in particular. Looking at other drawings and paintings by Lee, it appears that he was already practising figures in action, and evoking a lively mood in his work. However, the skeleton on the skateboard (2c) was qualitively different from the other paintings and drawings he made the same morning. This could be due to the aspects of the illustration that inspired it; the visual impact of its subject and the sheer enjoyment he had in recreating it first from memory and then from observation. Both seem to have sustained his concentration and enabled him to compose and paint with increased skill and confidence within his own system as well as allowing him to change some of his rules to incorporate aspects of the image from the book. He selected an appropriate challenge for himself and this enabled him to enlarge his previous drawing experience.

Some of the rather subtle qualities of this drawing in paint are more fortuitous than deliberate and owe much to the changing amount of paint Lee had on his brush and the speed and pressure he used to draw. It is important that even young children become aware that they can control the lightness or darkness of a painted line or mark using different amounts of paint and water. Where Lee pressed firmly with the brush there was a strong thicker line, where he drew lightly with the point, in the spider for example, there are small fine marks. The difference these effects make can be seen by looking at 2ci, which reproduces the format but not the painted quality of Lee's picture. It is important that children know that what they have drawn or painted can be described in terms other than those that simply name the objects or events they have represented. They need to build up a web of understanding about the way paint works, or the range and types of marks they can make (with ink, chalks, oil pastels, crayons and pencils on different types of paper, for example) and as they grow older they can deepen and extend their understanding and confidence in the same media. The growth of skills in using and handling materials goes hand in hand with developing ideas and images. Responsive drawing or painting requires sensitivity to the marks that are made on paper as well as to the qualities in the objects or scenes they refer to. If teachers can respond with sensitivity to the qualities in children's drawing (even when they are fortuitous, as may sometimes be the case with young children) they will be contributing to children's artistic learning.

Several of the drawings illustrated show the difference, between those made using felt pens (1a-c, 2a, 2f), using pencil with crayon (2d, 2e, 2g, 3e-j, 4b, 4f), using oil pastels (4a, 4c, 4e), or drawing with a fine paintbrush (2c). With felt pens it is more difficult to control the quality of a line and children need different pens to make thick and thin lines whereas with a soft pencil or suitably thin paint, pressure and speed can make subtle differences. Different patterns or arrangements of lines also create very different aesthetic effects and may be usefully highlighted in any discussion. The lion in 2f with straight lines for a mane and a straight tail was drawn by Isabel (aged 5 years 1 month) shortly after she had seen a male lion crouching on the ground eating a chicken carcass at the zoo. She thought the lion looked dangerous and the arrangement of the mane with jutting out lines certainly helps convey this impression. It can be compared with a lion she made up at 4 years 9 months. This lion (2d) has a mane of curved lines that almost revolves around his face and gives a more playful, friendly expression. The word 'impression' emphasizes that although the lines of the manes are indisputably straight or curved, the aesthetic effect of their impact may not be perceived by everyone in exactly the same way. This idea does not mean that aesthetic effects should not be discussed, in fact sensitive teachers have a vital role to play in heightening children's awareness of the aesthetic dimension in the natural environment, the work of artists and in children's own work (Smith, 1992).

It is often the aesthetic quality of a particular drawing that may lead to it being looked at more closely. Looking carefully at the way children construct figures or animals for example it becomes noticeable when a child has used a new and different system to construct a drawing. This may be as a result of the drawing, as has just been seen in the example of the lion (2d), being inspired by special events or circumstances. Carl's gorillas (2g) or Isabel's cat (2e) both stand out as being completely different from other drawings they did at the same time, both in structure and visual impact. In both these cases the children were inspired by powerful images, both direct and indirect, and the children who are not yet 5-years-old, have constructed their animals using a continuous line, a 'bounding outline' or 'embracing contour' as it has been called (Goodnow, 1977, Golomb, 1992). This system is generally used by much older children. Carl's gorilla on the left is drawn in profile using a single line. With the addition of lines representing fur, it is more difficult to see than the continuous line Isabel has used to draw the head and body of her cat. Carl (aged 4 years 11 months) was inspired to do his drawing (2g) from memory as a result of looking at and discussing illustrations and photographs of gorilla family groups in his reception class. The facility with which the animal on the left of the tree has been drawn may signal a particularly visual sensitivity and responsiveness to the characteristic movements of gorillas, and be an imaginative reconstruction from several in the book. It may equally reflect the effect of a single frozen image, already in two-dimensional form which makes it much easier to reproduce (Gardner, 1980, chapter 7). Whatever the exact source, Carl's drawing constitutes an achievement in his formal means of representation and expression.

The context of Isabel's cat drawing (2e, aged 4 years 9 months) is significant as it was made on one of the first occasions in her reception class when she was allowed to choose and to draw first before writing a sentence. Previously she had always been given a sentence by the teacher to copy and illustrate. She chose to make this drawing of her own cat from memory. Its bounding outline may be the result of her visual familiarity with the appearance of her cat, and her tactile familiarity with the feel of its shape and its texture. This much loved long-haired cat with its fluffy tail and jaunty step is conjured up by a particular quality of line, characterized by the speed and deftness of its making, which is echoed in the clouds and small figures in another part of the drawing (a boy falling off his bicycle). The added colour and texture in the cat and the pavement below is applied by vigorous crayoning. Isabel's tendency to 'scribble' was constantly highlighted by her teacher in a way that suggested that this was not the way to go about drawing. This is a difficulty that teachers face if they ask children to fill in and to keep within the outlines. This dominating aspect of 'colouring in' conflicts with what may be rough or jagged crayoning. This may not in fact be careless drawing, but drawing that actually conveys the irregular surface or outline of an object. Filling areas with scribbly texture can play an important part and may be a significant aspect of development in a child's work as will be seen in the last section of this chapter. In this picture it represents Isabel's first attempt, prompted by the chance to draw and write something of her own choice, to explore familiar aspects of her own environment; her black cat and its inner city street. She insisted on writing below 'my cat is black and black is my favourite colour'. What the image showed and what the writing said stood out from other work in Isabel's school book.

Closer investigation of the circumstances in which the drawings in illustrations 3 and 4 (children aged 4 to 6) were made allows the role of close observation and memory to be explored a little further. 3c shows several dinosaurs drawn by Neill. The one on the far right is quite different from the others. He drew this particular dinosaur to satisfy Ricky (3d) that he could draw a dinosaur 'properly'. Ricky was drawing a small plastic model dinosaur and protesting quite strongly that Neill's first dinosaur (at the top of 3c) didn't look like one. Neill was not particularly concerned by his protest but eventually he put the toy dinosaur near his paper and, after a brief discussion of its features with an adult, he drew it. Seeing that Ricky was satisfied, he continued to draw dinosaurs the way he had done initially (Korzenik, 1977; Thompson and Bales, 1991).

Neill and Ricky may have been drawing different species of dinosaur at the beginning of this incident but Ricky was judging Neill's dinosaurs by his own model (that walked in an upright position). There is a noticeable difference between Neill's first drawing which is a general representation of a dinosaur and his second drawing which is a more detailed depiction of a specific model. The profile drawing of the plastic dinosaur emerges with a continuous line fusing the head and body and the jagged spine, knobbly knees and claws are all clearly differentiated. Had this incident not occurred, Neill's ability to generate a different drawing system which describes specific features may not have been known. However he moved back to his less differentiated style to continue his drawing that was turning into a story. A generic dinosaur figure may have been in his mind for this purpose and appropriate for his drawing. He may in fact have been able to draw quite a detailed dinosaur from memory if he had been prompted to think of one that he knew in particular (Smith, 1983). The same difference between drawing from memory and drawing from close observation that Neill showed is clearly evident in the two drawings made by Penny. The first drawing (3h) was made in response to a request to draw herself from memory and the second drawing was done shortly afterwards while she looked in a small mirror. Unlike the first drawing, the second drawing (3j) was also preceded by a discussion of what sorts of features Penny and her group would draw and what sorts of shapes, lines and arrangements they would use to show them. There is a marked difference in the two drawings, and again had Penny been prompted in her memory drawing it may not have been quite so great. However, I think it is important that teachers recognize that each drawing system has its own purposes and values. Spare, diagrammatic drawing will continue to be an important strand in Neill and Penny's drawing 'repertoire', alongside drawing that develops more naturalistic features (Wolf and Perry, 1988; Gentle, 1985).

In both these cases the children would probably not have initiated an act of close observation without the prompting of another person. Sometimes it is much less obvious how much close observation children initiate as a result of challenges from other directions. Diaries, newsbooks and writing activities may reveal quite surprising incidences of careful observation. Joanna's diary (3a and 3b) underlines the importance of talking to children about their drawings as 3a is not particularly significant on its own. A student teacher had introduced a simple zig-zag diary to her class of 4 and 5-year-olds for them to record activities on each day of the week. Each day the class decided which of the day's activities to represent but on Friday they were allowed to choose any activity they liked. On Tuesday Joanna drew the teacher playing the piano and the children singing (3a). For the Friday drawing (3b), she explained that she had chosen to draw the Tuesday activity again. She hadn't got the teacher right on Tuesday as she had found it hard to show her playing the piano. She added, with obvious satisfaction, that on Friday when she had tried it again she had succeeded because in the meantime, she had another chance to see the piano being played. Then drawing from memory, she was able to show the piano's 'legs' (the black shapes beneath the teacher's outstretched arms), and the whole piano next to the teacher — a large yellow area of colouring visible either side of the teacher's body. Other children in the class included the piano in their Tuesday drawings. Joanna was not satisfied with her own drawing, and reconstructed it from knowledge in her memory as a result of observation rather than copying any of the other children's ways of showing the piano.

The drawings from a newsbook, completed once a week (3e, 3f, 3g), illustrate an interesting change in the means Greg uses to depict the same scene. The writing over a period of several weeks showed increasing complexity in what was said and how it was constructed. The drawings reveal Greg's mother, with disc in hand by his chair and computer desk (3e), and Greg, playing with his computer (3f). In 3f he is shown wedged between the chair and the desk. In 3g, although it is on a much smaller scale, he has drawn himself sitting on the chair at his desk and the chair has gained an extra structural component. Many teachers may be tempted to give only a cursory glance at drawings that illustrate children's writing and when they do make comments that show they may have a presentation framework in their minds. (Such a framework could give rise to comments on how effectively the page space has been filled, how neatly or faintly the illustration has been drawn, whether it is finished or needs colouring in or has been spoiled by 'scribble'.) That a child may have modified his repertoire of drawn figures to allow a figure to sit convincingly on a chair may pass unnoticed. As a result of needing more information to reconstruct his chair from memory, he may have looked more closely at it, but this too may pass unnoticed. Drawings illustrating writing are enormously rich sources of knowledge about children's spontaneous drawing activities but are often cited as evidence of lack of drawing ability or examples of stereotypical drawings. Often they reveal unusual and significant features that would not take form if it were not for the interest inspired by the combination of recalling a personal and meaningful experience through thinking, talking and in some cases writing about it first.

Building up a profile of children's drawing may reveal important information about the way that they draw from memory or observation; differences and change have been highlighted so far. However, it is also possible to recognize when young children are developing an individual personal style. This includes using media in particular ways and preferring certain arrangements and configurations to others, as well as choosing which aspects of an object or event to express and represent. Penny's drawings (3h and 3j) although different, share some common features. The firm way she uses her pencil to draw lines and to make solid shapes or the way she colours in areas with crayon are the same in both drawings. In the examples illustrated in 4a-f, the three children show interesting similarities of style and approach in both of their drawings. These were based on direct observation (hyacinths) and memories of a closely observed school event (toy theatre performance in the school playground). They were carried out with the encouragement and support of their student teacher.

Caroline's particular use of media in both drawings (4a and 4b) shows a delicate and sensitive touch. She also experiments with different effects, combining smudged areas of oil pastel with bolder strokes in the hyacinth drawing

(4a) and using different textures for crayoning the playground, van and sky in her drawing of a school event (4b). Zoë uses solid and bolder blocks of colour in both her drawings (4e and 4f), building up a very dense textured effect in the hyacinth flowerheads using one layer of colour on top of another (4e). The three pairs of drawings also reveal individual preferences for certain types of shapes and arrangement. David arranges the audience of school children in the playground in front of the theatre van, in careful lines (4d). In the same way he indicates the numerous flower heads of the hyacinth in short lines of alternating colour, indicating that they are all over the stem (4c). Caroline uses a multiplicity of shapes, echoing in each picture the range of content she includes. She adds a small round sun, a textured patch of sky and dots of rain to the Lyalinth drawing which already has clusters of flowers like starbursts and lines of leaves and stems opening out at the base of the flowers. The scent of the flowers is almost palpable (4a). Her theatre van has a balloon of smoke emerging diagonally upwards from its exhaust on one side and on the other, lines to show the sound of the accompanying music. The children's arms are raised and their hands drawn in star-like shapes (4b). In contrast Zoë emphasizes the outline of the objects in both her drawings (4e and 4f) by drawing them with strong simple shapes, avoiding too much detail. She establishes a powerful and deliberate relationship between the figures or flowers and their respective backgrounds and the spaces between the objects act as very positive shapes.

Until the student teacher paired up all the children's drawings she was unable to recognize these features fully. Establishing the similarities within these pairs of drawings (as one might highlight differences in another context) heightens understanding and appreciation of their formal aspects even though their contents are quite different. It is important to help children in their work by being sensitive to their individual styles and preferences, giving feedback and encouragement, and challenging them, particularly if they become too rigidly caught up in a style of working or too timid and closed to any further experimentation or development. Regular viewing of children's work soon identifies individual patterns and approaches, particularly when work is viewed from as wide a range of sources as possible.

A Case Study: Isabel (illustrations 5–8)

The drawings, paintings, writing and other materials in this case study emerged over time like an elaborate tapestry growing vertically and woven with many different threads from both home and school. One of the advantages of collections of children's work is that they enable us to 'gain a feeling for the processes of artistic growth. And because we know what has gone before, and what will follow, we acquire a sense of significance that is impossible to secure from the study of single context-free drawings' (Gardner, 1980, pp. 75–93, see also Golomb, 1992; Paine, 1981). Building up a longitudinal case study helps establish vital patterns of growth and also reveals the extent to which

Illustration 5 (Isabel)

a 5.2

b 5.11

c 5.11

d 5.11

e 5.11

Illustration 6 (Isabel)

a 5.11

b 6.0

c 6.4

d 6.4

e 6.4

f 7.4

g 7.4

Illustration 7 (Isabel)

a 8.8

b 8.6

c 9.10

d 9.10

Illustration 8 (Isabel)

a 8.9

b 8.5

c 10.9

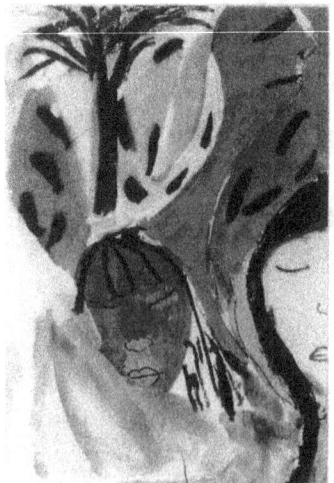

d 11.1

e 10.9

children are developing a broad drawing 'repertoire', rather than proceeding in some kind of linear fashion, to a particular 'end point' (Wolf and Perry, 1988).

The illustrations 5–8 show several strands in Isabel's growing drawing 'repertoire' from the ages of 5 to 11 years. Many of the individual, social and cultural factors that influence the imagery and drawing performance of children, can be seen in the examples of this particular child.[2] As each group of drawings is considered, the codes (drawing systems etc.) and contexts necessary for understanding the work will be explored.[3] The first group (illustrations 5 and 6) consists of a single drawing and three sets of drawings, each set having been carried out at approximately the same time. By looking at similarities and differences between these drawings and at the group as a whole, several aspects of Isabel's drawing systems, drawing style, imagery and artistic growth can be identified. A second group of drawings (illustrations 7 and 8) are from the later primary years and continue to explore some of the themes that emerge from the first group. One pair of drawings only will be the focus of this section.

The drawing of Isabel's summer holiday (5a, aged 5 years 2 months) provides a rich starting point in the first group. This biro pen drawing remained hidden in the back of an old drawing book, only to be discovered years after it was made. Unlike Jasvir's monster drawing, we do not depend on verbal comments, gestures and other cues to apprehend its meaning. The marks and lines and what they represent can be read quite easily on one level by having an understanding of the way young children draw and on a deeper level by recognizing the particular objects and events that the drawing refers to. Many drawings children make would, if closely investigated, yield similarly surprising evidence of just how richly children are making sense of, and responding to, their experiences through visual means. As in Isabel's case, this is more clearly seen if children's work is being collected systematically.

Isabel's summer holiday drawing is altogether more complex in arrangement and content than previous drawings she had made. It can be read almost like a boardgame or a storyboard. It represents her seaside holiday starting with the journey past Heathrow airport on the left and including at the top, the zoo she visited (with the lion 2f, that ate the chicken carcass). The seafront with bathing huts are shown on the right hand side leading to a carefully remembered schematic arrangement of the campus where she stayed, with its drive winding past fish ponds and trees, up to a grand house with several floors and balconies. The end of the holiday is continued into the top right area below the lion and shows Isabel and her mother waving to a friend before taking the train home. Unfortunately, it is not possible to know where on the paper this holiday drawing started. But drawing allows the possibility of moving backwards, forwards and around in time and space on a single page and also of building up layers of drawn experience in a way that underlines one of its fundamental differences from writing, as well as underlining its own vital role in children's learning. Drawing also allows great flexibility in both its form and content, and this example shows several drawing systems being used together to explore the world more fully. Characteristics seen in drawings discussed earlier in this chapter (lion 2d, cat 2e) are noticeably present.

Two other strands in her previous drawing experience come together in this elaborate example. By the end of her first year in school Isabel had begun to indicate the location of figures in relation to their environment using point-plot arrangements. She drew a rectangle for the park and plotted the position of herself and her friends playing football. She also drew herself and her friends at the funfair and used a fold-out arrangement to show them all swinging around on a carousel.[4] The holiday drawing is an orderly combination of vertical and horizontal spatial arrangements where the edges of the paper act as a coordinate frame (Matthews, 1991). A horizontal baseline is adopted for the zoo section at the top of the drawing and by turning the paper sideways it may be adopted for the seaside represented at the right-hand side and also probably for the airport scene opposite. The grand house consists of vertically arranged parts; a plan of its garden; the front face of the building; and the roof area with chimneys attached. Below the house, the ponds enclosing fish and lilies are also drawn in plan and in order to show herself and her friends, Isabel uses a fold-out arrangement. She attaches the figures at right angles to the outer edges of the pond and allows them to occupy the space on the surrounding area of the page. In another part of the drawing further above she has drawn the figures of herself and her mother inside and in front of the train (with smoke at one end and a flag at the other). There are no 'view-points' here, these are both convenient ways of representing her experience. She continued to use schematic and fold-out arrangements for specific purposes throughout the following year (see 6c) but then the fold-out system appears to have been replaced by a mainly vertical projective system (Willats, 1985) which remained in her repertoire throughout her primary years, suiting a range of functions.

Not only has Isabel thought carefully about the arrangement and particular content necessary to record objects and events from her holiday, but also through the aesthetic elements of line, shape and pattern she is able to celebrate her experience. The means by which her lions (2d and 2f) could appear fierce or friendly or her black cat (2e) convey something of its cheeky personality are available in this drawing. The sheer variety of lines and shapes in the drawing could be said to encapsulate something of the enjoyment of the holiday event represented. The joyful mood may be perceived partly as a result of the upward direction of many of the lines in the composition of the drawing but the sense of exuberance and motion is mainly conveyed by the repeated use of curly lines and an overall impression of circular (clockwise) movement. The curly lines were noticeable in her cat drawing (2c) and here they represent smoke from the chimneys, the sea curling around three sides of the paper and the railings encircling the garden of the grand house.

When Isabel as an 11-year-old was looking at a drawing of the same period as this one that included a similar garden and railings, she reflected that she had always drawn low curling railings, having been fascinated by them as a young child in London's many parks. What may be less recognizable but nevertheless of as much importance as such details, are the visual spatial aspects of the environment that a child has experienced. Isabel certainly attended to the railings, ducks, ponds, bridges and willow trees in London parks as her drawings and paintings show. But at the same time, in the park or elsewhere in the city, she was also constantly exploring a network of paths and routes, tracing and retracing her steps, and in company with adults, looking at maps and diagrams (mostly topographical in nature) identifying landmarks and pondering directions. These rich visual spatial experiences in the lives of children may be overlooked both when evidence of their existence emerges in spontaneous drawing (one of the 4-year-old children at Jasvir's table was drawing a recognizable map) or as a source to be tapped into and explored as an increasingly distinct genre in a child's drawing repertoire (McFee and Degge, 1992, Wolf and Perry, 1988).

Isabel's seaside holiday emerges as the most complex drawing she had made up to that time. She did not have an opportunity to create a similarly significant and complex drawing until nearly a year later (see 5b). In the case of both drawings (5a and 5b) she found herself in an artistically stimulating environment, where she had been inspired by seeing other children's artwork, adult students at work and examples of artists' work. She had also been given encouragement and feedback for her own drawing and painting by adults and other children. The set of drawings 5a-6b were all carried out, along with many others, in the same week (around her sixth birthday). Although closely related to earlier drawings done both at home and school they constitute an important burst of creative activity and exploration. They show features and themes already well established being reconstructed, elaborated, and reaching new levels of achievement whilst at the same time new ideas are emerging. Themes ranged from a circus experience she had been revisiting since she was 3-years-old, explored in a new range of media and on a large scale (5b); familiar figures from her environment (London punks) with newly differentiated features including a guitar (5c); a seated Teddy Bear (her first ever drawing and painting from observation 5d); Rapunzel, a favourite fairy-story character (her first ever seated figure drawn later the same day as the seated Teddy bear, 5e); another version of a familiar pond and fountain (6a) (first explored the previous year in 5a); cartoon characters Tom and Jerry (drawn back at school after her holiday, filling a whole page in her writing book, 6b).

Like the majority of drawings young children make at this time, 5a-6a are self-contained images, making little or no reference to objects or events outside the borders of the drawings themselves. In contrast, the drawing of Tom and Jerry (6b) is the first drawing Isabel made which shows only the lower half of a figure and deliberately uses the edges of the page as a frame to 'crop' the scene. This powerfully effective framing device familiar from television and comic strip illustrations as well as many other sources occurs more frequently than much literature on young children's drawing suggests (Wilson and Wilson,

157

1980). In classrooms where children are encouraged to make narrative picture sequences it occurs quite regularly. In Isabel's drawing it was not necessary to show the rest of the cartoon character because, as she explained 'you never see her face anyway'. This drawing was unusual in Isabel's writing book that year and apart from practising half-length figures, using a portrait format, the only occasion previously when she had used a similar cropping device in a drawing was the day she went to the cinema for the first time (aged 5 years 1 month) (Brown, 1988). (She drew a scene from *Jungle Book* immediately afterwards which included a cropped image of Mowgli hiding in the grass and the head and neck of a large smiling tiger 'looking into' the scene from the edge of the paper.) Not only is this drawing of Tom and Jerry striking in that it shows an unusually cropped figure, but it is also very dramatically arranged with a 'positively' empty space between the cat and the mouse. There is almost a sense that the cat is still in the process of being lifted up and away from the mouse (the writing said 'Tom wanted to catch Jerry'). This impression comes from the strong vertical emphasis in the legs, leading into the stripes of the skirt, and also in the cat's front paws and pointed ears. This sense of movement in the drawing is also triggered by the use of multiple lines for arms. A similar sense of movement is created in the cascading fountain (6a) by a similar repetition of sweeping lines.

Sweeping movement is also characteristic of the next set of drawings, 6c-6e, all carried out on the same day when Isabel was 6 years 4 months. The heightened quality of this set of drawings, like those in the set 5a-6b, illustrate 'that what happens "naturally" in the course of development is in no way equivalent to what can happen, given a particular educational regimen or in light of the messages embedded in a given cultural setting' (Gardner, 1988). The drawing 6e uses the framing convention of 6b and this was the first time Isabel had spontaneously used this device, working from direct observation (her fish tank). She has selected a portion of the tank and used the edges of the page to frame the scene. She drew rapidly using economical marks to indicate the fish and weed, crayoning vigorously with the oil pastels for the surrounding water. This remarkable drawing was preceded by another (6d), also drawn rapidly, with solid colouring of Nelson's column and the ornamental lions at its base and a burst of short marks around the top to represent the birds swarming in the air. Both these drawings with their vivid characterizations are the result of Isabel's heightened aesthetic awareness of her environment on that particular day after a visit to the National Gallery. This heightened environmental awareness is described by Rod Taylor (1992): 'something of what has been experienced within the art gallery affects the way we subsequently see the everyday world around us once outside the art gallery'.

The drawing of her cat by a fish pond (6c and Plate 1) was made earlier that day in the gallery, after she had been looking closely at paintings of Monet's garden at Giverny. She had responded to the two she liked best (the Japanese bridge and a close up view of the surface of the pond with irises against it) and made her own drawing combining elements from both pictures. The same spontaneous crayonning of the entire page with pastel that was seen in 6e was undoubtedly inspired by the examples all around her in the gallery. Covering the entire paper surface is commonly one of the first features that young children emulate when making their own responses to looking at artists' work, even in postcard reproduction. The arrangement of this drawing (6c and Plate 1) consists of the entire surface of a circular pond with her black cat in profile seated above it. The cat is hiding 'behind' a bush, watching fish in a pond. A tree in blossom is nearby and the coloured shapes of the blossom have been stirred into the swirl of coloured patches that make up the surface of the pond. A fringe of grass is folded out around its edge. Observing Monet closely has led Isabel to make this imaginary narrative scene employing many of her tried and tested drawing conventions but experimenting significantly with one new aspect; the depiction of reflections and movement in the surface of water with soft oil pastels. After this experience she immediately made two view-specific drawings of her immediate environment, one glimpsed and drawn from memory, one drawn from direct observation. In both she confidently extends her newly-acquired skills with soft pastels to capture both movement and reflections. In these drawings Isabel shows that as well as representing 'the theme or mood of a work of art' (DES, 1992), as in 6c, she is identifying with the purposes of an artist in a broader context in 6d and 6e.

The third set of drawings (6f and 6g) were carried out when Isabel was 7 years 4 months. The school drawing (6f) in pencil and felt pen was made to illustrate a favourite place, in her case 'a house in the country,' and accompanied a piece of writing. The drawing (6g) was made in response to an evening drive in the Devon countryside during the half-term holiday using pencil and pastels and was drawn from memory afterwards. It shows no specific place but is a composite arrangement of several places glimpsed during the journey. In that respect it is similar to 6f which is also a composite of features Isabel has chosen to highlight in her countryside idyll. The difference between these two drawings lies not only in what they are actually about but also in the entirely different ways in which they are drawn. The house in the country (6f) is easily dismissed as 'stereotyped' or taken as evidence of a lack of awareness of features that are clearly evident in 6g. This highlights the danger of choosing a single drawing on which to base an assessment of a child's work (Clements and Page, 1992). When 6f is viewed in the context of all her drawings, it appears more restrained and formally organized and is certainly neater than her usual drawings. This was induced by anxiety to please her new class teacher with neatness and at the same time be seen among her new class-mates as able to draw in a particular style. Isabel thought it one of her better drawings that year, partly because she gained teacher and peer-group approval through it, but also because she was able to respond to a favourite theme she had previously explored and would continue to explore. She enjoyed making this countryside fantasy picture with all its generic features. The bird perched on the sun and the animated scarecrow are characteristic of two important aspects of Isabel's individual personality; her sense of humour and her feeling for animation. Her strong sense of balance and pattern is also highlighted by the formal arrangement. Drawing 6g shows other personal characteristics that had emerged quite early; her aesthetic awareness and responsiveness to certain atmospheric effects (sky and water in particular), and more generally to lively movement. Isabel's sensitive handling of texture and colour in 6g is highly suggestive of the pale October sunset she had experienced. The use of scribbled texture over the spindly trees and roofs of the nestling houses evokes the sense of movement in a fleeting glimpse of the countryside, and the soft focus of the landscape allows the sunset to be the most important feature of the drawing.

It is only when looking across a child's work and including evidence as dissimilar as these two drawings, that a fuller picture of a child's repertoire emerges. Looking longitudinally it is important to see how both these drawings exemplify strands already developed in her repertoire and contain features that will be developed and extended in later years along with others not illustrated in these examples.

The second group of illustrations (7 and 8) include two drawings made within a few days of each other during a holiday in Durham (7c and 7d, 9 years 10 months). In a similar manner to the countryside drawings 6f and 6g, they explore two different aspects of city environment. 7d is an imaginary scene of life in the inner city, contemplated from a distance, whereas 7c was made on location, from direct observation and records a specific view of Durham cathedral and city. The drawing 7d is not unlike Jasvir's monster in jail in the way it allows Isabel to combine fantasy and reality. Through it she is able to explore some very real tensions and apprehensions in her own world, diffusing them in a humorous way. A man is walking his rottweiler to the 'dog's hairdresser' in Dog Street. A woman is emerging from a fish shop at the side and is about to step into a minicab. She has just bought herself a piranha fish in a small tank and is carrying it with both hands. Whilst the figures, the dogs and the building are drawn from the side, the pavement and minicab are drawn from above. This allows Isabel to describe the minicab more fully and to include a large graffiti symbol (a letter S) on its roof. She is also beginning to make it look more three dimensional (see the car in 7a, aged 8 years 5 months). She is venturing into new territory in that aspect of her drawing repertoire in both Dog Street and the cathedral drawing (7c). Before discussing that dimension of her work, it is important to consider the way she has created the powerfully tense and somewhat bizarre scene in 7d.

Few writers have explored the role of humour in children's drawing (Paine, 1989). It has already been seen in several of the young children's drawings in this chapter and in Isabel's case it appeared frequently from the earliest years but more consistently after the age of 7. Around the time she made the drawings 7b and 8a (between 8 years 6 months and 8 years 9 months) she had developed quite an anarchic spirit. Her favourite author was Roald Dahl and at the same time she was also exploring a cartoon style, which developed out of drawings like the 'house in the country' (6f) and reflected the influence of other children's drawings and also her own love of illustrators such as Quentin Blake. Her PE picture 8a, uses this style for showing a class of children out of control in the school hall, (the drawing illustrates a poem she had written exploring this fantasy) and even a visit to the National Gallery gave her the opportunity to revisit her favourite Monet painting, using a cartoon style to depict an amusing incident taking place on Monet's bridge at Giverny (7b).[5] Drawings like 7b and 8a are important in their own right as well as being links in the development of a more serious strand of humour, which in Isabel's case began to emerge visually in a drawing like Dog Street. She no longer requires speech bubbles and similar conventions to extend the narrative. She uses more formal means to highlight tension and incongruity.

In considering the aesthetic development of children's drawing, it is possible to see how by the middle primary years, children may have a considerable range of drawing means available to them (see especially Smith, 1992). New characteristics emerging in their use of line, shape, pattern and texture can evoke moods and describe aspects of the visual, tactile and spatial world by means previously unavailable. In Dog Street, which is drawn on a large scale, there is a new forcefulness and a slight awkwardness in some of the shapes and lines that are being explored and these allow figures, like the man in his striped suit to look slightly ridiculous. Isabel had always taken a keen interest in how she drew clothing and is using a deliberately formal arrangement of the costume and pose in this figure. The diagonal line of the dog's lead gives emphasis to the parallel line of the man's forward leg, suggesting a marching movement. She surrounds this tidy figure with the scrawl of advertising, notices and the graffiti on the shop door.

It is important at this point, as has already been seen with younger children, to distinguish intention from unintended outcomes. As children (and adults) at any stage in artistic production combine familiar and new ways of representing the world or expressing emotions or other sensory experiences, there may be ambiguities and unresolved tensions that characterize work at that stage. These are not deficits, they are the unmistakable signs of artistic life and growth. Sensitivity to what children are attempting to do remains as crucial as when children were younger and knowledge and understanding of the range of children's drawing systems for example, is essential if adults are to avoid discouraging and making negative assessments of children's understanding through drawing.

Such signs of growth are evident in part of the drawing of Dog Street. Isabel was already very adept at using overlapping shapes to indicate depth in space and at adjusting the scale of figures, buildings and other items to sustain this illusion (7a). She does this consistently in Dog Street except for the minicab in the side street. Here she attempts to make the minicab three dimensional by adjusting her previous rules to make the parts of the cab 'fit' together. Although she had previously explored volume in the mass of the hill in 8b (which looks very much more solid than the hill in 6g a year earlier) and was beginning to make figures and animals look more solid, she was still relying on showing a single face view of most regular 3-D shapes and only occasionally moving towards showing any other faces (top, sides). In the minicab she is successfully moving towards making the necessary adjustments to show not only the front and side of the vehicle but the top. She has temporarily ignored the scale she has established elsewhere in the picture (she drew this item last) although she manages to integrate it with the rest of the picture in the way she applies a pattern of lines and coloured shapes to the vehicle.

Although as a general rule Isabel had worked very little from direct observation in her drawing and painting, both at home and school, her keenly observant eye had informed much of her work from memory and imagination. The few occasions where she had been encouraged (by an adult or teacher) to draw from observation, it had affected her drawing from memory quite considerably. The seated figure of Rapunzel (5e) appeared the same day that she had at first struggled to make her Teddy Bear look as if it was sitting down. (After an adult had helped her see how she could make some fairly simple adjustments to her drawing rules to achieve this, she appeared to have internalized these changes so that they could then operate in a similar context.) At 7-years-old, drawing a self-portrait from close observation she managed (after discussion) to devise a new way of indicating nostrils effectively and this was immediately incorporated into her drawings of people from memory. Having drawn herself from observation appears to have heightened her sensitivity to other people's faces and her drawings from memory in the following days were noticeably more sensitive and showing evidence of thoughtful observation of a whole range of features. Rod Taylor's comment about the impact of art gallery experiences applies equally to other very powerful visual experiences whether at home, at school or in the local environment. The example of Isabel going to the National Gallery and seeing art, while powerfully affected by other 'frameworks' and responding accordingly (7b), is also a reminder of the reciprocal nature of art and experience (Goodman, 1969; Gombrich, 1977).

Although Isabel had never drawn anything in the built environment from direct observation, she had shown an interest in drawing buildings, including churches, monuments and bridges from an early age. She jumped at the suggestion that she should sit outside and draw the view of Durham Cathedral (on an A2 sheet of paper fixed to a drawing board). What factors could enable a child of 9 years 10 months to tackle such a challenge with enthusiasm and to complete the drawing 7c in one hour in the open air? There are obvious attitudes that need to be considered. She had available the attention span and powers of concentration to draw solidly in front of a motif that would command such attention and concentration. She had the encouragement of adult expectation but was under no pressure. Other personal factors may include the excitement of being on holiday and having had some new artistic experiences, a large sheet of good quality paper and a range of sharp pencils. However important these are, they are not enough to explain fully how she came to make this drawing.

What this drawing relies on first and foremost is Isabel's mind being able to inform her eye as she looks at the view in front of her. It is in the same way that she looked into her fish tank as a 6-year-old and selected certain features while rejecting others. It is in the same way that it was possible for her to organize, discriminate and make association with experiences from earlier that same day in the marks, lines and shapes she constructed to represent the fish tank. As Isabel asked questions and made comments as she drew 7c, it is possible to pinpoint some of the features in this drawing process. As she used the edges of her paper to mentally 'frame' the scene in front of her, she could be said to be using an internalized coordinate frame that her previous drawing experiences had established firmly in her mind, and this enabled her to make initial choices as to where she would place the general 'shape' of the scene she had chosen. As in many of her compositions she made a strong centrally placed feature (in this case the Cathedral tower) and this marker established a reference point for scale and measurement throughout the drawing. She did not need much questioning to help her break down the task in front of her into manageable steps and to start drawing. I would suggest her first-hand experience of views of Durham Cathedral from various points around the city in the previous days, as well as her familiarity with it through postcards and a calendar at home, played a part in helping her frame the scene readily. However she encountered two specific problems as she drew. When it came to the buildings in the city below the cathedral she was daunted at the prospect of drawing each one as individually as she had drawn the parts of the cathedral. At this stage in her drawing experience she needed help to see how she could simplify the building structures, representing their general appearance rather than attending to each individual building detail-by-detail.

Whether children work from memory or observation, it is the result of changes in their thinking rather than their looking on its own that effects their drawing development. This was highlighted particularly by Isabel's second difficulty which was trying to get the cathedral tower 'to look right'. She left the tower unfinished when she went home after drawing. (The two single lines that represent the left side and the rear edge of the top of the tower were missing.) From the hilly position where Isabel drew this scene, the top of the tower in fact appeared as a horizontal line as it was almost at eye level on the hill opposite. No amount of looking at the scene would make her drawing 'right', because her drawing of the slanted nave roof and other parts of the picture had suggested a higher view point than she actually had and that is also what the present tower top suggests. Isabel added the two final lines to the tower after she had read David Macaulay's book *Cathedral* and looked closely at the fascinating illustrations (Macaulay, 1974). Without hesitation she declared the two lines made her drawing 'look right'. There was no single illustration in the book that gave her the answer. Rather the wide range of different ways of looking at structures, drawn in much detail but with utmost clarity, helped her view her drawing as a whole and make the additional lines 'fit'. As much as the cathedral drawing appears to be from observation (and there is obviously much observed detail in it) it is also dependent on two important factors; Isabel's own drawing systems and what she can show with them as well as her personal style (preference for certain types of line, shape, pattern and composition, for example).

It is significant that after this experience Isabel used clearly parallel oblique lines with great confidence to present the receding edges of regular objects. In drawing the rest of the cathedral, Isabel also struggled to ensure that it hung together, in the way that she also had to get her minicab to work in 7d. In the cathedral drawing she compensates for the steep angle of the roof of the nave, the sloping angle of the windows and the two small towers in front of the nave, by drawing the far left outer tower of the cathedral at a sloping angle in the opposite direction. The trees and buildings below the cathedral almost act like buttresses to the cathedral itself and the west towers (right-hand side) are fused solidly with the houses below. Even the large bird perched on an aerial seems to add weight and stability to this corner of the scene. Despite some awkwardnesses and lines slanting in many and varied directions in parts of this drawing, the overall achievement is one of balance and unity.

Although these two drawings 7c and 7d represent only two types of drawing Isabel was making around her tenth birthday, it is valuable in conclusion to see how elements in both of them developed in her last year in primary school. Far from moving towards any single 'end point', Isabel continued to make sense of her world and the world of other artists, using a growing repertoire of skills to explore themes and ideas she had already contemplated as well as to develop new strands in her thinking. Her interest in clothing, costume and body adornment broadened out into a serious interest in fashion and textile design through innumerable sketches and visualizations, carried out mainly at home. The drawing 8c shows an imaginary figure wearing a hat Isabel has designed. Even though her main interest in this drawing was in the clothing this girl is wearing Isabel has paid careful attention to the way she has drawn the hair and it is quite clear how much her drawing skills are developing. The range and quality of line in this example, to render the form and texture of the hair and to indicate the form of the hat or head is significantly more subtle and sensitive than a year earlier. This is not so much in Isabel's case, the result of drawing from direct observation but much more from frequent close observation of people in her daily environment (particularly during her journeys to school by bus and train) as well as from designers fashion drawings. She continued to explore ideas inspired by artists work and still returned to Monet, from time to time. The watercolour study 8e is part of a series of sketches she made in preparation for a wallpaper/fabric design incorporating motifs such as lilies, leaves and goldfish.

The last example of her work 8d, is a reminder of the many strands that make up teachers understanding of children's drawing. These include the factors mentioned at the beginning of this section, such as the individual, social and cultural influences that shape children's drawing performance and most importantly the purposes and motives that children have for drawing. Goodman suggests that curiosity and enlightenment, understanding, the urge to know and the delight of discovery are primary forces in the use of symbols (Goodman, 1969; Gombrich, 1977). This framework allows us to look at children's symbol use from *their* point of view and to identify *their* learning through art. Isabel's enigmatic picture of two of her friends (8d) is also a reminder that what we bring to a child's work will affect the way we see it. That we may be reminded of work by Paul Gaugin or Sonia Boyce is in no way invalidated when we find she had never heard of these particular artists but if we fail to recognize the value that a piece of work like this may have in a child's construction of meaning, we may be missing a vital part in understanding the significance of children's drawing.

Notes

1 This incident shows Jasvir's intentions being confirmed *by* and *for* the girl next to him. See also Thompson and Bales (1991).
2 For a discussion of these factors in another setting see Court (1992) and Wilson and Litvoegt (1992).
3 Although not specifically related to children's drawings, the framework of thinking in the following chapter is very helpful: Gombrich (1982) 'The visual image: Its place in communication'.
4 For a discussion of schematic systems see Dubery and Willats (1983); Goodnow (1977) and Golomb (1992) among others discuss fold-out features in children's drawings. See also Smith (1983) pp. 62–4.
5 Isabel and her friend are standing on the bridge, having thrown their clothes into the pond. Isabel is wearing her bathing costume, her friend is saying 'I wish I'd brought my costume'. Isabel's mother is calling them from the bank. The clothes floating in the water are bonnets, ribbons, skirts and blouses and other nineteenth century costume. The boat that Monet painted is also seen floating in the pond and the oars are among the clothes. Isabel is using her knowledge of the historical context of Monet's picture from her reading of Bjork and Anderson (1987).

References

ARNHEIM, R. (1974) *Art and Visual Perception*, Berkeley, CA, University of California Press.
ATHEY, C. (1981) 'Parental involvement in nursery education', *Early Child Development and Care*, 7, pp. 353–67.
ATHEY, C. (1990) *Extending Thought in Young Children*, London, Paul Chapman Publishing Ltd.
ATKINSON, D. (1991) 'How children use drawing', *Journal of Art and Design Education*, 10, 1, pp. 57–72.
BJORK, C. and ANDERSON, L. (1987) *Linnea in Monet's Garden*, Stockholm, R and S Books.
BLANK, P., MASSEY, C., GARDNER, H. and WINNER, E. (1984) 'Perceiving what paintings express', in CROZIER, W.R. and CHAPMAN, A.J. (Eds) *Cognitive Processes and the Perception of Art*, Amsterdam, North-Holland.

BROWN, L.K. (1988) 'Fiction for children: Does the medium matter?', *Journal of Aesthetic Education*, 22, 1, pp. 35–44.
CLEMENTS, R. and PAGE, S. (1992) *Principles and Practice in Art*, Harlow, Oliver and Boyd.
COURT, E. (1992) 'Researching social influences in the drawings of rural Kenyan children', in THISTLEWOOD, D. (Ed) *Drawing, Research and Development*, Harlow, Longman.
DES (1992) *Art in the National Curriculum*, London, HMSO.
DES (1992) *Art in the National Curriculum: Non-statutory Guidance for Teachers* issued by the Curriculum Council for Wales, Cardiff, HMSO.
DUBERY, F. and WILLATS, J. (1983) *Perspective and Other Drawing Systems*, London, Herbert Press Ltd.
EGAN, K. (1992) *Imagination in Teaching and Learning*, London, Routledge.
GARDNER, H. (1980) *Artful Scribbles*, New York, Basic Books.
GARDNER, H. (1988) 'Towards more effective arts education', *Journal of Aesthetic Education*, 22, 1, pp. 157–67.
GENTLE, K. (1985) 'The assessment and evaluation of children's art', in GENTLE, K. *Children and Art Teaching*, London, Croom Helm, pp. 185–210.
GOLOMB, C. (1992) *The Child's Creation of a Pictorial World*, Berkeley, CA, University of California Press.
GOMBRICH, E.H. (1977) *Art and Illusion* (5th edn), Oxford, Phaidon Press.
GOMBRICH, E.H. (1982) *The Image and the Eye*, Oxford, Phaidon Press Ltd.
GOODMAN, N. (1969) *Languages of Art*, London, Oxford University Press.
GOODNOW, J. (1977) *Children's Drawing*, London, Penguin.
HUGHES, A. (1989) 'The copy, the parody and the pastiche', in THISTLEWOOD, D. (Ed) *Critical Studies in Art and Design Education*, Harlow, Longman, pp. 71–81.
KORZENIK, D. (1977) 'Saying it with pictures', in PERKINS, D. and LEONARD, B. (Eds) *The Arts and Cognition*, Baltimore, MD, Johns Hopkins University Press, pp. 192–207.
MACAULEY, D. (1974) *Cathedral*, London, William Collins, Sons & Co Ltd.
MCFEE, J.K. and DEGGE, R.M. (1992) *Art, Culture and Development*, Dubuque, IA, Kendall/Hunt Publishing Company.
MATTHEWS, J. (1988) 'The young child's early representation and drawing', in BLENKIN, G.M. and KELLY, A.V. (Eds) *Early Childhood Education: A Development Curriculum*, London, Paul Chapman, pp. 162–83.
MATTHEWS, J. (1991) 'How children map 3D volumes and scenes on to 2D surfaces', in JONES, L. (Ed) *Teaching Mathematics and Art*, Cheltenham, Stanley Thornes Publishing Ltd., pp. 9–20.
MATTHEWS, J. (1992) 'The genesis of aesthetic sensibility', in THISTLEWOOD, D. with COURT, E. and PAINE, S. (Eds) *Drawing, Research and Development*, Harlow, Longman.
PAINE, S. (1981) *Six Children Draw*, London, Academic Press.
PAINE, S. (1989) 'The role of humour in children's drawing experience', in DYSON, A. (Ed) *Looking, Making and Learning: Art and Design in the Primary School*, London, Kogan Page, pp. 98–109.
PIDGEON, S. (1992) 'Assessment at Key Stage 1: Teacher assessment through record-keeping', in BLENKIN, G.M. and KELLY, A.V. (Eds) *Assessment in Early Childhood Education*, London, Paul Chapman Publishing, pp. 122–43.
SMITH, N.R. (1982) 'The visual arts in early childhood education: Development and the creation of meaning', in SPODEK, B. (Ed) *Handbook of Research in Early Childhood Education*, New York, Free Press, pp. 295–317.
SMITH, N.R. (1983) *Experience and Art: Teaching Children to Paint*, New York, Teachers College Press.

SMITH, N.R. (1992) 'Development of the aesthetic in children's drawings', in THISTLEWOOD, D. et al (Eds) *Drawing, Research and Development*, Harlow, Longman.
TAYLOR, R. (1992) *Visual Arts in Education*, London, Falmer Press.
THOMPSON, C. and BALES, S. (1991) 'Michael doesn't like my dinosaurs: Conversations in a pre-school art class', *Studies in Art Education*, 32, 1, pp. 43–55.
WERNER, H. and KAPLAN, B. (1963) *Symbol Formation*, New York, John Wiley and Sons.
WILLATS, J. (1985) 'Drawing systems revisited: The role of denotation systems in children's figure drawing', in FREEMAN, N. and COX, M.V. (Eds) *Visual Order*, New York, Cambridge University Press, pp. 78–100.
WILLATS, J. (1992) 'What *is* the matter with Mary Jane's drawing?', in THISTLEWOOD, D. et al (Eds) *Drawing, Research and Development*, Harlow, Longman, pp. 141–52.
WILSON, B. (1992) 'Primitivisim, the avant-garde and the art of little children', in THISTLEWOOD, D. et al (Eds) *Drawing, Research and Development*, Harlow, Longman.
WILSON, B., HURWITZ, A. and WILSON, M. (1987) *Teaching Drawing from Art*, Worcester, MA, Davis Publications Inc.
WILSON, B. and LITVOEGT, J. (1992) 'Across time and cultures: Stylistic changes in the drawings of Dutch children', in THISTLEWOOD, D. et al (Eds) *Drawing, Research and Development*, Harlow, Longman, pp. 75–88.
WILSON, B. and WILSON, M. (1980) 'Cultural recycling: The use of conventional configurations, images and themes in the narrative drawings of American children', *Arts in Cultural Diversity*, INSEA 23rd World Congress, Sydney, Holt, Rinehart and Winston, pp. 277–81.
WINNER, E. (1982) *Invented Worlds*, Cambridge, MA, Harvard University Press.
WOLF, D. and PERRY, M.D. (1988) 'From endpoints to repertoires: Some new conclusions about drawing development', *Journal of Aesthetic Education*, 22, 1, pp. 17–34.

Acknowledgments

Children from: Ayresome Primary School, Brandon Infant School, Cheveley Park Primary School, Clavering Primary School, Cromwell Road Nursery, Oxbridge Lane Primary School, Ushaw Moor Infant School, West Ewell County First School, The following students/teachers: C. Abbott, J. Bulmer, S. Harrison, M. King, H. Monk, H. Richmond, and last, but not least Isabel. Photographs by J. Buckham and D. Hutchinson.

Chapter 11

Physical Education as a Specialist Subject

Pauline Wetton

Physical education is a subject which is unique because it is concerned almost exclusively with the physical child. Arguably, then, it should command a special place in the curriculum and have a specific purpose in education. In a broad and balanced programme for younger children, physical education will focus attention on:

1. the physical growth and development of children's bodies;
2. making children aware of the importance of an active lifestyle in the maintenance of good health;
3. increasing children's abilities in motor skills;
4. extending children's physical competence;
5. increasing children's body management.

Developing such a focus will enable physical education to make a distinctive contribution to a child's total education.

If children are to grow properly, remain healthy and become skilful enough to cope with their working and leisure lives, then physical education must be explored rigorously. However brilliant an individual's intellect, neglect of that individual's body will always hinder the highest capacity for academic and technical achievement. The following statement by the British Medical Association has as much truth today as it had in 1936 when it was first published:

> The aim of physical education is to obtain and maintain the best possible development and functioning of the body, and thereby to aid the development of mental capacity and character.

The accomplishment of such aims, however, is by no means an easy task especially for children, whose lifestyles are changing rapidly as we move towards the twenty-first century. These changing lifestyles have often meant more restrictions than freedom for children who need to be physically active. Whereas formerly they could play unsupervised in playgrounds, parks or even in the streets, social conditions today have made such informal opportunities for development and practice both unsuitable and unsafe. Even the school playground with its emphasis on TV-type enactment activity or role rehearsal soccer games favours the strongest and pushes all others to the periphery to pursue such physical activity as is possible in the space available (Practical Guides PE, 1992). Research shows that where activity is most expected it is sometimes least likely to occur (Sleap and Warburton, 1989). Children, for example, now walk less than they used to in simply getting to school. Traffic density and parental regard for general safety means that they are either transported to school by the ubiquitous motor car or accompanied by an adult, both 'methods' restricting their normal capacity for active movement! It is little wonder that as a result of these, and many more 'inactivity patterns', there is a growing concern for the ultimate health of the nation's young.

The advent of the National Curriculum for Physical Education (DES, 1992) however, has given teachers a wonderful and timely opportunity to redress the situation. Crucially, the emphasis in the documentation is on practical activity with a recommendation, for example, that younger children should have a physical education lesson once each day (DES, 1991). The attainment target goes further, stating that,

> pupils should be able to demonstrate the knowledge, skills and understanding involved in areas of activity encompassing athletic activities, dance, games activities, outdoor and adventurous activities and swimming.

It is also acknowledged in the documentation that the context and types of activity will vary, given different localities and environmental restrictions, but whatever activities schools select, they must be selected because of the opportunity which 'the activities afford for developing the children's physical competence and because they are considered valuable in their own right'. It goes without saying that younger children will need many opportunities to develop basic movement patterns in a variety of situations as they progress through a number of stages in their quest for this physical competence. To its credit, the National Curriculum provides teachers with a format of activities which will give children access to the development of these basic movement patterns. It is important, though, that teachers realize it is not only a matter of following the programmes of study provided by the NCC. They themselves must become fully conversant with the knowledge, skills and understanding necessary when presenting the six areas of activity in the National Curriculum. It is necessary for them to understand, for instance, how children grow and develop and in which order motor skills emerge so that tasks are presented when children are ready to acquire them. Teachers must also be knowledgeable about which factors may encourage or inhibit the acquisition of physical competence and bodily management. Most importantly, too, they should be aware of the increasing body of knowledge about physical activity and its relationship to a healthy lifestyle.

So how can teachers obtain the knowledge of physical development/ management/competence etc. which are the essential prerequisites for planning programmes for younger children? In this context, it might be useful to consider the five aims of physical education stated previously as a starting point and look at each of these in turn examining how they can inform the teacher's awareness of the growing child.

1 The physical growth and development of children's bodies

The growth of a child's body is a very regular and organized process, a product of the continuous and complex interaction of both heredity and environment. The genetic or hereditary factor is very important in both the child's growth process and in the child's eventual adult size. Put simply, children of the same chronological age do not necessarily grow at either an even rate or at the same rate. It follows, then, that children in the same class can often be observed to have different heights, weights and body shapes to each other which, quite naturally, will have important implications for class teachers who teach physical education. Activity tasks, for example, will need to be set which allow individual responses and all children to be active at their own developmental stage.

Environmental factors also need to be taken into account. Research has shown that climate and the season of the year can affect children's growth:

> ... it is the season of the year which exerts considerable influence on velocity of growth, at least in Western European children. Growth in height, for instance, is on average fastest in spring, and growth in weight is fastest in autumn. (Tanner, 1978)

Such research findings have implications for teachers of young children since growth in height and weight could alter the child's perception about a movement or a motor task which has already been acquired. It follows, for instance, that the child's new height/weight ratio may cause her/him to manage her/his body in a different way and may cause her/him to almost relearn the skill because of the fundamental adjustments which will need to be made. The practical implications for the teacher are self-evident — there will be a need to repeat lessons presented earlier so that each child has the opportunity to repractice that skill.

So, if a child is heavier, s/he has several adjustments to make if s/he has to land her/his 'new body' from a height such as is involved in jumping down from a gymnastic table.

Or, if a child's legs become longer, then s/he needs to alter the stride pattern, not only in physical education lessons but when walking round the classroom or the school corridor. For a short time, such adjustment might make the child appear to be 'clumsy'.

Physical Education as a Specialist Subject

Teachers also need to be aware of more obvious cultural factors which could have a detrimental effect on children's growth. Malnutrition, illness, psychological disturbance and lack of general exercise can all, in their various ways, undermine physical growth. Often these factors are inter-linked and the 'cure' for one can result in normal growth being quickly re-established. It is not always appreciated, either, that growth can be delayed if children are exposed to adult forms of exercise in their childhood years. Also, children who are involved in 'high performance' activities outside school, for example, gymnastics, run the risk of 'overload' on particular parts of the body which are vital for growth as a whole. The whole question of physical development would seem to be a matter of degree and balance but it is clear that regular exercise is vitally important in the whole process. Whereas inactivity can result in production of less bone mass leading to weakening and brittleness, for instance, exercise with even a small amount of stress, can lead to increases in bone width and strength (*ibid*). Muscular development too follows quite naturally from regular exercise. Physically active children, for example, have a higher proportion of lean body mass to body fat. Since a child's size and shape can be affected by body fat, then, there is no doubt that it is possible to arrest the development of fat cells during the growth of a child by not only cutting down on 'junk food' but more importantly, by using physical activity which places some stress on the body.

2 The importance of an active lifestyle in the maintenance of good health

The notion of, 'an active lifestyle in the maintenance of good health' must be approached with some caution in the context of early education. Unfortunately, being continuously on the move, or just taking part in a PE lesson does not necessarily ensure the maintenance of good health. Health benefits can only be achieved by doing physical activities regularly and for sustained periods of time (Biddle and Biddle, 1989). Such activities, known as health-related fitness (HRF) are intended to improve cardiorespiratory functioning, muscular strength and endurance, flexibility, and the composition of the body. Teachers should be aware of these important constituents of HRF and wherever possible should include relevant activities in PE lessons. In this way, the general health of the children being taught will be enhanced and some diseases prevented. A suitable selection might include, cardiorespiratory activities designed to control body weight and increase the function and condition of the heart and lungs, muscle stretching and strengthening to help maintain the flexibility and posture of the body and activities which place some stress on the bones and muscles in order to help the body to develop properly. Such activities would undoubtedly be of help to children regardless of their physical abilities. The essential message is that ALL children should not only take part in such activities but should be encouraged to improve their own capacity for exercise. The teacher's task would seem to be to make sure that children are educated about the benefits of HRF. The task is surely made easier when one considers that most young children, even those with special needs, are more than willing to take part in PE lessons and for the most part are motivated learners. If Plato is to be believed, 'Knowledge which is acquired under compulsion has no hold on the mind' then early childhood educators are clearly in a strong position to influence children's thinking about the importance of an active lifestyle in the maintenance of their health. (Teachers can find information on suitable HRF activities in the Biddle and Biddle, 1989; Biddle, 1987; Anderson, 1980; and HEA, 1990.)

3 Increasing children's abilities in motor skills

In their early years at school, children need as much fine motor, gross motor and locomotor practice as possible if they are to develop the motor coordination and manual dexterity needed, not only to grow and develop properly and remain healthy, but to acquire the essential skills of reading, writing and the manipulation of tools. Since it has been shown (Bruner, 1966; and Furth and Wachs, 1974) that there is a correlation between motor experience and cognitive development, then it seems axiomatic that children should be offered a rich, varied and stimulating motor skill acquisition programme. It is reassuring to know, incidentally, that the document, *Physical Education in the National Curriculum* (DES, 1992) gives teachers a broad and balanced programme which, if implemented correctly, will allow children to develop their motor abilities.

The exact process **whereby** children learn motor skills is not known. However, certain conditions have been shown to be effective in creating a suitable environment for learning to take place, and these are listed below:

(i) the learning situation should be fun;
(ii) adequate space should be available so that every child has the chance to practice her/his motor skills;
(iii) there should be flexibility in the structure of the lesson so that each child has time to practice at her/his own level of performance;
(iv) there should be enough equipment and a variety of equipment for each child's needs (including the needs of the disabled);
(v) the child must be developmentally 'ready' to acquire the skills s/he is expected to learn;
(vi) the teacher should ensure that each child achieves some success or some praise in each lesson. Some praise should be given for effort and improvement as well as achievement.

It is also possible to list a number of 'facts' which will assist teachers when planning their skill acquisition programmes, for example:

(i) The development of motor ability relies on physical maturation (Tanner, 1978).

(ii) Some skills (phylogenetic) are controlled chiefly by maturation whilst other skills (ontogenetic) can only be learned by guided experience and practice.
(iii) Children need to have the freedom to explore and experiment with a movement or a tool before being given a specific task.
(iv) Control of the larger muscle groups precedes control of the smaller muscle groups, for example, whole hands before fingers.
(v) A child's skill acquisition improves as her/his balance and strength improve.
(vi) Improvement occurs when a child is given frequent practice of the task for short periods of time (Steele, Warburton and Wetton, 1991).
(vii) The task should be goal-directed and the child should understand what s/he is required to do, and be motivated to do it.
(viii) There are large individual differences in the rate and extent of children's motor learning.
(ix) Eighty-four per cent of children are right-handed when assessed at the age of 4. Yet children in the 5–8 age group are much more likely to ambidextrous and therefore willing to use either hand or both hands when given a motor task (Belmont and Birch, 1963).
(x) 'Footedness' is established by the age of 5. Children seldom alter their preference for the use of a particular foot after this age.
(xi) Children in the age group 5–8 have no preference for the use of either eye.
(xii) Most 5 and 6-year-old children exhibit a mixed eye–hand preference i.e. left eye and right hand. Seven and 8-year-old children are evenly divided: 50 per cent exhibit a mixed eye–hand preference and 50 per cent have developed a 'pure' combination i.e. right eye and right hand or left eye and left hand.
(xiii) By $5^1/_2$–6 years of age, about 70 per cent of children are able to distinguish between the left and the right sides of their body and can identify body parts. However, 30 per cent are still unsure.
(xiv) Directionality in space is conceptualized later that conceptualization of the body (Swanson and Benson, 1955).
(xv) Cultural effects (i.e. more chances to practice) have resulted in boys being able to throw further than girls at each age (Steele, Warburton and Wetton, 1991).
(xvi) There are no sex-linked anatomical or physiological differences in motor ability potential (Tanner, 1978).

If one accepts that the above information is important, then the teacher has a crucial role to play in children's learning. It is the teacher, for example, who must continually offer the children the opportunity to practice particular tasks over a sustained period of time. In this way, each child will be maturationally ready to learn the task and will be equipped to acquire it.

The National Curriculum in PE offers teachers an attractive opportunity to help children acquire physical skills, skills which are necessary in order that the most fundamental 'educational' skills can be acquired or developed. To take a simple example: if a child is not yet able to manipulate a pencil, s/he will have the opportunity to develop the characteristics which may ultimately allow this to happen, for example, strengthening and moving the fingers by undertaking such physical tasks as rolling or throwing a ball, pulling and pushing the hands through water, climbing a climbing frame, carrying ropes, hoops and skittles and activating the fingers while dancing.

4 Extending children's physical competence

It might be supposed that if suitable conditions were present for children to grow and develop normally and to be healthy as well as to acquire motor skills when they were developmentally ready, then their physical competence would be almost automatically extended. Unfortunately this is not the case, mainly because of the wide-ranging differences among and between children of the same chronological age. Thus, expectations regarding the performance of individuals might not always be pitched as high as they should be. Nevertheless, it has been shown repeatedly that children are capable of high performance levels and although we might not want to turn our infant children into Olympic gymnasts or swimmers, we do have examples of outstanding capability from the very young. It is important to realize that most children, including those who are disabled, have the resources to perform high order motor skills. All that is necessary is for teachers to know when children are not only ready to acquire these skills, but when they can be pressed a little harder to achieve them.

The role of class teachers then becomes crucial. It is they who know the children very well. They know that the children in their care do not come from the same mould and they also know the strategies they must employ to persuade or cajole children to greater effort or better performance. It should never be the case that children are allowed to settle for second best and it is their job to see that this does not happen by providing motivation through enjoyable and worthwhile experiences in physical education situations.

5 Increasing children's body management

In the past, it has been reasonable for teachers to assume that by the time a child entered school s/he would have mastered the skills necessary to move about in the school environment. Such skills of body management would have been either learned at home, a pre-school institution or at both. These skills, for example, locomotion, postural adjustment, balance of the body etc. would give him/her an excellent chance of being able to cope with the normal activities in school such as negotiating spaces within the classroom, sitting on a chair or on the carpet and also performing competently when asked to do work in technological, musical or artistic activities from the curriculum.

Unfortunately, however, some children nowadays have not acquired these fundamental skills for a variety of reasons. Consequently, some schools will have to create an environment and a programme where suitable compensation can be made for these children, especially on school entry. Even after having done this, incidentally, there will still be some children who will never 'catch up' on these skills. It has been estimated, for instance, that 5 per cent of the whole school population experience motor problems and are deemed as being 'clumsy' (Groves, 1979), exhibiting problems with either gross or fine motor tasks. Although such children are not, at the present time, classed as having a special need in terms of the 1981 *Education Act*, unless some remedial help is given to them as early as possible the physical 'gap' between their ability and that of their peers will widen irretrievably. In PE lessons, then, teachers need not only to improve the body management skills of the 'clumsy' child, but to ensure the maintenance, development and extension of skills already acquired for all children. The achievement of such goals ought to result in children enjoying both social and recreational activities (in and out of school) and becoming competent in life activity generally.

Body management forms an important part of the National Curriculum in PE. There are six areas of activity in which children are given the opportunity to learn the skills involved:

(i) Games

    (a) sending, receiving and travelling with a ball
    (b) using a variety of equipment of different size and weight
    (c) dodging, swerving, chasing and negotiating space

(ii) Athletic activities

    (a) running, jumping and throwing
    (b) controlling speed, height and landings

(iii) Dance

    (a) developing control, poise, balance and elevation
    (b) coordinating a series of actions
    (c) turning, leaping, gesturing at different levels
    (d) developing rhythmic body movements

(iv) Swimming

    (a) controlling the body in water
    (b) floating, diving, manoeuvring

(v) Gymnastic activities

(a) acquiring bodily control, coordination and versatility
(b) climbing, balancing, swinging, rolling, jumping, landing
(c) various methods of travelling across, over and under a variety of pieces of equipment of different shapes and sizes
(d) travelling across equipment with a variety of surfaces
(e) lifting, carrying and manoeuvring equipment

(vi) Outdoor and Adventurous activities

(a) managing her/his body on various pieces of equipment such as slides, roundabouts and swings
(b) managing her/his body on various surfaces such as grass, tarmac, shale, stepping stones
(c) managing her/his body on a variety of natural obstacles such as hills, slopes, walls, fences and steps

If children are exposed to all these body management skills activities together with all the motor skill practices, then they should be competent not only to choose to enjoy these activities in their future recreational lives but also they will have acquired the necessary techniques to cope with most of the essential life skills. A complete list of all the life skills children need is inappropriate here but a sample of what physical education can help children to do is given below:

(i) Gymnastics: climbing ladder activity;
     Life skill: cleaning windows, hanging curtains, painting ceilings.
(ii) Gymnastics: lifting, carrying and manoeuvring gymnastic equipment;
     Life skill: moving furniture, carrying and lifting shopping, coping with gardening tasks.
(iii) Dance: negotiating the body in space;
     Life skill: coping with crowd situations at sporting events, railway stations, and walking in major city streets.

Conclusion

School gives some children, and their number is growing steadily, their only chance to develop their physical potential. Thus, physical education lessons are by their very nature crucially important. By giving their approval for the inclusion of PE in the National Curriculum in 1992, the government has endorsed the notion that the physical child is important. Children at the primary stage learn by doing and have an extreme motivation towards physical activity. What is more they enjoy it. It is vital that we respond with urgency to their needs if they are to be both physically healthy and competent.

References

ANDERSON, B. (1980) *Stretching*, London, Pelham.
BELMONT, L. and BIRCH, H.G. (1963) 'Lateral dominance and right, left awareness in normal children', *Child Development*, 34, 2, p. 257.
BIDDLE, S. (Ed) (1987) *Foundations of Health-Related Fitness in Physical Education*, London, The Ling Publishing House.
BIDDLE, S. and BIDDLE, G. (1989) 'Health-related fitness for the primary school in issues', in WILLIAMS, A. (Ed) *Issues in PE for the Primary Years*, London, Falmer Press.
BRITISH MEDICAL ASSOCIATION THE, 'Report of the committee on physical education', *British Medical Journal Supplement*, p. 150.
BRUNER, J. (1966) *Studies in Cognitive Growth*, New York, John Wiley.
DES (1991) *Physical Education for Ages 5–16*, London, HMSO.
DES (1992) *Physical Education in the National Curriculum*, London, HMSO.
FURTH, H.G. and WACHS, H. (1974) *Thinking Goes to School: Piaget's Theory into Practice*, London, Oxford University Press.
GROVES, L. (Ed) (1979) *Physical Education for Special Needs*, Cambridge, Cambridge University Press.
H.E.A. (1990) *Happy Heart 1*, London, HEA/Nelson.
PRACTICAL GUIDES, P.E. (1992) *Teaching Within the National Curriculum*, Leamington Spa, Scholastic Publications.
SLEAP, M. and WARBURTON, P. (1989) *Physical Activity Patterns in Primary School Children*, Interim Report to Happy Heart Project, London, PEA.
STEELE, J., WARBURTON, P. and WETTON, P. (1991) *Two Surveys of the Motor Performance of Infant Aged School Children*, DES Library.
SWANSON, R. and BENSON, A.L. (1955) 'Some aspects of the genetic development of right left discrimination', *Child Development*, 26, 2, p. 123.
TANNER, J.M. (1978) *Education and Physical Growth*, London, Hodder and Stoughton.

Chapter 12

Subject Knowledge in the Early Years: The Case of Religious Education

David Day and Elizabeth Ashton

The title of this chapter raises a crucial question. What exactly constitutes the subject matter of religious education in the schools of a pluralist society? Religions are vast, unwieldy affairs, with limitless ramifications. It was difficult enough to see how young children could have made much sense of one religion when Christianity was the only one likely to be encountered. In the present society at least six religions compete for the attention with numerous other variants, offshoots and hybrids. At first sight the area may seem far too complicated for the intellect of the very young child to comprehend.

It might also be argued that for most children religion is a remote phenomenon, far removed from their everyday experience. To ask them to engage with the subject is to invite bewilderment, boredom or verbalisms — the parroting of correct answers which have no grounding in lived experience.

It was with such anxieties in mind that an earlier fashion in religious education prescribed an almost exclusive focus on 'Life Themes' for the early years. Topics like 'homes', 'who am I?', 'hands' and 'people who help us' appeared more tractable than explicitly religious material. Every child had instant access to such domestic subject matter. Moreover, the general moral teaching which typically issued from these areas of inquiry had the additional advantage of bypassing the conceptual and theological difficulties which tended to be evoked by talk about God. Even at the time many teachers were unable to see anything particularly religious about these approaches, despite the assurances of the experts. Nevertheless the fashion prevailed with the result that it is not entirely inaccurate to describe infant RE from the mid-1960s as suffering from a colossal failure of nerve and an avoidance of the distinctive subject matter of religion.

The life themes of infant RE represent one answer to the question of the proper subject-matter. A more obvious and in many ways more defensible response was that which declined to ignore the observable aspects of religion. Despite the dominance of the theme, during the 1970s and 1980s many schools managed to include specifically religious material in their schemes of work, drawing the content from a variety of religions.

If anything, the Education Reform Act has encouraged this trend. The sections which deal with religious education require new Agreed Syllabuses to 'reflect the fact that the religious traditions in Great Britain are in the main Christian while taking account of the teaching and practices of the other principal religions represented in Great Britain' (DES, 1988). Both halves of this sentence drive new curriculum planning in the direction of the explicit treatment of religion. They shift the balance away from the general, values-related integrated theme towards recognizably religious subject-matter.

This development can be illustrated by those Agreed Syllabuses which have been published since the Act. They have not ignored the exploration of human experience but they have established that religious phenomena have a place at Key Stage 1. A few examples will demonstrate this point. The North Tyneside syllabus expects that pupils will be able to 'show some awareness of the major faiths in Great Britain: have some experience of places of worship, festivals, stories and artistic expression; recognize that major faiths have special books and ways of praying' (North Tyneside Local Education Authority, 1990). Sunderland requires pupils to celebrate 'major religious festivals both in school and places of worship in the neighbourhood' and instances Harvest, Christmas and Passover (Sunderland Local Education Authority, 1991). Cleveland's draft form, specifies the study of the 'significance of a special place and what kinds of special places are important in religion' giving Mecca, Jerusalem and Lourdes as examples (Cleveland Local Education Authority, 1991). Among Newcastle's Foundation Units can be found 'special prayers, the Lord's prayer', 'the story of Christmas and other major Christian festivals; Harvest festival', 'the Jewish festivals of Passover and Purim' (Newcastle upon Tyne Local Education Authority, 1990).

We can see from these examples that an answer to the question. 'What is the subject matter of religion?' is already being supplied in terms of the phenomena of religious rituals, festivals and practices. However, it is still important to try to meet the two objections raised at the beginning of this chapter. The first of these suggested that religion might be just too remote from the ordinary experience of the young child; the second, that religious language bristled with conceptual and theological difficulties which were beyond the capacities of infants.

In fact, the assumption that young children do not meet religion in the normal course of events is a precarious one to make. While it might be fairly argued that religious practice is a marginalized activity in our society, it does not follow that children have no contact at all with it. From the outset such a claim ignores that not inconsiderable group of children who are themselves members of faith communities. Even for those children who are not, it can be plausibly argued that in unsystematic and random ways they are likely to encounter religious phenomena. The ordinary business of living may confront the young child with religion in a variety of forms — a friend who goes to

179

Sunday school or to the mosque, the story of Christmas or Easter, the sight of a Sikh turban or a Muslim woman in traditional dress, a Salvation Army band, a family wedding or baptism. Nor is this just a matter of observing practices. The ideas with which religion deals may also come to consciousness — from hearing older children discuss the Devil in a horror film or through being told that Granny or the pet hamster have 'gone to be with Jesus'. Moreover, many young children pray and the problems of unanswered prayer can raise a bewildering array of theological issues. Thus religious practices and concepts rapidly become a part, even if not a major part, of the world of most children.[1]

In the light of this conclusion it is not difficult to argue that the explicit study of religion is the proper focus for primary RE and that subject knowledge understood in the most obvious way as the phenomena of religion should constitute the lesson content and area of inquiry. The first attempts to meet this remit filled the classrooms with a glorious variety of stimulus material. Teachers presented their classes with content drawn from a number of faiths. Infants engaged with festivals, food, rituals, dress, songs, stories and artefacts. They cooked and sang and played and acted and painted.

More recently unease has been expressed about the lasting value of this kind of energetic activity. Was there a danger that the meaning and point of religion was being lost beneath the weight of stimulating and colourful customs? Did this kind of RE ever get round to raising the issue of God, or of helping children to understand the feelings of awe and commitment which underpinned the practice? The term 'multifact RE' was coined — a curriculum described with some justification as 'the sterile cavalcade of outlandish phenomena' (Minney, 1992). Brenda Watson (1987) has commented sharply but perceptively:

> There has been a precipitate rush to remodel syllabuses and examination work within the wider mould without appreciating the dangers. These include the superficiality of what has been lampooned with some accuracy as a 'Cook's Tour' of religions. (p. 145)

In the face of these reservations, some may well be tempted to abandon the study of explicit religion altogether and retreat to the familiar and reassuring life theme, the exploration of infant experience. Others may persist with religion but narrow the focus to an exclusive concentration on Christian studies. Neither represents a particularly constructive response.

Much more positive is the approach adopted by the Birmingham University team which produced the 'Gift to the Child' project (Grimmitt *et al*, 1991). This does constitute a radically novel way of introducing young children to religion, persisting with the use of explicitly religious material, while trying to avoid methods which are purely descriptive. The basic outlines of the strategy are as follows:

> The project assumes that young children can benefit from exposure to real religious content, drawn from a variety of faith traditions. For

The Case of Religious Education

instance, in the project handbook the authors use as exemplar material Nanak's song, Bernadette of Lourdes, the Muslim call to prayer, the story of Jonah, Angels, Ganesha and Hallelujah.

It further assumes that the way religious material is pursued in a classroom must be determined ultimately by educational rather than by religious concerns. This does not mean that the teacher will distort or deny the way the material is handled by the faith in question. But the use made of the phenomenon may not be restricted solely to that faith's self-understanding. Behind this possibility lies another axiom, namely, that in the classroom it is proper that religion should have an instrumental or functional purpose. That is, it should be good for something. This explains the Project's title. Every piece of religious content has a 'gift' to impart to the child. The gift may be of a religious nature (and may even nourish a child in its own faith) but it may just as well have a more general educational or personal value. The units trialled by the team are all capable of articulation within well established theories of human development; each in its own way can contribute to the young child's psychological growth.

The gift is not imparted automatically, however. It is dependent on the child's interaction with the material. This has led the project team to develop a fourfold strategy for encouraging children to engage with religious items. The stages are labelled engagement, discovery, contextualization and reflection and are to a large extent self-explanatory. Their use is intended to evoke responses which range from the spontaneous reactions and first impressions aroused by curiosity as the item is disclosed and introduced to a reflective stage where children, now having some idea of the context and position of the item within the community of faith are encouraged 'to give full rein to their emotions and their ideas in the light of their experience of the religious material'. (Grimmitt, 1992)

Michael Grimmitt, the Project Director is at pains to stress that the gifts emerge through interaction between item and child; thus they cannot be prespecified or predetermined. It is not possible to predict the results of the dialogue. It is likely, however, that they will be of a very diverse kind and extend far beyond the conventional understanding of the objectives of teaching religion. In fact the project sees the religious material as making its major contribution to the personal and emotional development of the child. Thus the gifts take the form of evoking questions, fostering imagination, empathy and identification, and contributing to the formation of values and personal beliefs.

Here then is an approach which sets subject knowledge at the heart of religious education but in a new way. It accepts the importance of religion as a distinctive perspective on the world, selects explicit examples of the phenomenon, handles them educationally, ensures that the treatment takes account of the abilities and interests of young children and makes a contribution to their personal development. The strategy is a taxing one but does not present the teacher with impossible demands. However, it does require her to be familiar with the subject matter, to be skilled in the process so as to facilitate maximum interaction and to have confidence both in the capacity of the material to provoke a rich response and in young children's competence to handle it.

We may approach the question of the subject matter of religious education from a different direction however. RE need not be only a matter of examining other people's religious content. The term might also be held to point to a process — that of learning to think and talk about religion for oneself. The skills of reflecting on religious questions and articulating those reflections is precisely what doing theology — 'God talk' — entails. Such a process presupposes the capacity to develop language which is able to explore religious ideas and those experiences which are capable of a religious interpretation.

Many writers on RE recoil at this point. The idea that young children could make any sense of such essentially abstract concepts as 'God', 'heaven', 'eternity' seems far-fetched. They are simply not ready for the metaphors and images of religious language. The term 'ready' recalls the influential work of Goldman (1964 and 1965) whose findings on religious thinking have dominated the infant classroom for nearly thirty years. His researches seemed to show that young children were unable to think in abstract and that their ability to deal with religious ideas and writings, particularly as expressed in the Bible, could not be developed until they had reached the time of adolescence: thus intellectual capacity was closely linked with biological maturity. Even a recent text like that of Kerry and Tollitt (1987) can repeat the confident assertion:

> Ageing but still useful researches by Ronald Goldman demonstrated that Piagetian insights could be obtained about the processes by which children learn about religion. Since religious education demands a grasp of quite difficult concepts and of abstract notions much of it cannot be grasped by infants. At this age it is often safer to stick to the moral issues and to the concepts that derive from these issues. (p. 90)

However, the theories of Piaget whose researches provided the foundation for Goldman's ideas, have now been seriously challenged. Petrovich (1989) pointed out that young children's literalist understanding of religious concepts is something which is learned from adults, rather than being a way of thought intrinsic to childhood:

> Contrary to Piaget's argument that anthropomorphism is a spontaneous mental tendency in young children, this study presents evidence that the child's representation of God as man is a direct outcome of religious instruction.

The Case of Religious Education

Additionally, conversations recorded by classroom teachers working with young children have given support to the theory that even infant-aged children, if given appropriate opportunities and suitable stimulation and teaching are able to express themselves in abstract (Ainsworth, 1983).

When young children participate in free play in the school playground, an individual child can become the symbol of a whole nation at war! It is equally common to see preschool children pretending to be mothers, fathers, or shop-keepers, themselves becoming symbols of those whom they experience in their everyday lives. Toys such as dolls, pistols and cars are also symbolic of the 'real thing' and even the 2-year-old child perceives the symbolic nature of the toy being used. To the child, the symbolic world of 'make-believe' operates adjacent to the real world of which it is an imitation, and that imitation is both a product of the child's imaginative powers and is understood as such by him/her. As pointed out by Donaldson (1978) children learn by experience and are able to understand abstract phenomena if such makes 'human sense' to them. Kieran Egan (1991) has further argued that it is the structure around which children process their thinking that enables them to cope with ideas which are out of their experience; if the structure of lesson material is familiar, they are able to cope with many new, unfamiliar situations and details.

To create symbols and to begin to manipulate them is to begin to engage in abstract thought. The young child's inner world is highly creative and it is this tremendously exciting potential for creative thought which should be used as a foundation upon which to base religious education. If Petrovich is correct and young children's literalist understandings are the direct outcome of their interaction with adults, both in and out of school, their creative capacity is not only being misused but in addition may even be suppressed in that unhelpful spatial concepts of God and heaven are being introduced and reinforced constantly. This vivid imaginative capacity of childhood should be developed adequately from the early years of schooling by introducing language which is highly symbolic and poetic, such as metaphor and simile. Such should be applied to the child's own creative efforts, thus helping forward the thinking process.

An example of how this could be done during work planned to teach concepts of God, could be to encourage young children to act out the Biblical story of the Good Shepherd; young children are quick to understand that God is something like the shepherd in the story; how may be drawn from the children in subsequent discussion and, perhaps, artwork. Although shepherds are remote from the experience of many young children, it is the structure of the story which enables them to relate to it: the Good Shepherd is based upon the binary opposites as described by Egan which provide the structure for young children's thinking processes. Hence the story is a narrative which evolves around the opposites of safety/danger and lost/found. Most young children experience being lost in large supermarkets and the joy of being reunited with their mother; many have lost things and have experienced relief upon finding them. This is the underlying thought structure which allows them to transfer knowledge, and because of the excitement with which such structures are saturated, that is the unknown outcomes, the children are motivated to transfer their experiences from one situation to another.

Additionally, young children are able to participate in this type of suggested lesson because they are accustomed to creative pretend play as outlined above, and they know from their role-play that the child being, say, mother, is only *like* mother in certain ways, such as looking after children, going shopping, or whatever activities are enacted in the game. They are able to be introduced to the way in which religious people understand what is called in English 'God' in a similar way and are quite able to appreciate the symbolic nature of the language being used.

By such teaching, which not only is based upon children's experiences and ways of thinking but which also extends their ideas, the use of metaphor in religious expression is introduced from a very early age. For the work to be effective, however, the taught skills need constant reinforcement and the children encouraged to discuss their own ideas about God, including as of necessity controversial aspects of the whole area of religious faith. The children may be introduced to such questions as whether everything in the world is beautiful, and why it is that nasty things such as germs exist which cause colds to develop. Such discussions help guard against the sentimentality which is easily fostered by an overemphasis upon such hymns as 'All Things Bright and Beautiful' and which is unhelpful in developing realistic questioning which comprises the type of 'ultimate questions' which young children are so frequently heard to be asking.

Closely associated with children's capacity to think and act in abstract is their ability to philosophize. This ability was recognized by Gareth Matthews who records many conversations he had with the very young. He points constantly towards the necessity of recognizing the young child's efforts to think philosophically and creatively and also to being alert for opportunities arising whereby their efforts may be helped to develop creatively. (Matthews, 1980).[2]

An example quoted by Matthews potentially raises the question of metaphysics: could there be a dimension to material life which exists alongside it and yet which is additional to it?

> Ursula (3 years 4 months): 'I have a pain in my tummy.' Mother: 'You lie down and go to sleep and your pain will go away.' Ursula: 'Where will it go?' She might have been puzzled, even worried ('Will it go under my bed?') Certainly children do worry about such matters ... because (the book suggests that) Ursula was happy, confident, curious and playful, I suspect that the question was a playful one ... Ursula's question is an invitation to philosophical reflection. (*ibid*, p. 17)

How could such a question be usefully adopted for religious education? Although a question is usually thought of as demanding an answer, it is true that there are some questions which have no answers. They are, therefore, really invitations to further questioning. This is the method of philosophical reflection and it is important to recognize questions of this nature when they arise and to help children further in their reflection upon them rather than to attempt to provide answers. This point is made by Watson (1987) when discussing children's reactions to situations when they are motivated to make statements about God:

> Catherine, when the hen's eggs in the incubator failed to hatch, complained 'But I prayed to God about them and I asked Him to make them hatch.' There were tears in her eyes and she almost stamped her foot. (p. 211)

Brenda Watson points out that if not dealt with adequately, such reactions may lead to serious misunderstandings and the development of unhelpful concepts of God: that is, in this case God is a kind of magician who will sometimes interfere with scientific laws at a simple request. She states that:

> the teacher is therefore faced with a highly responsible task, to be able, at a second's notice, to turn a chance remark into valuable theological, philosophical and scientific education. (*ibid*, p. 212)

What is required is some statement which encourages the child to think more deeply. In this case, perhaps, inviting the child to consider the mystery which exists at the heart of the universe and life on earth and how some things can be very puzzling. Thus, the child may be helped to understand how it is not possible for us always to have what we desire, sometimes for reasons which elude us at the time. Any attempt to offer a simplistic answer is to suppress further opportunities for reflective thought and a deepening understanding.

Children sometimes engage in very creative thinking which, if shared with an adult, offers much potential for development into spiritual questioning and searching. For example, a 5-year-old child told her teacher she had visited her grandmother the previous day and had watched her shovelling coals from the coal-house for the fire. The child said she had wondered if the coals had tried to stop themselves from falling onto the shovel because they were afraid of being burnt or of leaving their friends! She also had wondered if the coals remaining in the coalhouse had spoken to each other of their escape! Such imaginative thought could easily be turned into religious education — for example, by discussing what life is really and whether the kind of life enjoyed by humans is similar to that of other living things. An 8-year-old child wrote a story about a walk in the garden and she described how she had wondered if the yellow centre of the daisies had watched her feet coming across the grass and if they had worried about being trodden upon. Such ideas could easily be developed into discussion of some religious themes such as rebirth and efforts to attain to the perfect freedom known as Nirvana.

It is certain that this creative world of children ought to be drawn upon by teachers in their education and looked upon as being an important resource or starting-point for religious education. If this is not done and the ideas of children are suppressed, a kind of emotional and reflective impasse is reached which prevents the development of further thinking, and has the effect, too, of encouraging young children to abandon creative reflection as something undesirable — usually described as daydreaming or being inattentive in class. As Matthews (1980) notes:

> Young children are indeed, ... emotional beings. But they are more than that. They are, and have a right to be, thinking beings as well. A child whose literary diet includes tales of great emotional significance but no tales of intellectual adventure is disadvantaged and deprived ... (p. 82)

The alternative is to enable children to build upon their rich, creative potential thereby forming foundations upon which a serious study of religion may be based later.

It is by such teaching that religious education may become recognized as being fundamental, or basic, to the school curriculum. Religions throughout the world point to the mystery which is the focus of all reflective thought and which is also at the heart of genuine religious understanding. This is not to state that religion should in the future, as it perhaps was in the past, be understood in terms of imperialism, whereby religion would dominate and control curriculum development. Religious education, or in its broader terms the human capacity to perceive the mystery which is at the heart of creation and form concepts concerning it, may be found within the thought processes of young children as they attempt to make sense of the world. This capacity to reflect upon metaphysical questions is an ability which ought to be taken seriously and given a place in the centre of the curriculum since it is this principle which revitalizes the energy and creative enthusiasm upon which future progress will be based.

Notes

1. For numerous examples of young children's encounters with, and thoughts about, religion see Madge (1965) and Herbert (1983).
2. For numerous examples of children's ability to reflect upon and discuss religious questions see Hull (1991).

References

AINSWORTH, D. (1983) *Religion and the Intellectual Capacities of Young Children*, Farmington Discussion Paper No. 1, Oxford, The Farmington Institute.

CLEVELAND LOCAL EDUCATION AUTHORITY (1991) *Agreed Syllabus for Religious Education*, Draft 4, Cleveland County Council, September.
DES (1988) *Education Reform Act*, Section 8.3, London, HMSO.
DONALDSON, M. (1978) *Children's Minds*, London, Fontana.
EGAN, K. (1991) *Primary Understanding*, London, Routledge.
GOLDMAN, R. (1964) *Religious Thinking from Childhood to Adolescence*, London, Routledge and Kegan Paul.
GOLDMAN, R. (1965) *Readiness for Religion*, London, Routledge and Kegan Paul.
GRIMMITT, M. (1992) 'The use of religious phenomena in schools: Some theoretical and practical considerations', *British Journal of Religious Education* 13, 2, spring, p. 84.
GRIMMITT, M., GROVE, J., HULL, J. and SPENCER, L. (1991) *A Gift to the Child: Religious Education in the Primary School*, London, Simon and Schuster.
HERBERT, C. (1983) *Listening to Children: A Fresh Approach to Religious Education in the Primary Years*, London, C10 for General Synod Board of Education.
HULL, J.M. (1991) *God-talk with Young Children*, Birmingham Papers in Religious Education No. 2, Derby, University of Birmingham, School of Education and Christian Education Movement.
KERRY, T. and TOLLITT, J. (1987) *Teaching Infants*, Oxford, Blackwell.
MADGE, V. (1965) *Children in Search of Meaning*, London, SCM Press.
MATTHEWS, G. (1980) *Philosophy and the Young Child*, Cambridge, MA, Harvard University Press.
MINNEY, R. (1992) 'Otto's contribution to religious education', in ASTLEY, J. and DAY, D. (Eds) *The Contours of Christian Education*, Great Wakering, McCrimmons, chapter 15.
NEWCASTLE UPON TYNE LOCAL EDUCATION AUTHORITY (1990) *Agreed Syllabus for Religious Education*, Newcastle LEA, p. 11.
PETROVICH, O. (1989) 'An examination of Piaget's theory of childhood artificialism', University of Oxford, unpublished PhD thesis from the conclusion.
NORTH TYNESIDE LOCAL EDUCATION AUTHORITY (1990) *Investigating Understanding and Caring: Agreed Syllabus for Religious Education*, North Tyneside LEA, p. 10.
SUNDERLAND LOCAL EDUCATION AUTHORITY (1991) *Learning to Live: Agreed Syllabus for Sunderland*, Sunderland, LEA, p. 15.
WATSON, B.G. (1987) *Education and Belief*, Oxford, Blackwell.

Chapter 13

The Role of Subject Knowledge

Carol Aubrey

The chapters in this book represent a growing educational research interest which is investigating the nature of teaching particular subject matter at particular stages, in this case, in the early years. Noted in the first chapter, for instance, was the work of Grossman *et al* (1989) which is building up a picture of the relationship between teachers' knowledge and beliefs about teaching particular subjects and the way these are taught. Under consideration by these writers, too, is the way subject knowledge changes and develops with experience.

Whilst individual contributors to this book may differ in the precise views they hold with respect to the role of instruction, overwhelmingly their own subject knowledge provides a major source upon which they draw in the consideration of what it means to teach subjects to young children. Through their detailed consideration of teachers' pedagogical subject knowledge the contributors address many complementary themes and issues and in so doing highlight the importance of teachers being knowledgeable about the subjects they teach. In addition, and especially in view of the age of the children concerned, the contributors discuss subject content which is organized to encourage children's own construction of knowledge. What is known about the development of children's ideas about the subject in question thus provides one basis for guiding instruction.

Chapter 1 emphasized the crucial role of language in the transmission of culture to the child, first in the family and with peers, and later with teachers in school. Natural language has a central role in supporting social communication and in representing the child's growing experience. The social origins of cognition and the role of teaching in leading development is central. As the chapters in this book have shown, however, even if speech remains by far the most important cultural instrument, other sign systems or cultural artefacts may have played an important role in the child's pre-school development such as song, drawing or dance. Furthermore by the end of the early years of schooling the teaching of school subjects will have promoted cognitive development, in particular, children's reflection on and control of learning, which is broader in effect than on the subject under consideration and this can be built on in other areas of the curriculum (Vygotsky, 1934 in Van der Veer and Valsiner, 1991).

Linda Thompson's chapter 2 develops the debate about early years schooling by attempting to unwrap what might be meant by a working knowledge of language structure and an appreciation of the variety of ways meaning is made, as well as the implications of such a descriptive model of linguistic development for the class teacher.

Peter Millward's chapter 3 explores the way drama relates to the everyday world of the child's experience and how it connects with the subjects of the formal curriculum. He concludes that the link between the child's everyday life and the formal structure of subject knowledge is the teacher. Knowledge of drama is knowing about relationships: relationships between everyday life and make-believe discourse; relationships between subject knowledge and personal understanding; and about relationships between teachers and children. It also means knowing about the possibilities for these relationships.

Deirdre Pettitt's chapter 4 about writing continues with an exploration of helping children to become better as writers whilst using what they already know about speaking and writing, which is considerable. She notes teachers must make their own knowledge about writing explicit in order to enable children to construct writing coherently. Writing helps to clarify thought: it is a tool for thinking and learning across the curriculum. As the writer playfully comments, in writing what we think we know we find out what we do not as we struggle with meaning!

Through the consideration of aspects of knowing and understanding mathematics Carol Aubrey's chapter 5 highlights the importance of teachers' mathematical subject knowledge and children's growing competence to use and apply mathematics to their social and physical world. Since for home and school the medium of mathematics teaching is language a goal of mathematics teaching is for children to think and reason quantitatively and to communicate these ideas as mathematically literate adults.

Rosemary Feasey's chapter 6 reiterates the role of the teacher in making sense of curriculum areas and the multi-dimensional experiences children bring from home into the school context. Unless the teacher's understanding of the nature of science and associated concepts is sufficient she will not be able to sustain the complexity of accommodating the demands of the science curriculum to the informal knowledge and understanding children bring into school. Complementary aspects of skills, processes, knowledge and understanding science are considered in the context of providing a challenging framework to science teaching in the early years.

In Deirdre Pettitt's chapter 7 she continues to explore the theme of what teachers themselves need to know, in this case, about the subject of history, historical principles and methodology, in order to support and extend young children's developing personal sense of history and time.

Joy Palmer's chapter 8 considers how the teacher can incorporate children's early learning about the natural and physical environment and their developing sense of place within the context of a well-defined curriculum for geography and environmental education. The writer shows how a 'sense of place' can be developed in a reception class and considers teaching and learning about distant lands in a year 2 class. In each case the children's developing knowledge is sensitively supported and developed by the teacher who builds on existing knowledge and, at times, constructively challenges.

Coral Davies' chapter 9 approaches the music education of young children through the consideration of the musical development of their songs which, she finds, in many ways is analogous to language acquisition. She advocates that teachers use children's songs and experience of singing them to construct their musical language and making their own expressive statements. This will provide an early intuitive understanding and a foundation for later knowledge *about* music.

Jennifer Buckham's chapter 10 again suggests that we must deepen our own knowledge and awareness of patterns of development in children's art work, recognizing its multiple strands and processes and guarding against the notion that development is linear or has a defined end point in visual accuracy. This means looking closely at children's many ways of working, recording systematically to uncover patterns in work and, thereby, constructing a personal knowledge base about children's art. Through this the teacher will be able increasingly to recognize, confirm, support and extend children's work.

Pauline Wetton's chapter 11 argues for a special place in the curriculum and a special purpose in education for physical education which requires teachers must gain both knowledge of physical activity and its relationship to a healthy life-style. Knowledge about growth and development, the role of an active life-style, increasing motor skills, extending physical competence and increasing body management are all essential in supporting children to grow physically, remain healthy and become skilful.

Finally in chapter 12 David Day and Elizabeth Ashton consider what constitutes the subject matter of religious education and argue for the explicit study of religion. The subject content may be specifically religious concerning faith's self understanding. This requires the development of a language which can explore religious ideas and experience and which is capable of religious interpretion. The subject content may be of educational or personal value, making a contribution to the personal and emotional development of the child, fostering imagination, empathy and identification, and contributing to the formation of values and personal beliefs. The writers conclude that the child's understanding is a direct outcome of religious instruction and that it is the teacher's task to support, encourage and deepen, to build on children's rich creative potential as a foundation for later, serious religious study.

As noted in chapter 1, Shulman (1986) has called the subject knowledge which concerns all of these writers **pedagogical content knowledge** and has described three components. These are: knowledge about the subject; knowledge of children's existing knowledge and beliefs about the subject; and knowledge of effective ways to represent the subject matter to children, through well-selected explanations, demonstrations, models and examples. Whilst the National Curriculum determines what content will be included in the curriculum, that content does not in itself provide the goal for instruction. Different teachers will hold different beliefs about the subjects involved and will provide very different learning experiences in the pursuit of common curriculum goals. The writer's own recent work in this area is beginning to show that experienced teachers may differ widely in the way these three components are combined in their teaching, and that this may well be associated with their knowledge of the subject and their beliefs concerning the nature of learning and teaching. Inevitably teachers will differ in their familiarity with and skill in teaching across different subjects, as well as different topics within the same subject.

Whilst the nature and depth of subject knowledge required by teachers to teach subjects in the early years may be still open to debate, the feasibility of all teachers possessing well-organized and available subject knowledge across all areas of the National Curriculum is probably less open to dispute. This raises questions for teacher education. What is the optimum subject knowledge for teachers? To what extent can pedagogical subject knowledge be formally taught at the pre-service level? How can experienced teachers be helped to extend their subject knowledge?

The Role of the Teacher

Brophy (1989 and 1991) has demonstrated, particularly in the subjects of science, mathematics and English that where teachers' knowledge is rich and better-integrated and more accessible they tend to teach more dynamically, represent the subject in more varied ways, encourage and respond more fully to children's questions and comments. Where knowledge is more limited, there is more emphasis on facts, more reliance on subject texts for content, more time spent by pupils in working individually and less in interactive discourse.

All the individual contributors to this book stress the importance of providing instruction which facilitates conceptual understanding of knowledge as opposed to the practice of skills in isolation and, hence, the importance of teaching subject content in contexts which are meaningful to young children. The teaching of coherent subject matter organized around key concepts, linking what is to be taught to what children know already, is a common theme. The need to challenge children's misconceptions has been associated particularly with the teaching of science as children are encouraged to reconstruct their understanding of the world on the basis of new evidence. Joy Palmer draws particular attention to this in her chapter on geography and environmental education.

Whilst it is generally accepted that children must have the opportunity to integrate new knowledge with existing ideas, the extent to which it is possible to access individual pupil knowledge and competences which are brought to the learning situation and to take account of these in classroom teaching is less clear. The writer's own work in the area of accessing the informal mathematical understanding young children bring into school has shown on the one hand, children already possess a rich mathematical knowledge and on the other, teachers neither attempt to access this, nor even seem aware of its existence. As one busy teacher reasonably noted, she had neither the time to elicit such information nor to utilize it, if acquired. Where a communicable knowledge-base of early development within subject domains exists already, however, and the previous chapters give some indication of the extent to which this is the case, there are strong grounds for supporting the view that it should provide a basis both for curriculum planning and for engaging in interactive teaching which offers some opportunity to determine pupils' current understandings and beliefs, errors and misconceptions. The provision of a rich and deep subject knowledge may, however, lead to the coverage of *less* subject content which the National Curriculum does not allow!

The Role of the Learner

A recurrent theme from the growing knowledge base of the early development within subject domains, and a common theme of this book, has been children's active sense-making in the construction of subject knowledge. This calls for the provision of learning experiences which stress conceptual understanding and application of skills to real-life situations.

Doyle (1983) has distinguished among four types of classroom task with associated demands. The first type, a **memory task**, calls for children to recognize or reproduce information already acquired. The second type, a **procedural task**, involves the exercise of learned routines, for instance, algorithms in mathematics. The third type of task calls for **comprehension** to transfer or apply knowledge, to problem-solve or draw inferences, and the fourth type, an **opinion task**, requires a personal response or view. Clearly the views of subject development put forward in this book would support an emphasis on the two latter tasks. Doyle (1986), however, has shown such tasks may be resisted as they carry ambiguity and risk within the context of the school's accountability system. One strategy that children adopt is to seek more information about the task from the teacher and, in the process, convert it into a memory or procedural task which Bennett *et al.* (1984) have shown to be prevalent in first school classrooms.

An alternative to simplifying task demand is to provide 'scaffolded' instruction in which attempts are made to support a group or class of children to carry out a task or solve a problem which would be beyond their independent means. This has been called 'cognitive strategy instruction'. Wang and Palinscar (1989) reviewing the related research, suggest a sequence of stages: assessment, introduction, modelling and guided practice, independent application and instruction for maintenance and transfer. Obviously the way this would be interpreted in art and music, for instance, would not be the same as in science or mathematics.

In the **assessment** stage the teacher assesses the children's current strategies through questions, observation of problem solving and by setting 'thinking aloud' tasks. The **introduction** stage provides explicit information on what is to be learned, what problem is to be set and why, or how it will be used. In the **guided practice and modelling** stage the teacher models 'think aloud' strategies or otherwise demonstrates what is to be done and in the early stages, leads, coaches and provides feedback to children's early efforts, as well as opportunities for transfer. It requires of the teacher, detailed knowledge of the learning process, provision of appropriate 'scaffolding' which is gradually withdrawn as children gain independence. In chapter 1, attention was drawn to the role the supportive adult provides to the young child's early learning. Perhaps, cognitively guided instruction offers one means of providing a similar instructional mode for the learning of subjects in school.

In fact this model of instruction is very compatible with conceptions of learning and teaching subject knowledge which have been developed throughout this book. The assessment stage focuses on children's existing knowledge and problem solving strategies in providing the basis for planning future learning. It thus allows young learners' naive, earlier experiences to play an important role in the acquisition of new knowledge. The introduction provides the context and the purpose to the activity being carried out and guided practice allows the experienced adult to provide a leading and supportive teaching role. The task demand is simplified and aid is given to allow children to respond independently. At the same time learning is extended and children's responses are elaborated in a shared context. As children internalize this scaffold, as Wertsch (1979) has noted, what was once 'interpersonal' becomes 'intrapersonal' and by such means self-regulation is developed.

In common with the main theme of the book pedagogical subject knowledge is central to both the planning of teaching goals and to the effectiveness of the procedures used. It may also be significant that the model of instruction has much in common with features associated with effective teaching techniques identified by Alexander, Rose and Woodhead (1992) who stated:

> the research evidence demonstrates very clearly that the level of cognitive challenge provided by the teacher is a significant factor in performance. One way of providing challenge is to set pupils demanding tasks. But equally it is important for teachers to organize their classrooms so that they have the opportunity to interact with their pupils: to offer explanations which develop thinking, to encourage speculation and hypothesis through sensitive questioning, to be creative, above all, a climate of interest and purpose. (paragraph 105, p. 27)

Clearly much still needs to be learned about the impact of subject knowledge on teaching in the early years. Already we have a considerable knowledge base which deserves to be made more widely available and which has the potential to enrich the pedagogical subject knowledge base of early years teaching.

References

ALEXANDER, R., ROSE, J. and WOODHEAD, C. (1992) *Curriculum Organisation and Classroom Practice in Primary School — A Discussion Paper*, London, HMSO.
BENNETT, N. et al (1984) *The Quality of Pupil Learning Experience*, Hillsdale, NJ, Lawrence Erlbaum.
BROPHY, J. (Ed) (1989) *Advances in Research on Teaching*, Vol. 1. Greenwich, CT, JAI Press Inc.
BROPHY, J. (Ed) (1991) *Advances in Research on Teaching*, Vol. 2. Greenwich, CT, JAI Press Inc.
DOYLE, W. (1983) 'Academic work', *Review of Educational Research*, 53, 2, pp. 159–99.
DOYLE, W. (1986) 'Classroom organisation and management', in WITTROCK, M. (Ed) *Handbook on Research on Teaching*, pp. 292–431.
DOYLE, W. (1986) 'Content representation in teachers' definitions of academic work', *Journal of Curriculum Studies*, 18, 4, pp. 365–379.
GROSSMAN, P.L., WILSON, S.M. and SHULMAN, L.S. (1989) 'Teachers of substance: Subject matter knowledge for teaching', in REYNOLDS, M.C. (Ed) *Knowledge Base of the Beginning Teacher*, Oxford, Pergamon Press.
SHULMAN, L.S. (1986) 'Those who understand: Knowledge growth in teaching', *Educational Researcher*, February, pp. 4–14.
VAN DER VEER, R. and VALSINER, J. (1991) *Understanding Vygotsky: A Quest for Synthesis*, Oxford, Blackwell.
WANG, M.C. and PALINSCAR, A.S. (1989) 'Teaching students to assume an active role in their learning', in REYNOLDS, M.C. (Ed) *Knowledge Base for the Beginning Teacher*, Oxford, Pergamon Press.
WERTSCH, J. (1979) 'From social interaction to high psychological processes: A clarification and application of Vygotsky's theory', *Human Development*, 22, pp. 1–22.

Notes on Contributors

Elizabeth Ashton has wide experience in primary school teaching, particularly in socially disadvantaged areas of North Tyneside. She has a Teacher's Certificate (Distinction in History) from the Institute of Education, Newcastle upon Tyne, BA (Open University) and MA (Dunelm) for a thesis concerning primary school children's religious concepts. In January 1992 she was appointed Lecturer in Religious Education at the University of Durham.

Carol Aubrey is a Senior Lecturer in the School of Education at the University of Durham and was until recently Director of the PGCE Primary. She trained and worked as a primary school teacher before taking up a research post to work on a Leverhulme Project at the University of Aston in Birmingham from 1977 to 1980. The outcome of this was a portfolio of teaching materials for children with specific learning difficulties (dyslexia) in ordinary classrooms, (LDA, 1981). After working as an Educational Psychologist in the early 1980s, she became a Lecturer in Education at University College, Cardiff from 1986 to 1988. She has written extensively on special education and school psychology, for example, *Consultancy in the UK: Its Role and Contribution to Educational Change* (1990, Falmer Press). A major research interest for the last three years has been the investigation of informal mathematical knowledge young children bring into school which has led to a recent ESRC award.

Jennifer Buckham is an artist and art-educator and has had experience of teaching all age groups of children. She taught for thirteen years in both primary and secondary schools in Nairobi and London before moving into higher education. She worked as a lecturer at Kingston Polytechnic and the University of Exeter before joining the School of Education in Durham. Her main area of research is concerned with children's drawing development and repertoire. She has built up an extensive collection and record of children's work in both Kenyan and British contexts and has a particular interest in individual case studies. She is currently involved in two longitudinal projects.

Notes on Contributors

Coral Davies is Lecturer in Music Education at the University of Durham where she contributes to the initial teacher education courses, primary and secondary. She has extensive experience of in-service education, and work with children in and out of school. Her interest in young children's invented songs was first stimulated by work with the Durham Youth Opera, founded by Richard Addison in the 1970s. She has recently completed a doctorate on the same subject at the University of York.

David Day is a Senior Lecturer in Religious Education at the University of Durham School of Education and Principal of St. John's College. He was previously Senior Lecturer in Theology and Religious Studies at Derby Lonsdale College of Higher Education and is currently Chair of the Durham County Council Standing Advisory Council on Religious Education. He is the author of articles in *Spectrum* and *British Journal of Religious Education*, and of the study, *Jeremiah: Speaking for God in a Time of Crisis* (1987, Leicester, Intervarsity). He is co-author of *Teenage Beliefs* (1991, Oxford, Lion) and co-editor of *The Contours of Christian Education* (Great Wakering, McCrimmons).

Rosemary Feasey is a former Deputy Headteacher of a primary school. Before becoming a Lecturer in Education at the University of Durham she was an Advisory Teacher for Science. She is one of the Directors of the *Exploration of Science Project* and has been involved in extensive research and writing for the National Curriculum Council. Her research interests focus on children's handling of investigations and the role of the teacher in science.

Peter Millward is Director of the BA (Ed) Course in the University of Durham. He is a member of the School of Education Language Team and teaches on the BA (Ed) and PGCE Primary Language and Drama courses. He supervises research students engaged in higher degrees in language and drama and contributes to the MA programme. He has managed a variety of in-service courses for practising teachers. He is the University representative on the Cleveland Education Committee and on the Cleveland Consultative Committee on In-service Education. He has been responsible for managing two evaluations commissioned by Durham Education Authority: 'An Evaluation of "Towards a Language Policy"' (1989) and 'An Evaluation of "Science and Cross-curricular Links"' (1990). His research interests are in the field of child language and drama: *Language of Drama* (doctoral thesis, 1988), *Drama as a Well-made Play* (Language Arts, 1990), *Children Talking About Poetry* (with Linda Thompson, 1991).

Joy Palmer is Senior Lecturer in Education at the University of Durham, where she was until recently Director of the BA (Ed) course and lectures in environmental issues. She has Masters degrees in educational psychology and curriculum theory from the Universities of Birmingham and Stanford; and a PhD from the University of Durham. She is past Chair of the National Association for Environmental Education and a member of the IUCN Commission on Education and Communication. She has published extensively in the areas of primary curriculum (notably geography and environmental education) and environmental issues.

Deirdre Pettitt is a Lecturer in the School of Education at the University of Durham and Deputy Director of the BA (Ed) Course with Peter Millward. She trained and worked as an infant teacher before moving into higher education at the University of East Anglia, where she was Director of the Early Years teacher education courses (1985 to 1987). Her major research interest is in early years and she is co-author of a book on beginning writing. For the last three years she has worked with Carol Aubrey on the investigation of informal mathematical knowledge children bring to school. A book she has most recently written with Joy Palmer is *Topic Work in the Early Years — 4–8* (1993, London, Routledge).

Linda Thompson is a Lecturer in Education at the University of Durham. She coordinates the English Language courses within the School of Education. She has taught in primary schools in the UK, as well as training teachers of English in the Netherlands and Sweden. Her main research project is an investigation of ethnic identity and language choice among bilingual nursery school children. Other research interests include Children's Understanding of Poetry. Her publications include: *Language and Culture* (1993 Clevedon, Multilingual Matters) for which she is joint editor and *Children Talking about Poetry* (with Peter Millward) in H. Constable and S. Farrow (Eds) *Changing Classroom Practice* (1993, London, Falmer Press).

Pauline Wetton lectures in Physical Education in the Early Years (3–8 years) at the University of Durham School of Education. Her main research interests are in the motor performance of children (3–8 years) and in curriculum development in nursery and infant schools. Her publications include: *Bright Ideas: Games for PE* (1989 Leamington Spa, Scholastic Publications), *Physical Education in the Nursery and Infant School* (1989, London, Routledge and Kegan Paul) and *Practical Guides PE: Teaching Within the National Curriculum* (1992 Leamington Spa, Scholastic Publications). In addition she writes regularly for *Child Education*, Scholastic Publications.

Index

Abelson, R. 14, 16
ability 84, 92, 168, 171, 175, 181
abstract thought 182–4
activity
  drama 29–30, 34–5
  English 23
  geographic 110–11
  mathematical 57–9
  musical 119
  physical 168–71
  religious education 179
  scientific 74–7, 80–1, 83–6
  social 8
addition 60–4, 69
aestheticism 146
Alexander, Robin 1, 18, 25, 42, 73, 76, 80, 81, 82, 84, 92, 101, 193
algebra 54, 66
Anderson, B. 10, 172
art 3, 8, 50, 80, 111, 133–65, 190
artefacts, use as resource 97–8, 116, 179
Ashton, Elizabeth 178–86, 190
assessment 20–1, 46, 52, 86–7, 103, 117, 134, 193
attainment 67, 92
  targets 85, 91, 93–4, 98–9, 103, 106, 109, 114, 119, 169
attitude 4, 7–8, 19, 107–10, 115, 117
Aubrey, Carol 1–11, 30, 53–70, 188–94
audience, writing for 42, 45–9

Bateson, G. 14, 15
behaviour 9, 15–16, 20

belief 15, 69, 79, 82, 181, 190–2
Bennett, N. *et al* 53, 192
Bereiter, C. 9, 10, 49, 51
bias 115–16
Bolton, G. 29, 30, 31, 33, 34, 35
Brophy, J. 7, 191
Bruner, J.S. 8, 9, 34, 37, 90, 172
Buckham, Jennifer 133–65, 190
Bullock Report (1975) 17, 25

Carlsen, W.S. 5, 68
Carpenter, T.P. 10, 56, 63, 64, 69
case study, drawing 150–65
child centred learning 80
Chomsky, N. 19–20
Cockcroft, W.H. 53–4, 57, 67
cognitive strategy instruction 192–3
colouring in 147
communication 8, 188–9
  drama 30, 33–4, 36
  English 19–21, 24
  geography 108, 113
  history 96
  mathematics as 54–5, 57–60, 69
competence, physical 168, 174, 176
composing 121–3, 131
comprehension task 192
concept
  development of 4–5, 191–2
  geography 111, 117
  history 89–91, 96, 99
  maths 56–9, 61
  physical 173

religious 178, 182–3, 185–6
scientific 76–7, 81–2, 84–5, 189
writing 43
content
   drama 29–30
   English 29
   geography 105–6, 108
   history 93, 98–9
   mathematics 53–5
   religious 178–9, 181
   teaching and 188, 190–2
   writing 42–3
contextualization, every day 32–9
contextualization of learning 2, 5–9, 15, 20–1, 30–1, 65, 83–4, 92, 110, 116–17, 134, 140, 169, 181, 190–1, 193
Coulthard, R.M. 15, 67
counting 65, 139
cross-curricular learning 106–8, 110, 113, 116
culture 8, 15, 31–2, 36, 57, 120, 125, 128–9, 171, 173, 188
curriculum development 24–5, 54, 65–6, 73–4, 79–80, 82, 89, 92, 101–2, 119, 193

data handling 54–5, 60, 66, 78
Davidson, L. 119, 120, 121
Davies, Coral 119–31, 190
Day, David 178–86, 190
Degge, R.M. 144, 157
development, child 5, 8–10, 188, 190
   art 133, 137, 147, 150, 155, 157–8, 160–1, 164
   drama 37
   English 22
   geography 112
   history 92, 95
   mathematics 56
   music 119–20, 128, 130–1
   physical education 168–71
   religious education 181–2
   science 76, 82
   writing 42–3
Donaldson, M. 9, 92, 183
Dowling, K. 119, 121
drama 29–39, 189
drawing 8, 50, 111, 133–65

Edwards, D. 31, 33, 36, 56
Egan, Kieran 76, 81, 96, 140, 183
emotion 9, 137–8, 140, 156
English 3, 14–26, 35, 99–100, 189, 191
environment
   and drawing 140, 144–7, 158–60, 162, 164
   and physical development 170, 175
environmental education 105–17, 190
expectation 15
experience 5–7, 10, 188
   drama and 30–4, 36–7, 39
   drawing and 133, 140, 144–5, 149, 155–7, 161–4
   English and 15, 23
   geography and 110–13
   mathematics and 55, 59, 65
   physical education and 174
   religious education and 178–80, 183–6
   writing and 43
expertise, subject 1–2, 25, 73–5
Exploration of Science Project 77–8, 80, 85

fair testing 77–8, 85
Feasey, Rosemary 73–87, 189
Fennema, E. 10, 63, 64, 69
fieldwork 108–10, 116–17
Foulds, K. 77, 78, 80, 85
frame song 125–9
frames 15–16

Gallistel, C.R. 10, 65
Gardner, H. 119, 120, 131, 138, 144, 147, 150, 158
Garrett, P. 16, 23
geography 101, 105–17, 190
Gift to the Child project 180–1
Gillet, J.W. 42, 45
Ginsburg, H.P. 61, 65
goals, learning 2, 18, 37, 43, 48–9, 95, 175, 193
Golomb, C. 134, 138, 146, 150
Gombrich, E.H. 138, 162, 165
Goodman, N. 140, 162, 164–5
Gott, R. 75, 77, 78, 80, 83, 85
grammar 18–19, 42–6
graphs 59–60
Grossman, P.L. 3, 4, 5, 188

Index

Harlen, W. 4–5, 81
health 168–9, 171–2, 176
health-related fitness (HRF) 171–2
Heathcote, Dorothy 30, 32, 37
history 3, 5, 23, 89–103, 189
   drama in 29, 34–5
home 7–9, 57–8, 63, 67, 81, 189
Hughes, M. 9, 58, 59, 61, 92
humour 160–1
Hymes, D. 19–20

initiation-response-evaluation (IRE) 67–8
intonation 44
investigation 75, 80, 83–6

James, C. 16, 23

Kaput, J.J. 9, 60
Karmiloff-Smith, A. 21–2
key stages
   drama 29, 34–5
   geography 105–6
   history 91–5, 98–9, 102
   mathematics 54–5
   music 123, 128–9, 131
   religious education 179
Kingman Report (1988) 17–18
knowledge about language (KAL) 16, 18–20, 25
knowledge of child 9–11, 188, 192, 193
   drama 30, 36, 39
   geography 107–9, 112, 114–15, 117
   mathematics 67, 69
   music 123
   science 78, 81, 83, 85
   writing 43
   see also previous knowledge
knowledge, musical 129, 131
knowledge of teacher 1–5, 188, 189, 191
   art 134, 190
   drama 35
   English 23–4
   history 92–5, 97, 103
   mathematics 66–9
   physical education 169–70
   religious education 182
   science 73–6, 78, 80–2, 84–7
   writing 43, 46, 52

Kozulin, A. 8, 57
Kress, G. 44, 47

language 8–9, 188
   awareness 18, 22, 188
   in drama 31, 33, 39
   in English 15–19, 21–4
   in geography 111
   in history 91, 96, 102
   in mathematics 54–5, 57–9, 61, 65, 67–9, 189
   in music 119, 121, 123, 129, 131, 190
   in religious education 179, 182–4, 190
   in science 78, 80
   in writing 43–5
learning
   child 7–9
   drama and 36–7
   in English 23–4, 26
   mathematics and 55–65
   writing and 42–3
Lesh, R. 9, 59
life style 168–72
linguistic performance and competence 19–20
literature 3, 5
Little, V. 97, 100

McFee, J.K. 144, 157
make-believe 33–4, 39, 183
management, body 168–70, 174–6
mapwork 108, 111–13
mathematics 5, 7, 10, 23, 29, 53–70, 77–8, 80, 91–2, 100, 113, 189, 191
   drama and 35–6
Matthews, D. 8–9
Matthews, Gareth 184, 186
Matthews, J. 134, 137, 138, 139, 156
measurement 55–7, 66, 75, 77–8, 83–4, 91
media, use of art 145, 149–50
melody development 120–1, 124–6, 128
memory 144–8, 163
   task 192
Mercer, N. 31, 33, 36, 56
metalinguistic awareness 16, 19, 21–3
Millward, Peter 29–39, 189
models for writing 47–9
Moog, H. 120, 121

Index

Moser, J.M. 60, 64
music 119–31, 190

National Curriculum 1–2, 4–6, 191–2
  art 133
  drama 29, 34
  English 17–18, 20, 25
  geography 105–7
  history 89, 91, 94, 101
  mathematics 54, 66
  music 131
  physical education 169, 172–3, 175–6
  science 73–4, 84–5, 87
  writing 41, 52
Nuffield Junior Science Project 80
number 54–9, 61, 63–5, 66

observation 76–7, 79, 83, 85, 113, 144–5, 148, 158, 162–4
opinion task 192

Paine, S. 150, 160
Palinscar, A.S. 192
Palmer, Joy 101, 105–117, 189, 191
performance drama 29, 34–5
Perry, M.D. 134, 138
Peterson, P.L. 10, 63, 64, 69
Pettitt, Deidre 41–52, 89–103, 189
philosophizing 184–6
physical education 168–76, 190
physiognomic perception 138–9
Piaget, J. 10, 56, 76, 77, 79, 90, 112, 129, 182
place, sense of 110–17, 190
planning
  geography 107, 110, 115–16
  history 102
  physical education 172–4
  religious education 179–80
  science 82, 86–7
  writing 49–51
play 8, 21, 23, 34, 66, 80, 183–4
Plowden Report (1967) 79–80
pluralism 178–9, 181
Pratt, C. 21, 22
previous knowledge 2, 4, 9, 11, 189–93
  English 18
  geography 115–16
  history 95–6, 98–9, 101–2
  mathematics 57–8, 61, 63, 66–7, 69
  science 73, 78, 81, 83, 85, 87
problem solving 53–5, 57, 59, 64–5, 69, 78, 113, 193
process 74–5, 77–8, 80, 82–3, 85, 92, 94, 110, 137, 192
profile, art 149–50
programmes of study 93–4, 99, 106, 169

reading 46–8, 92, 95–6, 102
reflection 33, 140, 181–2, 185–6
relationship between child and teacher 37–9, 67, 133–4, 189
religious education 1, 178–86, 190
representation 9, 111, 121
  drawing and 133–4, 137–8, 156, 159, 163
  mathematics as 59–65
resources
  art 133
  geography 108, 112, 117
  history 95–8
role
  child 31
  drawing 155
  education 9
  knowledge 2
  learner 192–4
  school 67
  teacher 1, 25, 31, 81, 86, 133, 146, 173–4, 191–3
  teacher in drama 37–8
Rose, J. 1, 18, 25, 73, 76, 80, 81, 82, 84, 92, 101, 193

Scardamalia, M. 9, 10, 49, 51
Schank, R. 14, 16
schema theory 10, 14–15
science 3–7, 10–11, 23, 48, 55, 73–87, 113, 189, 191
scripts 15–16
sensitivity 144–6, 149–50
shape and space 54–5, 58–9, 66, 155–7
sharing 46
Shulman, L.S. 2, 3, 4, 5, 190
Sinclair, J.M. 15, 67
skill, development 4–5, 191, 192
  drama 29
  drawing 133, 137, 145, 147, 150, 155, 157–8, 160–1, 164

201

Index

geography 108–10, 112–14, 117
history 89, 92, 99
mathematics 53–4, 57, 66, 68–9
physical education 168, 170, 172–6
religious education 184
science 74–8, 80, 82–5
writing 43
Smith, Nancy R. 133, 134, 138, 146, 148, 161
song 119–31, 179, 190
specialism, subject 1, 6, 25–6, 93–4, 119
speech and writing 43–7
Steffe, L.P. 63, 69
story
and myth 96–7, 99–100
song 121–4, 127–9
telling 47–8, 137, 179
subtraction 60–4, 66, 69
Swanwick, K. 128–9
symbolism 137–8, 140
systems, drawing 155–61, 164

Tanner, J.M. 170, 172, 173
Taylor, Rod 158, 162
teaching methods 1–6, 11
drama 29, 37–8
English 17–18
history 99–100
mathematics 56–7, 65–70
science 79–82, 85–7
writing 42, 45–7, 49–51
Temple, C. 42, 45
Thompson, Linda 10, 14–26, 189
Thornton, S.J. 90, 91
time in history, role of 90–1, 94, 100–1, 189
Tizard, B. 9, 23, 58, 66

topic work 1, 54, 66, 80, 87, 99, 101–3, 106–7, 110, 114, 116–17
training, teacher 1, 3, 6–7, 18, 24–5

understanding
science 73, 75–6, 82–3, 189
teacher 3–4, 11, 78, 82, 85, 90, 134, 164–5, 169
understanding of child 2, 5–6, 8, 189, 192
drama 29–30, 34–7
drawing 140, 145
English 18, 24
geography 107–10, 113–14
history 90
mathematics 53, 55, 61, 63, 68–9
music 119, 121, 128–9, 131
science 73, 81, 84
using and applying mathematics 54

Vukelick, R. 90, 91
Vygotsky, L.S. 8, 31, 37, 57, 189

Walkerdine, V. 56, 58, 69
Warburton, P. 169, 173
Watson, Brenda G. 180, 185
Wells, Gordon 8, 9, 30, 41, 57, 67, 96
Wetton, Pauline 168–76, 190
Willats, J. 137, 139, 156
Willes, M.J. 15, 31, 67
Wilson, B. 133, 134, 144, 157
Wilson, M. 133, 144, 157
Wilson, S.M. 3, 4, 5
Winner, E. 134, 138
Wolf, D. 134, 138, 148, 155, 157
Woodhead, C. 1, 18, 25, 73, 76, 80, 81, 82, 84, 92, 101, 193
writing 41–52, 92, 102, 113, 155, 189

Zweng, M. 64

For Product Safety Concerns and Information please contact our EU representative GPSR@taylorandfrancis.com
Taylor & Francis Verlag GmbH, Kaufingerstraße 24, 80331 München, Germany

www.ingramcontent.com/pod-product-compliance
Lightning Source LLC
Chambersburg PA
CBHW061445300426
44114CB00014B/1839